ABOUT THIS PUBLICATION

FOR SERVICE ASSISTANCE

Customer Service
1.704.898.0770

North Carolina General Statues is published by The Muliti-Media Group of Greater Charlotte in Charlotte, North Carolina. Copyright 2015 by the Multi-Media Group of Greater Charlotte. This book or parts thereof may not be reproduced in any form, stored in a retrieval system, or transmitted in any form by any means—electronic, mechanical, photocopy, recording or otherwise—without prior written permission of the publisher, except as provided by United States of America copyright law.

The records required by U.S. Code 2257(a) through (c) and the pertinent regulations 28 C.F.R. Cli. 1, Part 75 with respect to this publication and all materials associated with such records are maintained by The Multi-Media Group of Greater Charlotte, Publisher and available for review by Attorney General.

www.visionbooks.org

Copyright © 2015 by MMGGC
All rights reserved!

TID: 5107887
ISBN (10) digit: 150324430X
ISBN (13) digit: 978-1503244306

123-4-56789-01239-Paperback
123-4-56789-01239-Hardback

First Edition

090520140547

Printed in the United States of America

2015 EDITION

North Carolina Criminal Law And Procedure-Pamphlet # 83

Printed In conjunction with the Administration of the Courts

North Carolina Criminal Law and Procedure
Pamphlet Reference Guide

Chapters	Pamphlet
Chapter 1 Civil Procedure	1
Chapter 1 Civil Procedure (Continue)	2
Chapter 1A Rules of Civil Procedure	2
Chapter 1B Contribution.	2
Chapter 1C Enforcement of Judgments.	2
Chapter 1D Punitive Damages.	2
Chapter 1E Eastern Band of Cherokee Indians.	2
Chapter 1F North Carolina Uniform Interstate Depositions and Discovery Act.	2
Chapter 2 - Clerk of Superior Court [Repealed and Transferred.]	3
Chapter 3 - Commissioners of Affidavits and Deeds [Repealed.]	3
Chapter 4 - Common Law	3
Chapter 5 - Contempt [Repealed.]	3
Chapter 5A - Contempt	3
Chapter 6 - Liability for Court Costs	3
Chapter 7 - Courts [Repealed and Transferred.]	3
Chapter 7A – Judicial Department	3
Chapter 7A – Continuation (Judicial Department)	4
Chapter 7A – Continuation (Judicial Department)	5
Chapter 7B - Juvenile Code	5
Chapter 8 - Evidence	6
Chapter 8A - Interpreters for Deaf Persons [Recodified.]	6
Chapter 8B - Interpreters for Deaf Persons	6
Chapter 8C - Evidence Code	6
Chapter 9 - Jurors	6
Chapter 10 - Notaries [Repealed.]	6
Chapter 10A - Notaries [Recodified.]	6
Chapter 10B - Notaries	6
Chapter 11 - Oaths	6
Chapter 12 - Statutory Construction	6
Chapter 13 - Citizenship Restored	6
Chapter 14 - Criminal Law	7
Chapter 14 –Criminal Law (Continuation)	8
Chapter 15 - Criminal Procedure	9
Chapter 15A - Criminal Procedure Act (Continuation)	10
Chapter 15A - Criminal Procedure Act (Continuation)	11
Chapter 15B - Victims Compensation	11
Chapter 15C - Address Confidentiality Program	11
Chapter 16 - Gaming Contracts and Futures	11
Chapter 17 - Habeas Corpus	11

Chapter 17A - Law-Enforcement Officers [Recodified.]	11
Chapter 17B - North Carolina Criminal Justice Education and Training System [Recodified.] Chapter 17C - North Carolina Criminal Justice Education and Training Standards Commission	11 11
Chapter 17D - North Carolina Justice Academy	11
Chapter 17E - North Carolina Sheriffs' Education and Training Standards Commission	11
Chapter 18 - Regulation of Intoxicating Liquors [Repealed.]	12
Chapter 18A - Regulation of Intoxicating Liquors [Repealed.]	12
Chapter 18B - Regulation of Alcoholic Beverages	12
Chapter 18C - North Carolina State Lottery	12
Chapter 19 - Offenses against Public Morals	12
Chapter 19A - Protection of Animals	12
Chapter 20 - Motor Vehicles	13
Chapter 20 - Motor Vehicles (Continuation)	14
Chapter 20 - Motor Vehicles (Continuation)	15
Chapter 20 - Motor Vehicles (Continuation)	16
Chapter 21 - Bills of Lading	17
Chapter 22 - Contracts Requiring Writing	17
Chapter 22A - Signatures	17
Chapter 22B - Contracts Against Public Policy	17
Chapter 22C - Payments to Subcontractors	17
Chapter 23 - Debtor and Creditor	17
Chapter 24 – Interest	17
Chapter 25 – Uniform Commercial Code	18
Chapter 25 – Uniform Commercial Code (Continuation)	19
Chapter 25A – Retail Installment Sales Act	20
Chapter 25B - Credit	20
Chapter 25C - Sales of Artwork	20
Chapter 26 - Suretyship	20
Chapter 27 - Warehouse Receipts [Repealed.]	20
Chapter 28 - Administration [Repealed.]	20
Chapter 28A - Administration of Decedents' Estates	20
Chapter 28B - Estates of Absentees in Military Service	20
Chapter 28C - Estates of Missing Persons	20
Chapter 29 - Intestate Succession	21
Chapter 30 - Surviving Spouses	21
Chapter 31 - Wills	21
Chapter 31A - Acts Barring Property Rights	21
Chapter 31B - Renunciation of Property and Renunciation of Fiduciary Powers Act	21
Chapter 31C - Uniform Disposition of Community Property Rights at Death Act	21
Chapter 32 - Fiduciaries	21
Chapter 32A - Powers of Attorney	21
Chapter 33 - Guardian and Ward [Repealed and Recodified.]	21

Chapter 33A - North Carolina Uniform Transfers to Minors Act	21
Chapter 33B - North Carolina Uniform Custodial Trust Act	21
Chapter 34 - Veterans' Guardianship Act	22
Chapter 35 - Sterilization Procedures	22
Chapter 35A - Incompetency and Guardianship	22
Chapter 36 - Trusts and Trustees [Repealed.]	22
Chapter 36A - Trusts and Trustees	22
Chapter 36B - Uniform Management of Institutional Funds Act [Repealed.]	22
Chapter 36C - North Carolina Uniform Trust Code	22
Chapter 36D - North Carolina Community Third Party Trusts, Pooled Trusts	23
Chapter 36E - Uniform Prudent Management of Institutional Funds Act	23
Chapter 37 - Allocation of Principal and Income [Repealed.]	23
Chapter 37A - Uniform Principal and Income Act	23
Chapter 38 - Boundaries	23
Chapter 38A - Landowner Liability	23
Chapter 39 - Conveyances	23
Chapter 39A - Transfer Fee Covenants Prohibited	23
Chapter 40 - Eminent Domain [Repealed.]	23
Chapter 40A - Eminent Domain	23
Chapter 41 - Estates	23
Chapter 41A - State Fair Housing Act	23
Chapter 42 - Landlord and Tenant	23
Chapter 42A - Vacation Rental Act	23
Chapter 43 - Land Registration	23
Chapter 44 - Liens	24
Chapter 44A - Statutory Liens and Charges	24
Chapter 45 - Mortgages and Deeds of Trust	24
Chapter 45A - Good Funds Settlement Act	24
Chapter 46 - Partition	24
Chapter 47 - Probate and Registration	25
Chapter 47A - Unit Ownership	25
Chapter 47B - Real Property Marketable Title Act	25
Chapter 47C - North Carolina Condominium Act	25
Chapter 47D - Notice of Settlement Act [Expired.]	25
Chapter 47E - Residential Property Disclosure Act	25
Chapter 47F - North Carolina Planned Community Act	25
Chapter 47G - Option to Purchase Contracts	25
Chapter 47H - Contracts for Deed	25
Chapter 48 - Adoptions	26
Chapter 48A - Minors	26
Chapter 49 - Bastardy	26
Chapter 49A - Rights of Children	26
Chapter 50 - Divorce and Alimony	26
Chapter 50A - Uniform Child-Custody Jurisdiction and	

Enforcement Act	26
Chapter 50B - Domestic Violence	26
Chapter 50C - Civil No-Contact Orders	26
Chapter 51 - Marriage	26
Chapter 52 - Powers and Liabilities of Married Persons	27
Chapter 52A - Uniform Reciprocal Enforcement of Support Act [Repealed.]	27
Chapter 52B - Uniform Premarital Agreement Act	27
Chapter 52C - Uniform Interstate Family Support Act	27
Chapter 53 - Banks	27
Chapter 53A - Business Development Corporations and North Carolina Capital Resource Corporations	28
Chapter 53B - Financial Privacy Act	28
Chapter 54 - Cooperative Organizations	28
Chapter 54A - Capital Stock Savings and Loan Associations [Repealed.]	28
Chapter 54B - Savings and Loan Associations	29
Chapter 54C - Savings Banks	29
Chapter 55 - North Carolina Business Corporation Act	30
Chapter 55A - North Carolina Nonprofit Corporation Act	31
Chapter 55B - Professional Corporation Act	31
Chapter 55C - Foreign Trade Zones	31
Chapter 55D - Filings, Names, and Registered Agents for Corporations, Nonprofit Corporations, and Partnerships	31
Chapter 56 - Electric, Telegraph and Power Companies [Repealed.]	31
Chapter 57 - Hospital, Medical and Dental Service Corporations [Recodified.]	31
Chapter 57A - Health Maintenance Organization Act [Recodified.]	31
Chapter 57B - Health Maintenance Organization Act [Recodified.]	31
Chapter 57C - North Carolina Limited Liability Company Act.	31
Chapter 58 - Insurance.	32
Chapter 58 - Insurance (Continuation)	33
Chapter 58 - Insurance (Continuation)	34
Chapter 58 - Insurance (Continuation)	35
Chapter 58 - Insurance (Continuation)	36
Chapter 58 - Insurance (Continuation)	37
Chapter 58 - Insurance (Continuation)	38
Chapter 58A - North Carolina Health Insurance Trust Commission [Recodified.]	38
Chapter 59 - Partnership.	39
Chapter 59B - Uniform Unincorporated Nonprofit Association Act.	39
Chapter 60 - Railroads and Other Carriers [Repealed and Transferred.]	39
Chapter 61 - Religious Societies	39
Chapter 62 - Public Utilities	39

Chapter 62 - Public Utilities (Continuation)	40
Chapter 62A - Public Safety Telephone Service And Wireless Telephone Service	40
Chapter 63 - Aeronautics	40
Chapter 63A - North Carolina Global TransPark Authority	40
Chapter 64 - Aliens	40
Chapter 65 – Cemeteries	40
Chapter 66 - Commerce and Business	41
Chapter 67 - Dogs	41
Chapter 68 - Fences and Stock Law	41
Chapter 69 - Fire Protection	41
Chapter 70 - Indian Antiquities, Archaeological Resources and Unmarked Human Skeletal Remains Protection	42
Chapter 71 - Indians [Repealed.]	42
Chapter 71A - Indians	42
Chapter 72 - Inns, Hotels and Restaurants	42
Chapter 73 - Mills	42
Chapter 74 - Mines and Quarries	42
Chapter 74A - Company Police [Repealed.]	42
Chapter 74B - Private Protective Services Act [Repealed.]	42
Chapter 74C - Private Protective Services	42
Chapter 74D - Alarm Systems	42
Chapter 74E - Company Police Act	42
Chapter 74F - Locksmith Licensing Act	42
Chapter 74G - Campus Police Act	42
Chapter 75 - Monopolies, Trusts and Consumer Protection	42
Chapter 75A - Boating and Water Safety	43
Chapter 75B - Discrimination in Business	43
Chapter 75C - Motion Picture Fair Competition Act	43
Chapter 75D - Racketeer Influenced and Corrupt Organizations	43
Chapter 75E - Unlawful Activities in Connection With Certain Corporate Transactions	43
Chapter 76 - Navigation	43
Chapter 76A - Navigation and Pilotage Commissions	43
Chapter 77 - Rivers, Creeks, and Coastal Waters	43
Chapter 78 - Securities Law [Repealed.]	43
Chapter 78A - North Carolina Securities Act	43
Chapter 78B - Tender Offer Disclosure Act [Repealed.]	43
Chapter 78C - Investment Advisers	43
Chapter 78D - Commodities Act	43
Chapter 79 - Strays [Repealed.]	43
Chapter 80 - Trademarks, Brands, etc.	44
Chapter 81 - Weights and Measures [Recodified.]	44
Chapter 81A - Weights and Measures Act of 1975.	44
Chapter 82 - Wrecks [Repealed.]	44
Chapter 83 - Architects [Recodified.]	44

Chapter 83A - Architects	44
Chapter 84 - Attorneys-at-Law	44
Chapter 84A - Foreign Legal Consultants	44
Chapter 85 - Auctions and Auctioneers [Repealed.]	44
Chapter 85A - Bail Bondsmen and Runners [Recodified.]	44
Chapter 85B - Auctions and Auctioneers	44
Chapter 85C - Bail Bondsmen and Runners [Recodified.]	44
Chapter 86 - Barbers [Recodified.]	44
Chapter 86A - Barbers	44
Chapter 87 - Contractors	44
Chapter 88 - Cosmetic Art [Repealed.]	44
Chapter 88A - Electrolysis Practice Act	44
Chapter 88B - Cosmetic Art	45
Chapter 89 - Engineering and Land Surveying [Recodified.]	45
Chapter 89A - Landscape Architects	45
Chapter 89B - Foresters	45
Chapter 89C - Engineering and Land Surveying	45
Chapter 89D - Landscape Contractors	45
Chapter 89E - Geologists Licensing Act	45
Chapter 89F - North Carolina Soil Scientist Licensing Act	45
Chapter 89G - Irrigation Contractors	45
Chapter 90 - Medicine and Allied Occupations	45
Chapter 90 - Medicine and Allied Occupations (Continuation)	46
Chapter 90 - Medicine and Allied Occupations (Continuation)	47
Chapter 90 - Medicine and Allied Occupations (Continuation)	48
Chapter 90A - Sanitarians and Water and Wastewater Treatment Facility Operators	48
Chapter 90B - Social Worker Certification and Licensure Act	48
Chapter 90C - North Carolina Recreational Therapy Licensure Act	48
Chapter 90D - Interpreters and Transliterators	48
Chapter 91 - Pawnbrokers [Repealed.]	48
Chapter 91A - Pawnbrokers Modernization Act of 1989	48
Chapter 92 - Photographers [Deleted.]	48
Chapter 93 - Certified Public Accountants	48
Chapter 93A - Real Estate License Law	49
Chapter 93B - Occupational Licensing Boards	49
Chapter 93C - Watchmakers [Repealed.]	49
Chapter 93D - North Carolina State Hearing Aid Dealers and Fitters Board.	49
Chapter 93E - North Carolina Appraisers Act	49
Chapter 94 - Apprenticeship	49
Chapter 95 - Department of Labor and Labor Regulations	49
Chapter 95 - Department of Labor and Labor Regulations (Continuation)	50
Chapter 96 - Employment Security	50
Chapter 97 - Workers' Compensation Act	50
Chapter 97 - Workers' Compensation Act (Continuation)	51

Chapter 98 - Burnt and Lost Records	51
Chapter 99 - Libel and Slander	51
Chapter 99A - Civil Remedies for Criminal Actions	51
Chapter 99B - Products Liability	51
Chapter 99C - Actions Relating to Winter Sports Safety and Accidents	51
Chapter 99D - Civil Rights	51
Chapter 99E - Special Liability Provisions	51
Chapter 100 - Monuments, Memorials and Parks	51
Chapter 101 - Names of Persons	51
Chapter 102 - Official Survey Base	51
Chapter 103 - Sundays, Holidays and Special Days	51
Chapter 104 - United States Lands	51
Chapter 104A - Degrees of Kinship	51
Chapter 104B - Hurricanes or Other Acts of Nature	51
Chapter 104C - Atomic Energy, Radioactivity and Ionizing Radiation [Repealed and Recodified.]	51
Chapter 104D - Southern States Energy Compact	51
Chapter 104E - North Carolina Radiation Protection Act	51
Chapter 104F - Southeast Interstate Low-Level Radioactive Waste Management Compact [Repealed]	51
Chapter 104G - North Carolina Low-Level Radioactive Waste Management Authority Act of 1987 [Repealed]	51
Chapter 105 - Taxation	51
Chapter 105 - Taxation (Continuation)	52
Chapter 105 - Taxation (Continuation)	53
Chapter 105 - Taxation (Continuation)	54
Chapter 105A - Setoff Debt Collection Act	55
Chapter 105B - Defaulted Student Loan Recovery Act	55
Chapter 106 - Agriculture	55
Chapter 106 - Agriculture (Continue)	56
Chapter 106 - Agriculture (Continue)	57
Chapter 107 - Agricultural Development Districts [Repealed.]	57
Chapter 108 - Social Services [Repealed and Recodified.]	57
Chapter 108A - Social Services	57
Chapter 108B - Community Action Programs	58
Chapter 108C Medicaid and Health Choice Provider Requirements.	58
Chapter 108D Medicaid Managed Care for Behavioral Health Services.	58
Chapter 109 - Bonds [Recodified.]	58
Chapter 110 - Child Welfare	58
Chapter 111 - Aid to the Blind	58
Chapter 112 - Confederate Homes and Pensions [Repealed.]	58
Chapter 113 - Conservation and Development	58
Chapter 113 - Conservation and Development (Continuation)	59

Chapter 113A - Pollution Control and Environment	59
Chapter 113A - Pollution Control and Environment (Continuation)	60
Chapter 113B - North Carolina Energy Policy Act of 1975	60
Chapter 114 - Department of Justice	60
Chapter 115 - Elementary and Secondary Education [Repealed.]	60
Chapter 115A - Community Colleges, Technical Institutes, and Industrial Education Centers [Repealed.]	60
Chapter 115B - Tuition and Fee Waivers	60
Chapter 115C - Elementary and Secondary Education	60
Chapter 115C - Elementary and Secondary Education (Continuation)	61
Chapter 115C - Elementary and Secondary Education (Continuation)	62
Chapter 115C - Elementary and Secondary Education (Continuation)	63
Chapter 115D - Community Colleges	63
Chapter 115E - Private Educational Facilities Finance Act [Recodified]	63
Chapter 116 - Higher Education	63
Chapter 116 - Higher Education (Continuation)	63
Chapter 116A - Escheats and Abandoned Property [Repealed.]	64
Chapter 116B - Escheats and Abandoned Property	64
Chapter 116C - Continuum of Education Programs	64
Chapter 116D - Higher Education Bonds	64
Chapter 116E - Education Longitudinal Data System	64
Chapter 117 - Electrification	64
Chapter 118 - Firemen's and Rescue Squad Workers' Relief and Pension Funds [Recodified.]	64
Chapter 118A - Firemen's Death Benefit Act [Repealed.]	64
Chapter 118B - Members of a Rescue Squad Death Benefit Act [Repealed.]	64
Chapter 119 - Gasoline and Oil Inspection and Regulation	64
Chapter 120 - General Assembly	65
Chapter 120 - General Assembly (Continuation)	66
Chapter 120 - General Assembly (Continuation)	67
Chapter 120C - Lobbying	67
Chapter 121 - Archives and History	67
Chapter 122 - Hospitals for the Mentally Disordered [Repealed.]	67
Chapter 122A - North Carolina Housing Finance Agency	67
Chapter 122B - North Carolina Agricultural Facilities Finance Act [Repealed.]	67
Chapter 122C - Mental Health, Developmental Disabilities, and Substance Abuse Act of 1985	67
Chapter 122C - Mental Health, Developmental Disabilities, and Substance Abuse Act of 1985 (Continuation)	68

Chapter 122D - North Carolina Agricultural Finance Act	68
Chapter 122E - North Carolina Housing Trust and Oil Overcharge Act	68
Chapter 123 - Impeachment	69
Chapter 123A - Industrial Development [Repealed.]	69
Chapter 124 - Internal Improvements	69
Chapter 125 - Libraries	69
Chapter 126 - State Personnel System	69
Chapter 127 - Militia [Repealed.]	69
Chapter 127A - Militia	69
Chapter 127B - Military Affairs	69
Chapter 127C - Advisory Commission on Military Affairs	69
Chapter 128 - Offices and Public Officers	69
Chapter 128 - Offices and Public Officers (Continuation)	70
Chapter 129 - Public Buildings and Grounds	70
Chapter 130 - Public Health [Repealed.]	70
Chapter 130A - Public Health	70
Chapter 130A - Public Health (Continuation)	71
Chapter 130A - Public Health (Continuation)	72
Chapter 130B - Hazardous Waste Management Commission [Repealed.]	72
Chapter 131 - Public Hospitals [Repealed.]	72
Chapter 131A - Health Care Facilities Finance Act	72
Chapter 131B - Licensing of Ambulatory Surgical Facilities [Repealed.]	72
Chapter 131C - Charitable Solicitation Licensure Act [Repealed.]	72
Chapter 131D - Inspection and Licensing of Facilities	72
Chapter 131E - Health Care Facilities and Services	72
Chapter 131E - Health Care Facilities and Services (Continuation)	73
Chapter 131F - Solicitation of Contributions	73
Chapter 132 - Public Records	73
Chapter 133 - Public Works	74
Chapter 134 - Youth Development [Recodified.]	74
Chapter 134A - Youth Services [Repealed.]	74
Chapter 135 - Retirement System for Teachers and State Employees; Social Security; Health Insurance Program for Children	74
Chapter 135 - Retirement System for Teachers and State Employees; Social Security; Health Insurance Program for Children	75
Chapter 136 - Transportation	75
Chapter 136 - Transportation (Continuation)	76
Chapter 137 - Rural Rehabilitation [Repealed.]	76
Chapter 138 - Salaries, Fees and Allowances	76
Chapter 138A - State Government Ethics Act	76

Chapter 139 - Soil and Water Conservation Districts	76
Chapter 140 - State Art Museum; Symphony and Art Societies	76
Chapter 140A - State Awards System	76
Chapter 141 - State Boundaries	76
Chapter 142 - State Debt	76
Chapter 143 - State Departments, Institutions, and Commissions	77
Chapter 143 - State Departments, Institutions, and Commissions (Continuation)	78
Chapter 143 - State Departments, Institutions, and Commissions (Continuation)	79
Chapter 143 - State Departments, Institutions, and Commissions (Continuation)	80
Chapter 143A - State Government Reorganization	80
Chapter 143B - Executive Organization Act of 1973	80
Chapter 143B - Executive Organization Act of 1973 (Continuation)	81
Chapter 143B - Executive Organization Act of 1973 (Continuation)	82
Chapter 143C - State Budget Act	83
Chapter 143D - The State Governmental Accountability and Internal Control Act	83
Chapter 144 - State Flag, Official Governmental Flags, Motto, and Colors	83
Chapter 145 - State Symbols and Other Official Adoptions.	83
Chapter 146 - State Lands	83
Chapter 147 - State Officers	83
Chapter 148 - State Prison System	84
Chapter 149 - State Song and Toast	84
Chapter 150 - Uniform Revocation of Licenses [Repealed.]	84
Chapter 150A - Administrative Procedure Act [Recodified.]	84
Chapter 150B - Administrative Procedure Act	84
Chapter 151 - Constables [Repealed.]	84
Chapter 152 - Coroners	84
Chapter 152A - County Medical Examiner [Repealed.]	84
Chapter 152A - County Medical Examiner [Repealed.] (Continuation)	84
Chapter 153 - Counties and County Commissioners [Repealed.]	84
Chapter 153A - Counties	84
Chapter 153A - Counties (Continue)	85
Chapter 153B - Mountain Resources Planning Act	85
Chapter 153C - Uwharrie Regional Resources Act	85
Chapter 154 - County Surveyor [Repealed.]	85
Chapter 155 - County Treasurer [Repealed.]	85

Chapter 156 - Drainage	85
Chapter 156 – Drainage (Continuation)	86
Chapter 157 - Housing Authorities and Projects	86
Chapter 157A - Historic Properties Commissions [Transferred.]	86
Chapter 158 - Local Development	86
Chapter 159 - Local Government Finance	86
Chapter 159 - Local Government Finance (Continuation)	87
Chapter 159A - Pollution Abatement and Industrial Facilities Financing Act [Unconstitutional.]	87
Chapter 159B - Joint Municipal Electric Power and Energy Act	87
Chapter 159C - Industrial and Pollution Control Facilities Financing Act	87
Chapter 159D - The North Carolina Capital Facilities Financing Act	87
Chapter 159E - Registered Public Obligations Act	87
Chapter 159F - North Carolina Energy Development Authority [Repealed.]	87
Chapter 159G - Water Infrastructure	87
Chapter 159H - [Reserved.]	87
Chapter 159I - Solid Waste Management Loan Program and Local Government Special Obligation Bonds	87
Chapter 160 - Municipal Corporations [Repealed And Transferred.]	87
Chapter 160A - Cities and Towns	88
Chapter 160A - Cities and Towns (Continuation)	89
Chapter 160B - Consolidated City-County Act	89
Chapter 160C - Baseball Park Districts [Repealed.]	90
Chapter 161 - Register of Deeds	90
Chapter 162 - Sheriff	90
Chapter 162A - Water and Sewer Systems	90
Chapter 162B Continuity of Local Government in Emergency.	90
Chapter 163 Elections and Election Laws.	90
Chapter 163 Elections and Election Laws. (Continuation)	91
Chapter 164 Concerning the General Statutes of North Carolina.	92
Chapter 165 Veterans.	92
Chapter 166 Civil Preparedness Agencies [Repealed.]	92
Chapter 166A North Carolina Emergency Management Act.	92
Chapter 167 State Civil Air Patrol [Repealed.]	92
Chapter 168 Persons with Disabilities.	92
Chapter 168A Persons With Disabilities Protection Act.	92

Chapter 143C.

State Budget Act.

Article 1.

General Provisions.

§ 143C-1-1. Purpose and definitions.

(a) Title of Chapter. - This Chapter is the "State Budget Act" and may be cited by that name.

(b) The provisions of this Chapter shall apply to every State agency, unless specifically exempted herein, and to every non-State entity that receives or expends any State funds. No State agency or non-State entity shall expend any State funds except in accordance with an act of appropriation and the requirements of this Chapter. The provisions of Chapter 120 of the General Statutes shall continue to apply to the General Assembly and to control its expenditures and in the event of a conflict with this Chapter, the provisions of Chapter 120 of the General Statutes shall control. Nothing in this Chapter abrogates or diminishes the inherent power of the legislative, executive, or judicial branch.

(c) Purpose. - This Chapter establishes procedures for the following:

(1) Preparing the recommended State budget.

(2) Enacting the State budget.

(3) Administering the State budget.

(d) Definitions. - The following definitions apply in this Chapter:

(1) Appropriation. - An enactment by the General Assembly authorizing the withdrawal of money from the State treasury. An enactment by the General Assembly that authorizes, specifies, or otherwise provides that funds may be used for a particular purpose is not an appropriation.

(1a) Authorized budget. - The certified budget with changes authorized by the Director of the Budget through authority granted in G.S. 143C-6-4 or other statutes.

(1b) Availability. - The total anticipated cash available within a fund for appropriation purposes, including unreserved fund balance and all revenue and receipts anticipated in a fiscal year.

(2) Biennium. - The two fiscal years beginning on July 1 of each odd-numbered year and ending on June 30 of the next odd-numbered year.

(3) Budget. - A plan to provide and spend money for specified programs, functions, activities, or objects during a fiscal year.

(4) Budget year. - The fiscal year for which a budget is proposed and enacted.

(5) Capital improvement. - A term that includes real property acquisition, new construction or rehabilitation of existing facilities, and repairs and renovations.

(6) Capital Improvements Appropriations Act. - An act of the General Assembly containing appropriations for one or more capital improvement projects.

(7) Certified budget. - The budget as enacted by the General Assembly including adjustments made for (i) distributions to State agencies from statewide reserves appropriated by the General Assembly, (ii) distributions of reserves appropriated to a specific agency by the General Assembly, and (iii) organizational or budget changes mandated by the General Assembly.

(7a) Continuation budget. - That part of the Recommended State Budget necessary to continue the same level of services in the next biennium as is provided in the current fiscal year, including (i) mandated Social Security rate adjustments; (ii) annualization of programs and positions; (iii) enrollment adjustments for public schools and Medicaid; (iv) reductions to adjust for items funded with nonrecurring funds during the prior fiscal biennium; (v) increases to adjust for nonrecurring reductions during the prior fiscal biennium; and (vi) if deemed necessary by the Director, other adjustments such as inflation, building reserves, and equipment replacement.

(8) Controller. - The Office of the State Controller.

(9) Current Operations Appropriations Act. - An act of the General Assembly estimating revenue availability for and appropriating money for the current operations of State government during one or more budget years.

(10) Departmental receipt. - Fees, licenses, federal funds, grants, fines, penalties, tuition, and other similar collections or credits generated by State agencies in the course of performing their governmental functions that are applied to the cost of a program administered by the State agency or transferred to the Civil Penalty and Forfeiture Fund pursuant to G.S. 115C-457.1, and that are not defined as tax proceeds or nontax revenues. Departmental receipts may include moneys transferred into a fiscal year from a prior fiscal year.

(11) Director. - The Director of the Budget, who is the Governor.

(12) Encumbrance. - A financial obligation created by a purchase order, contract, salary commitment, unearned or prepaid collections for services provided by the State, or other legally binding agreement.

(13) Fiscal period. - A fiscal biennium beginning in odd-numbered years or the first or second fiscal year within a fiscal biennium.

(14) Fiscal year. - The annual period beginning July 1 and ending on the following June 30.

(15) Fund. - A fiscal and accounting entity with a self-balancing set of accounts recording cash and other resources, together with all related liabilities and residual equities or balances, and changes therein, for the purpose of carrying on stated programs, activities, and objectives of State government.

(16) General Fund Operating Budget. - The sum of all appropriations from the General Fund for a fiscal year, except appropriations for (i) capital improvements, including repairs and renovations, and (ii) one-time expenditures due to natural disasters or other emergencies shall not be included.

(16a) Increase the scope. - With respect to a capital improvement project, either increasing the square footage of a capital improvement project by more than ten percent (10%) of the amount authorized or programming new functions into the project.

(17) Information technology. - As defined in G.S. 147-33.81(2).

(18) Non-State entity. - Any of the following that is not a State agency: an individual, a firm, a partnership, an association, a county, a corporation, or any other organization or group acting as a unit. The term includes a unit of local government and public authority.

(19) Nontax revenue. - Revenue that is not a tax proceed or a departmental receipt and that is required by statute to be credited to a fund.

(20) Object or line item. - An expenditure or receipt in a recommended or enacted budget that is designated in the Budget Code Structure of the North Carolina Accounting System Uniform Chart of Accounts prescribed by the Office of the State Controller.

(21) Performance information. - The organizational structure, agency activity statements, performance indicators, and analyses of program efficiency and effectiveness.

(22) Public authority. - A municipal corporation that is not a unit of local government or a local governmental authority, board, commission, council, or agency that (i) is not a municipal corporation and (ii) operates on an area, regional, or multiunit basis, and the budgeting and accounting systems of which are not fully a part of the budgeting and accounting systems of a unit of local government.

(23) Purpose or program. - A group of objects or line items for support of a specific activity outlined in a recommended or enacted budget that is designated by a nine-digit fund code in accordance with the Budget Code Structure of the North Carolina Accounting System Uniform Chart of Accounts prescribed by the Office of the State Controller.

(24) State agency. - A unit of the executive, legislative, or judicial branch of State government, such as a department, an institution, a division, a commission, a board, a council, or The University of North Carolina. The term does not include a unit of local government or a public authority.

(25) State funds. - Any moneys including federal funds deposited in the State treasury except moneys deposited in a trust fund or agency fund as described in G.S. 143C-1-3.

(26) State resources. - All financial and nonfinancial assets of the State.

(27) State revenue. - An increase, other than interfund transfers and debt issue proceeds, in the financial assets of any State governmental or proprietary fund.

(28) Statutory appropriation. - An appropriation that authorizes the withdrawal of funds from the State treasury during fiscal years extending beyond the current fiscal biennium, without further act of the General Assembly.

(29) Unit of local government. - A municipal corporation that has the power to levy taxes, including a consolidated city-county, as defined by G.S. 160B-2(1), and all boards, agencies, commissions, authorities, and institutions thereof that are not municipal corporations.

(30) Unreserved fund balance. - The available cash balance effective June 30 after excluding documented encumbrances, unearned revenue, statutory requirements, and other legal obligations to a fund's cash balance as determined by the State Controller. Beginning unreserved fund balance equals ending unreserved fund balance from the prior fiscal year. (2006-66, s. 6.19(h); 2006-203, s. 3; 2006-221, s. 3A; 2006-259, s. 40(h); 2007-393, s. 2; 2010-31, s. 30.8; 2013-360, s. 6.12(a), (b), (h), (i).)

§ 143C-1-2. Appropriations: constitutional requirement; reversions.

(a) Appropriation Required to Withdraw State Funds From the State Treasury. - In accordance with Section 7 of Article V of the North Carolina Constitution, no money shall be drawn from the State treasury but in consequence of appropriations made by law. A law enacted by the General Assembly that authorizes the expenditure of money from the State treasury is an appropriation; however, an enactment by the General Assembly that authorizes, specifies, or otherwise provides that funds may be used for a particular purpose is not an appropriation.

(b) Reversions. - Unless otherwise provided by law, at the end of the fiscal year the unexpended, unencumbered balance of an appropriation reverts to the fund from which the appropriation was made; except that (i) an appropriation to the General Assembly shall not revert unless otherwise provided by the Legislative Services Commission, (ii) an appropriation for a capital improvement project shall revert as provided by G.S. 143C-8-11, and (iii) an appropriation for the implementation of information technology (IT) projects shall not revert until the project is implemented or abandoned. (2006-203, s. 3.)

§ 143C-1-3. Fund types.

(a) Types. - The Controller shall account for State resources through use of the fund types listed in this subsection. The Controller may not establish a fund type that differs from the listed fund types unless the Governmental Accounting Standards Board has approved the use of the different fund type.

The fund types are described as follows, except that where a conflict exists between a description used in this section and the definition of the corresponding fund type issued by the Governmental Accounting Standards Board, it is presumed that the definition issued by the Governmental Accounting Standards Board shall prevail.

Governmental Funds.

(1) Capital Projects Funds. - Accounts for financial resources to be used for the acquisition or construction of major capital facilities other than those financed by proprietary funds or in trust funds for individuals, private organizations, or other governments. Capital outlays financed from general obligation bond proceeds should be accounted for through a capital projects fund.

(2) Debt Service Funds. - Accounts for the accumulation of resources for, and the payment of, general long-term debt principal and interest.

(3) General Fund. - Accounts for all financial resources except those required to be reported in another fund.

(4) Special Revenue Funds. - Accounts for the proceeds of specific revenue sources, other than trusts for individuals, private organizations, or other governments or for major capital projects, that are legally restricted to expenditure for specified purposes.

(5) Permanent Funds. - Accounts for resources that are legally restricted to the extent that only earnings, and not principal, may be used for purposes that support the reporting government's programs.

Proprietary Funds.

(6) Enterprise Funds. - Accounts for any activity for which a fee is charged to external users for goods or services. Activities are required to be reported as enterprise funds if any one of the following criteria is met. Each of these criteria should be applied in the context of the activity's principal revenue sources.

a. The activity is financed with debt that is secured solely by a pledge of the net revenues from fees and charges of the activity.

b. Laws or regulations require that the activity's costs of providing services, including capital costs, be recovered with fees and charges rather than with taxes or similar revenues.

c. The pricing policies of the activity establish fees and charges designed to recover its costs, including capital costs.

(7) Internal Service Funds. - Accounts for any activity that provides goods or services to other funds, departments, or agencies of the primary government and its component units, or to other governments, on a cost-reimbursement basis. Internal service funds should be used only if the reporting government is the predominant participant in the activity. Otherwise, the activity should be reported as an enterprise fund.

Agency and Trust Funds.

(8) Agency Funds. - Accounts for resources held by the reporting government in a purely custodial capacity. Agency funds typically involve only the receipt, temporary investment, and remittance of fiduciary resources to individuals, private organizations, or other governments.

(9) Investment Trust Funds. - Accounts for the external portion of investment pools reported by the sponsoring government.

(10) Pension and Other Employee Benefit Trust Funds. - Accounts for resources that are required to be held in trust for the members and beneficiaries

of defined benefit pension plans, defined contribution plans, other postemployment benefit plans, or other employee benefit plans.

(11) Private-Purpose Trust Funds. - Accounts for all other trust arrangements under which principal and income benefit individuals, private organizations, or other governments.

(b) Designation. - If State resources are designated by law as a fund or an account within a fund and there is a conflict between the legal designation and the appropriate accounting designation of the State resources, then the Controller shall determine the appropriate designation of the State resources based on the intended use and financial treatment of the State resources as set out in the law establishing the fund or account. The Controller shall determine the fund type of all separate funds and account for them accordingly. The Controller shall keep the total number of funds to the minimum number practical.

(c) Notwithstanding subsections (a) and (b) of this section, funds established for The University of North Carolina and its constituent institutions pursuant to the following statutes are exempt from Chapter 143C of the General Statutes and shall be accounted for as provided by those statutes, except that the provisions of Article 8 of Chapter 143C of the General Statutes shall apply to the funds: G.S. 116-35, 116-36, 116-36.1, 116-36.2, 116-36.4, 116-36.5, 116-36.6, 116-44.4, 116-68, 116-220, 116-235. (2006-203, s. 3; 2013-360, s. 6.12(c).)

§ 143C-1-4. Interest earnings credited to the General Fund; interest earnings on Highway Fund and Highway Trust Fund credited to those funds.

(a) Interest Earnings Credited to the General Fund. - Unless otherwise provided by law, interest earned on all funds shall be credited to the General Fund.

(b) Exception for Interest Earnings on Highway Fund and Highway Trust Fund. - Interest earned by the Highway Fund and the Highway Trust Fund shall be credited to the Highway Fund and the Highway Trust Fund respectively. (2006-203, s. 3.)

§ 143C-1-5. Chapter is applicable to The University of North Carolina.

Except as expressly provided in G.S. 143C-1-3(c) or otherwise expressly provided by law, The University of North Carolina shall be subject to the provisions of this Chapter in the same manner and to the same degree as other State agencies. (2013-360, s. 6.12(d).)

Article 2.

Director of the Budget.

§ 143C-2-1. Governor is Director of the Budget.

(a)   Governor is Director of the Budget. - The Governor is the Director of the Budget. In that capacity, the Governor is required by Article III, Section 5(3) of the North Carolina Constitution to prepare and recommend a budget and to administer the budget as enacted by the General Assembly. The Governor's powers under this Chapter extend to all agencies, institutions, departments, bureaus, boards, and commissions of the State of North Carolina under whatever name now or hereafter known. The Governor may delegate the authority to perform a power or duty of the Director under this Chapter to the Office of State Budget and Management or to one or more persons.

(b)   State Agencies and Non-State Entities to Provide Information Requested by the Director; Examination of Persons and Agencies by Director. - Upon request, all State agencies and non-State entities subject to this act shall furnish the Director, in the form and at the time requested by the Director, any information desired by the Director in relation to their respective activities or fiscal affairs so long as the information is not confidential pursuant to federal or State law. The Director may subpoena and examine under oath any person directly or indirectly responsible for the operations of any executive State agency or any non-State entity subject to the provisions of this Chapter.

(c)   Governor May Request State Auditor to Audit State Agency or Non-State Entity Receiving State Funds. - As authorized by G.S. 147-64.6(c)(3), the Governor may request the State Auditor to make an audit of or cause an audit to be made of the books and accounts of any State agency and may require that the cost of the audit be borne by the State agency. The Governor may also request the State Auditor to make an audit of or cause an audit to be made of the books and records of any non-State entity receiving State funds pursuant to the State Auditor's authority granted in G.S. 147-64.7. (2006-203, s. 3.)

§ 143C-2-2. Collection of State Budget Statistics.

The Director shall coordinate the efforts of governmental agencies to collect, disseminate, and analyze economic, demographic, and social statistics pertinent to State budgeting. The Director shall do all of the following:

(1) Prepare and release the official demographic and economic estimates and projections for the State.

(2) Conduct special economic and demographic analyses and studies to support statewide budgeting.

(3) Develop and coordinate cooperative arrangements with federal, State, and local governmental agencies to facilitate the exchange of data to support State budgeting.

(4) Report major trends that influence revenues and expenditures in the State budget in the current fiscal year and that may influence revenues and expenditures over the next five fiscal years. (2006-203, s. 3.)

§ 143C-2-3. Fiscal analysis required for any State agency bill that affects the budget.

A State agency proposing a bill that affects the State budget shall prepare a fiscal analysis for the bill and submit the analysis to the Fiscal Research Division upon introduction of the bill. The fiscal analysis shall estimate the impact of the legislation on the State budget for the first five fiscal years the legislation would be in effect. (2006-203, s. 3.)

§ 143C-2-4. Director of the Budget may direct State Treasurer to borrow money for certain payments.

The Director of the Budget, by and with the consent of the Governor and Council of State, may authorize and direct the State Treasurer to borrow in the name of the State, in anticipation of the collection of taxes, such sum as may be necessary to make the payments on the appropriations as even as possible and to preserve the best interest of the State in the conduct of the various State agencies during each fiscal year. (2006-203, s. 3.)

§ 143C-2-5. Grants and contracts database.

(a) The Director of the Budget shall require the Office of State Budget and Management, with the support of the Office of Information Technology Services, to build and maintain a database and Web site for providing a single, searchable Web site on State spending for grants and contracts to be known as NC OpenBook.

(b) Each head of a principal department listed in G.S. 143B-6 shall conduct a review monthly of all State contracts and grants administered by that principal department.

(c) All State institutions, departments, bureaus, agencies, or commissions subject to the authority of the Director of the Budget that maintain a Web site shall be required to include an access link to the NC OpenBook Web site on the home page of the agency Web site. Each agency shall also prominently display a search engine on the agency Web site home page to allow for ease of searching for information, including contracts and grants, on the agency's Web site. (2010-169, s. 9.)

§ 143C-2-6. Contents of database and Web site.

(a) The Office of State Controller, the Department of Administration, and the Office of Information Technology Services shall provide the Office of State Budget and Management with the statewide information on State contracts necessary for the development and maintenance of the database and Web site required by this Article, with the information updated at least monthly.

(b) The Office of State Budget and Management shall work with the Office of the State Auditor and the Grant Information Center to incorporate data on grants into the database and Web site required by this Article. All State institutions, departments, bureaus, agencies, or commissions subject to the authority of the Governor shall make necessary changes to existing reporting processes for contracts and grants to ensure the goals of this Article are met.

(c)   All State contracts and grants awarded in amounts in excess of ten thousand dollars ($10,000) shall be included in the database and Web site required by this Article. The following information shall be provided for each contract or grant:

(1)   The name of the entity receiving the award.

(2)   The amount of the award or estimated award.

(3)   Information on the award, including type of transaction, funding agency, and duration of the contract or grant.

(4)   The location of the entity receiving the award.

(5)   Background information on the entity receiving the award.

(6)   Time lines for anticipated completion of the work required.

(7)   Expected outcomes of the contract or grant and specific deliverables required.

(8)   Contact information for the responsible State government officer or administrator of the contract or grant. (2010-169, s. 9.)

Article 3.

Development of the Governor's Recommended Budget.

§ 143C-3-1. Budget estimate for the legislative branch.

The Legislative Services Officer shall give the Director an estimate of the financial needs of the legislative branch for the upcoming fiscal period in accordance with the schedule prescribed by the Director. The estimates for the legislative branch shall be approved and certified by the President Pro Tempore of the Senate and the Speaker of the House of Representatives. The estimates shall be itemized in accordance with the accounting classifications adopted by the Controller. The Director shall include the estimates in the budget the Director submits to the General Assembly. The Director may recommend changes to these estimates in the budget submitted to the General Assembly. (2006-66, s. 6.19(g); 2006-203, s. 3; 2006-221, s. 3A; 2006-259, s. 40(g).)

§ 143C-3-2. Budget estimate for the judicial branch.

The Administrative Officer of the Courts shall give the Director an estimate of the financial needs of the judicial branch for the upcoming fiscal period in accordance with the schedule prescribed by the Director. The estimates for the judiciary shall be approved and certified by the Chief Justice. The estimates shall be itemized in accordance with the accounting classifications adopted by the Controller. The Director shall include these estimates for the judicial branch in the budget the Director submits to the General Assembly. The Director may recommend changes to these estimates in the budget the Director submits to the General Assembly. (2006-203, s. 3; 2007-393, s. 3.)

§ 143C-3-3. Budget requests from State agencies in the executive branch.

(a)   General Provisions. - A State agency that is not in the legislative or judicial branch of government shall submit its budget requests for the upcoming fiscal period to the Director in accordance with the schedule prescribed by the Director. The Director shall give each State agency instructions to be used in estimating the funds required to provide necessary State government programs and capital improvements. The estimates shall be itemized in accordance with the accounting classifications adopted by the Controller and shall be approved and certified by the respective head or responsible officer of the agency submitting them.

(b)   University of North Carolina System Request. - Notwithstanding the requirement in G.S. 116-11 that the Board of Governors prepare a unified budget request for all of the constituent institutions of The University of North Carolina, repairs and renovations, capital fund requests, and information technology requests shall comply with subsections (c), (d), and (e) of this section.

(c) Repairs and Renovations Funds Request. - In addition to any other information requested by the Director, any State agency proposing to repair or renovate an existing facility shall accompany that request with all of the following:

(1) A description of current deficiencies and proposed corrections with a review and evaluation of that proposal prepared by the Department of Administration.

(2) An estimate of project costs approved by the Department of Administration.

(3) A certification of project feasibility as described in G.S. 143-341, except that in the case of a project of The University of North Carolina for which advance planning has not been completed, the request may be submitted without this certification.

(4) An explanation of the method by which the repair or renovation is to be financed.

(d) Capital Funds Request. - In addition to any other information requested by the Director, any State agency proposing to (i) acquire real property, (ii) construct a new facility, (iii) expand the building area (sq. ft.) of an existing facility, or (iv) rehabilitate an existing facility to accommodate new or expanded uses shall accompany that request with all of the following:

(1) An estimate of its space needs and other physical requirements, together with a review and evaluation of that estimate prepared by the Department of Administration, except that in the case of a project of The University of North Carolina for which advance planning has not been completed, the estimate of space needs may be a preliminary estimate.

(2) An estimate of project costs and cash flow requirements approved by the Department of Administration.

(3) A certification of project feasibility as described in G.S. 143-341, except that in the case of a project of The University of North Carolina for which advance planning has not been completed, the request may be submitted without this certification.

(4) An explanation of the method by which the acquisition, construction, or rehabilitation is to be financed.

(5) An estimate of maintenance and operating costs, including personnel, for the project, covering the first five years of operation.

(6) An estimate of revenues, if any, to be derived from the project, covering the first five years of operation.

This subsection does not apply to requests for State resources for railroad, highway, or bridge construction or renovation.

(e) Information Technology Request. - In addition to any other information requested by the Director, any State agency requesting significant State resources, as defined by the Director, for the purpose of acquiring or maintaining information technology shall accompany that request with all of the following:

(1) A statement of its needs for information technology and related resources, including expected improvements to programmatic or business operations, together with a review and evaluation of that statement prepared by the State Chief Information Officer.

(2) A statement setting forth the requirements for State resources, together with an evaluation of those requirements by the State Chief Information Officer that takes into consideration the State's current technology, the opportunities for technology sharing, the requirements of Article 3D of Chapter 147 of the General Statutes, and any other factors relevant to the analysis.

(3) A statement by the State Chief Information Officer that sets forth viable alternatives, if any, for meeting the agency needs in an economical and efficient manner.

(4) In the case of an acquisition, an explanation of the method by which the acquisition is to be financed.

This subsection shall not apply to requests submitted by the General Assembly or the Administrative Office of the Courts. (2006-203, s. 3; 2007-117, s. 5(a); 2011-145, s. 30.12(a); 2013-360, s. 6.12(j).)

§ 143C-3-4. Budget requests from non-State entities.

Unless otherwise provided by law, budget requests from non-State entities shall be submitted to the Director or to a State agency designated by the Director. A State agency designated to receive a budget request from a non-State entity shall evaluate the request and forward its evaluation to the Director in accordance with procedures established by the Director. This section does not apply to the General Assembly or to actions of the General Assembly to appropriate funds to non-State entities. (2006-203, s. 3.)

§ 143C-3-5. Budget recommendations and budget message.

(a)   Budget Proposals. - The Governor shall present budget recommendations, consistent with G.S. 143C-3-1, 143C-3-2, and 143C-3-3 to each regular session of the General Assembly at a mutually agreeable time to be fixed by joint resolution.

(b)   Odd-Numbered Years. - In odd-numbered years the budget recommendations shall include the following components:

(1)   A Recommended State Budget setting forth goals for improving the State with recommended expenditure requirements, funding sources, and performance information for each State government program and for each proposed capital improvement. The Recommended State Budget may be presented in a format chosen by the Director, except that the Recommended State Budget shall clearly distinguish program continuation requirements, program reductions, program eliminations, program expansions, and new programs, and shall explain all proposed capital improvements in the context of the Six-Year Capital Improvements Plan and as required by G.S. 143C-8-6.

(1a)   The Governor's Recommended State Budget shall include a continuation budget, which shall be presented in the budget support document pursuant to subdivision (2) of this subsection.

(2)   A Budget Support Document showing, for each budget code and purpose or program in State government, accounting detail corresponding to the Recommended State Budget.

a. The Budget Support Document shall employ the North Carolina Accounting System Uniform Chart of Accounts adopted by the State Controller to show both uses and sources of funds and shall display in separate parallel columns all of the following: (i) actual expenditures and receipts for the most recent fiscal year for which actual information is available, (ii) the certified budget for the preceding fiscal year, (iii) the currently authorized budget for the preceding fiscal year, (iv) program continuation requirements for each fiscal year of the biennium, (v) proposed expenditures and receipts for each fiscal year of the biennium, and (vi) proposed increases and decreases.

b. The Budget Support Document shall include detailed information on recommended expenditures for capital improvements as required by G.S. 143C-8-6.

c. The Budget Support Document shall include accurate projections of receipts, expenditures, and fund balances. Estimated receipts, including tuition collected by university or community college institutions, shall be adjusted to reflect actual collections from the previous fiscal year, unless the Director recommends a change that will result in collections in the budget year that differ from prior year actuals, or the Director otherwise determines there is a more reasonable basis upon which to accurately project receipts. Revenue and expenditure detail provided in the Budget Support Document shall be no less detailed than the two-digit level in the North Carolina Accounting System Uniform Chart of Accounts as prescribed by the State Controller.

d. The Budget Support Document shall clearly identify all proposed expenditures supported by existing or proposed appropriations, including statutory appropriations.

(3) A Current Operations Appropriations Act that makes appropriations for each fiscal year of the upcoming biennium for the operating expenses of all State agencies as contained in the Recommended State Budget, together with a Capital Improvements Appropriations Act that authorizes any capital improvements projects.

(4) The biennial State Information Technology Plan as outlined in G.S. 147-33.72B to be consistent in facilitating the goals outlined in the Recommended State Budget.

(5)   A list of budget adjustments made during the prior fiscal year pursuant to G.S. 143C-6-4 that are included in the proposed continuation budget for the upcoming fiscal year.

(c)   Even-Numbered Years. - In even-numbered years, the Governor may recommend changes in the enacted budget for the second year of the biennium. These recommendations shall be presented as amendments to the enacted budget and shall be incorporated in a recommended Current Operations Appropriation Act and a recommended Capital Improvements Appropriations Act as necessary. Any recommended changes shall clearly distinguish program reductions, program eliminations, program expansions, and new programs, and shall explain all proposed capital improvements in the context of the Six-Year Capital Improvements Plan and as required by G.S. 143C-8-6. The Governor shall provide sufficient supporting documentation and accounting detail, consistent with that required by G.S. 143C-3-5(b), corresponding to the recommended amendments to the enacted budget.

(d)   Funds Included in Budget. - Consistent with requirements of the North Carolina Constitution, Article 5, Section 7(1), the Governor's Recommended State Budget, together with the Budget Support Document, shall include recommended expenditures of State funds from all Governmental and Proprietary Funds, as those funds are described in G.S. 143C-1-3, and all funds established for The University of North Carolina and its constituent institutions that are subject to this Chapter. Except where provided otherwise by federal law, funds received from the federal government become State funds when deposited in the State treasury and shall be classified and accounted for in the Governor's budget recommendations no differently than funds from other sources.

(e)   Availability Estimates. - The recommended Current Operations Appropriations Act shall contain a statement showing the estimates of General Fund availability, Highway Fund availability, and Highway Trust Fund availability upon which the Recommended State Budget is based.

(f)   Budget Message. - The Governor's budget recommendations shall be accompanied by a written budget message that does all of the following:

(1)   Explains the goals embodied in the recommended budget.

(2)   Explains important features of the activities anticipated in the budget.

(3) Explains the assumptions underlying the statement of revenue availability.

(4) Sets forth the reasons for changes from the previous biennium or fiscal year, as appropriate, in terms of programs, program goals, appropriation levels, and revenue yields.

(5) Identifies anticipated sources of funding for major spending initiatives.

(6) Prepares a fiscal analysis that addresses the State's budget outlook for the upcoming five-year period. This fiscal analysis shall include detailed estimates for five years for any proposals to create new or significantly expand programs and for proposals to create new or change existing law.

(g) Different Gubernatorial Administrations. - For years in which there will be a change in gubernatorial administrations, the incumbent Governor shall complete the budget recommendations and budget message by December 15 and deliver them to the Governor-elect. (2006-203, s. 3; 2007-393, s. 4; 2012-194, s. 34; 2013-360, s. 6.12(e), (k).)

Article 4.

Budget Requirements.

§ 143C-4-1. Annual balanced budget.

The budget recommended by the Governor and the budget enacted by the General Assembly shall be balanced and shall include two fiscal years beginning on July 1 of each odd-numbered year. Each fiscal year and each fund shall be balanced separately. The budget for a fund is balanced when the beginning unreserved fund balance for the fiscal year, together with the projected receipts to the fund during the fiscal year, is equal to or greater than the sum of appropriations from the fund for that fiscal year. (2006-203, s. 3.)

§ 143C-4-2. Savings Reserve Account and appropriation of General Fund unreserved fund balance.

(a) Creation and Source of Funds. - The Savings Reserve Account is established as a reserve in the General Fund. The Controller shall reserve to the Savings Reserve Account one-fourth of any unreserved fund balance, as determined on a cash basis, remaining in the General Fund at the end of each fiscal year.

(b) Use of Funds. - The Savings Reserve Account is a component of the unappropriated General Fund balance. Funds reserved to the Savings Reserve Account shall be available for expenditure only upon an act of appropriation by the General Assembly.

(c) Goal for Savings Reserve Account Balance. - The General Assembly recognizes the need to establish and maintain sufficient reserves to address unanticipated events and circumstances such as natural disasters, economic downturns, threats to public safety, health, and welfare, and other emergencies. It is a goal of the General Assembly and the State to accumulate and maintain a balance in the Savings Reserve Account equal to or greater than eight percent (8%) of the prior year's General Fund operating budget. (2006-203, s. 3.)

§ 143C-4-3. Repairs and Renovations Reserve.

(a) Creation and Source of Funds. - The Repairs and Renovations Reserve is established as a reserve in the General Fund. The State Controller shall reserve to the Repairs and Renovations Reserve one-fourth of any unreserved fund balance, as determined on a cash basis, remaining in the General Fund at the end of each fiscal year.

(b) Use of Funds. - The funds in the Repairs and Renovations Reserve shall be used only for the repair and renovation of (i) State facilities and related infrastructure that are supported from the General Fund or (ii) State Information Technology Services facilities and related infrastructure. Funds from the Repairs and Renovations Reserve shall be used only for the following types of projects:

(1) Roof repairs and replacements;

(2) Structural repairs;

(3) Repairs and renovations to meet federal and State standards;

(4)   Repairs to electrical, plumbing, and heating, ventilating, and air-conditioning systems;

(5)   Improvements to meet the requirements of the Americans with Disabilities Act, 42 U.S.C. § 12101, et seq., as amended;

(6)   Improvements to meet fire safety needs;

(7)   Improvements to existing facilities for energy efficiency;

(8)   Improvements to remove asbestos, lead paint, and other contaminants, including the removal and replacement of underground storage tanks;

(9)   Improvements and renovations to improve use of existing space;

(10)   Historical restoration;

(11)   Improvements to roads, walks, drives, utilities infrastructure; and

(12)   Drainage and landscape improvements.

Funds from the Repairs and Renovations Reserve shall not be used for new construction or the expansion of the building area (sq. ft.) of an existing facility unless required in order to comply with federal or State codes or standards.

(c)   Use of Funds. - Funds Available Only Upon Appropriation. - Funds reserved to the Repairs and Renovations Reserve shall be available for expenditure only upon an act of appropriation by the General Assembly.

(d)   Allocation and Reallocation of Funds for Particular Projects. - Any funds in the Repairs and Renovations Reserve that are allocated to the Board of Governors of The University of North Carolina or to the Office of State Budget and Management may be allocated or reallocated by those agencies for repairs and renovations projects so long as all of the following conditions are satisfied:

(1)   Any project that receives an allocation or reallocation satisfies the requirements of subsection (b) of this section.

(2)   If the allocation or reallocation of funds from one project to another under this section is two million five hundred thousand dollars ($2,500,000) or more for a particular project, the Office of State Budget and Management or the

Board of Governors, as appropriate, consults with the Joint Legislative Commission on Governmental Operations prior to the expenditure or reallocation.

(3)   If the allocation or reallocation of funds from one project to another under this section is less than two million five hundred thousand dollars ($2,500,000) for a particular project, the allocation or reallocation of funds is reported to the Joint Legislative Commission on Governmental Operations within 60 days of the expenditure or reallocation.

(e)   Repealed by Session Laws 2013-360, s. 6.12(l), effective July 1, 2013. (2006-203, s. 3; 2011-145, s. 30.11(a); 2012-142, s. 26.11; 2013-360, ss. 6.12(l), 36.5(d).)

§ 143C-4-4. Contingency and Emergency Fund.

(a)   Creation. - The Contingency and Emergency Fund is established within the General Fund. The General Assembly shall appropriate a specific amount to this fund for contingencies and emergencies in the Current Operations Appropriations Act or other appropriations bill.

(b)   Authorized Uses. - Notwithstanding any other provision of law, funds appropriated to the Contingency and Emergency Fund may be used only for expenditures required: (i) by a court or Industrial Commission order, (ii) to respond to events as authorized under G.S. 166A-19.40(a) of the North Carolina Emergency Management Act, or (iii) for other statutorily authorized purposes or other contingencies and emergencies.

(c)   Request for Allocation. - A State agency may request an allocation from the Contingency and Emergency Fund by submitting a request in writing to the Director along with any information required by the Director. If the Director approves the request, the Director shall present the request, together with a recommendation, to the Council of State for its approval. If the Council of State approves the request, the Director shall order the Controller to allocate the funds requested. The Director shall report on the request at the next scheduled meeting of the Joint Legislative Commission on Governmental Operations. (2006-203, s. 3; 2012-12, s. 2(v).)

§ 143C-4-5. Non-State match restrictions.

Whenever money is required to match an appropriation made for a specific purpose by the State of North Carolina, the recipient of the appropriation shall actually receive as a gift, grant, earnings in actual money, or a pledge that can be used as collateral in any prudent loan transaction, the matching amount required. The recipient shall retain the matching amount received in its possession until spent for that purpose and shall spend an equal percentage of the appropriation and of the matching amount each time an expenditure is made, unless the individual appropriation requires otherwise. (2006-203, s. 3.)

§ 143C-4-6. General Fund operating budget size limited.

(a) Size Limitation. - Except as otherwise provided in this section, the General Fund operating budget each fiscal year shall not be greater than seven percent (7%) of the projected total State personal income for that fiscal year.

(b) Increase in Size Limitation. - To the extent that any percent increase in appropriations for a fiscal year for (i) Medicaid, (ii) operation of prisons, or (iii) operation of the courts or (iv) the costs of providing health insurance for teachers and State employees, exceeds the percent increase in State personal income growth for the same period, the limitation on the size of the General Fund operating budget provided in subsection (a) of this section for that fiscal year shall be increased by the dollar amount represented by the excess percentage. For all subsequent fiscal years, the percent limitation contained in subsection (a) shall then be increased to reflect that dollar adjustment.

(c) Fiscal Reports. - The Office of State Budget and Management and the Fiscal Research Division of the General Assembly shall each submit a tentative estimate of total State personal income for the upcoming fiscal year to the General Assembly no later than February 1 of each year. The Office and the Fiscal Research Division shall each submit a final projection of total State personal income for the upcoming fiscal year to the General Assembly no later than May 1 of each year. The General Assembly shall use the lower of the two final projections to calculate the limitation on the size of the General Fund operating budget provided in this section. (2006-203, s. 3; 2007-393, s. 5.)

§ 143C-4-7. Limit on number of permanent positions budgeted.

The total number of permanent budgeted positions established in State agencies shall not be increased by the end of any State fiscal year by a greater percentage rate of change than the percentage rate of change of the residential population growth for the State of North Carolina. The Office of State Budget and Management shall be responsible for computing the annual percentage rates of change for each measure. The population growth rate shall be computed by averaging the annual residential population growth rate in each of the preceding 10 fiscal years as stated in the annual estimates of residential population in North Carolina made by the United States Census Bureau. The growth rate of the number of budgeted positions shall be computed by averaging the annual rate of growth of State budgeted positions in each of the preceding 10 fiscal years. The total number of permanent budgeted positions established in State agencies shall be computed by adding the total number of budgeted Full-Time Equivalents from all fund types. This section does not apply to State-funded positions supported by the State in a local public school system or local community college institution. (2006-203, s. 3.)

Article 5.

Enactment of the Budget.

§ 143C-5-1. Rules for the introduction of the Governor's appropriations bills.

The Current Operations Appropriations Act recommended by the Governor and the Capital Improvements Appropriations Act recommended by the Governor shall be introduced by the chairs of the committee on appropriations in each house of the General Assembly. This section shall be considered and treated as a rule of procedure in the Senate and House of Representatives unless provided otherwise by a rule of either branch of the General Assembly. (2006-203, s. 3.)

§ 143C-5-2. Order of appropriations bills.

Each house of the General Assembly shall first pass its version of the Current Operations Appropriations Act on third reading and order it sent to the other chamber before placing any other appropriations bill on the calendar for second reading. This section does not apply to the following bills:

(1)   An appropriations bill to respond to an emergency as defined by G.S. 166A-19.3.

(2)   An appropriations bill making adjustments to the current year budget.

(3)   An appropriations bill authorizing continued operations at current funding levels. (2006-203, s. 3; 2012-12, s. 2(w).)

§ 143C-5-3. Availability statement required.

The Current Operations Appropriations Act enacted by the General Assembly shall state the General Fund, Highway Fund, and Highway Trust Fund availability used as basis for appropriations from those funds. (2006-203, s. 3.)

§ 143C-5-4. Enactment deadline.

The General Assembly shall enact the Current Operations Appropriations Act by June 15 of odd-numbered years and by June 30 of even-numbered years in which a Current Operations Appropriations Act is enacted. (2006-203, s. 3.)

§ 143C-5-5. Committee report used to construe intent of budget acts.

A committee report incorporated by reference in the Current Operations Appropriations Act or the Capital Improvements Appropriations Act and distributed on the floor of the House of Representatives and of the Senate as part of the explanation of the act is to be construed with the appropriate act in interpreting its intent. If a report conflicts with the act, the act prevails. The Director of the Fiscal Research Division of the Legislative Services Commission shall send a copy of the reports to the Director. (2006-203, s. 3.)

Article 6.

Administration of the Budget.

Part 1. Certification and Administration of the Budget.

§ 143C-6-1. Budget enacted by the General Assembly; certified budgets of State agencies.

(a) Governor to Administer the Budget as Enacted by the General Assembly. - In accordance with Section 5(3) of Article III of the North Carolina Constitution, the Governor shall administer the budget as enacted by the General Assembly. All appropriations of State funds now or hereafter made to the State agencies and non-State entities authorize expenditures only for the (i) purposes or programs and (ii) objects or line items enumerated in the Recommended State Budget and the Budget Support Document recommended to the General Assembly by the Governor, as amended and enacted by the General Assembly in the Current Operations Appropriations Act, the Capital Improvements Appropriations Act, or any other act affecting the State budget. The Governor shall ensure that appropriations are expended in strict accordance with the budget enacted by the General Assembly.

(b) Departmental Receipts. - Departmental receipts collected to support a program or purpose shall be credited to the fund from which appropriations have been made to support that program or purpose. A State agency shall expend departmental receipts first, including receipts in excess of the amount of receipts budgeted in the certified budget for the program or purpose, and shall expend other funds appropriated for the purpose or program only to the extent that receipts are insufficient to meet the costs anticipated in the certified budget.

Except as authorized in G.S. 143C-6-4, excess departmental receipts shall not be used to increase expenditures for a purpose or program.

(c) Certification of the Budget. - The Director of the Budget shall certify to each State agency the amount appropriated to it for each program and each object from all funds included in the budget as defined in G.S. 143C-3-5(d). The certified budget for each State agency shall reflect the total of all appropriations enacted for each State agency by the General Assembly in the Current Operations Appropriations Act, the Capital Improvements Appropriations Act, and any other act affecting the State budget. The certified budget for each State agency shall follow the format of the Budget Support Document as modified to reflect changes enacted by the General Assembly. (2006-203, s. 3; 2013-360, s. 6.12(m).)

§ 143C-6-2. Methods to avoid deficit.

(a) Appropriations. - Each appropriation is maximum and conditional. The expenditures authorized by an appropriation from a fund shall be made only if necessary and only if the aggregate revenues to the fund during each fiscal year of the biennium, when added to any unreserved fund balance from the previous fiscal year, are sufficient to support the expenditures.

(b) Revenue Collections. - The Director, with the assistance of the Secretary of Revenue and other officials collecting or receiving appropriated State revenue, shall continuously survey the revenue collections. If the Director finds that revenues to any fund, when added to the beginning unreserved fund balance in that fund, will be insufficient to support appropriations from that fund, the Director shall immediately notify the General Assembly that a deficit is anticipated. The Director shall consult with the Chief Justice to identify expenditure reductions and other lawful measures the Chief Justice and Judicial Branch can implement to reduce expenditures. The Director shall report in a timely manner to the General Assembly a plan containing the expenditure reductions and other lawful measures as the Director is implementing in order to avert the deficit.

(c) Local Governments Funds. - In exercising the powers contained in Section 5(3) of Article III of the North Carolina Constitution, the Governor shall not withhold from distribution funds that have been collected by the State on behalf of local governments or funds that the General Assembly has appropriated to local governments unless the Governor has exhausted all other sources of revenue of the State including any appropriated surplus remaining in the treasury at the beginning of the fiscal period.

In accordance with Section 19 of Article I of the North Carolina Constitution and the Due Process Clause of the United States Constitution, the State is prohibited from taking local tax revenue. This subsection does not authorize the Governor to withhold revenues from taxes levied by units of local governments and collected by the State. (2006-203, s. 3; 2007-393, s. 6.)

§ 143C-6-3. Allotments.

To receive the operating funds appropriated to it, a State agency shall submit to the Director, at intervals and in a format prescribed by the Director, a request for an allotment of the amount estimated to be required for the agency's operating costs during the ensuing fiscal period. The Director shall approve or modify the allotment requests, and the State Controller shall implement the allotments as approved or modified by the Director. (2006-203, s. 3.)

§ 143C-6-4. Budget Adjustments Authorized.

(a) Findings. - The General Assembly recognizes that even the most thorough budget deliberations may be affected by unforeseeable events; therefore, under the limited circumstances set forth in this section, the Director is authorized to adjust the enacted budget by making transfers among lines of expenditure, purposes, or programs or by increasing expenditures funded by departmental receipts.

(b) Budget Adjustments. - Notwithstanding the provisions of G.S. 143C-6-1, a State agency may, with approval of the Director of the Budget, spend more than was appropriated in the certified budget by adjusting the authorized budget for all of the following:

(1) Line items within programs. - An object or line item within a purpose or program so long as the total amount expended for the purpose or program is no more than was authorized in the certified budget for the purpose or program.

(2) Responses to extraordinary events. - A purpose or program if the overexpenditure of the purpose or program is:

a. Required by a court or Industrial Commission order;

b. Authorized under G.S. 166A-19.40(a) of the North Carolina Emergency Management Act; or

c. Required to call out the North Carolina National Guard.

(3) Responses to unforeseen circumstances. - A purpose or program not subject to the provisions of subdivision (b)(2) of this subsection, if each of the following conditions is satisfied:

a. The overexpenditure is required to continue the purpose or programs due to complications or changes in circumstances that could not have been foreseen when the budget for the fiscal period was enacted.

b. The scope of the purpose or program is not increased.

c. The overexpenditure is authorized on a one-time nonrecurring basis for one year only, unless the overexpenditure is the result of (i) salary adjustments authorized by law or (ii) the establishment of time-limited positions funded with agency receipts.

(b1) If the overexpenditure would cause a department's total requirements for a fund to exceed the department's certified budget for a fiscal year for that fund by more than three percent (3%), the Director shall consult with the Joint Legislative Commission on Governmental Operations prior to authorizing the overexpenditure.

(b2) Subsection (b) of this section shall not be construed to authorize budget adjustments that cause General Fund expenditures, excluding expenditures from General Fund receipts, to exceed General Fund appropriations for a department.

(c) Overexpenditures Reported. - The Director shall report quarterly, beginning October 31, to the Joint Legislative Commission on Governmental Operations on overexpenditures approved by the Director under subdivisions (2) and (3) of subsection (b) of this section.

(d) Overexpenditures in Senate Budget. - The President Pro Tempore of the Senate may approve expenditures for more than was authorized in the enacted budget for objects or line items in the budget of the Senate.

(e) Overexpenditures in House of Representatives Budget. - The Speaker of the House of Representatives may approve expenditures for more than was authorized in the enacted budget objects or line items in the budget of the House of Representatives.

(f) Transfers Between Line Items or Programs in General Assembly Budget Other Than Senate and House of Representatives. - Expenditures exceeding amounts authorized for programs, objects, or line items in the budget of the General Assembly other than those of the Senate and House of Representatives shall be approved jointly by the President Pro Tempore of the Senate and the Speaker of the House of Representatives.

(g) Transfers in The University of North Carolina Budget. - Transfers or changes within the budget of The University of North Carolina may be made as provided in Article 1 of Chapter 116 of the General Statutes.

(h) Transfers Within the Office of the Governor. - Transfers or changes as between objects or line items in the budget of the Office of the Governor may be made by the Governor. (2006-203, s. 3; 2007-117, s. 4; 2009-281, s. 1; 2011-183, s. 127(c); 2012-12, s. 2(x); 2013-360, s. 6.12(n).)

§ 143C-6-5. No expenditures for purposes for which the General Assembly has considered but not enacted an appropriation; no fee increases that the General Assembly has rejected.

(a) Notwithstanding any other provision of law, no funds from any source, except for gifts, grants, or funds allocated from the Repair and Renovations Account in accordance with G.S. 143C-4-3, funds allocated from the Contingency and Emergency Fund in accordance with G.S. 143C-4-4, and funds exempted from Chapter 143C in accordance with G.S. 143C-1-3(c) may be expended for any new or expanded purpose, position, or other expenditure for which the General Assembly has considered but not enacted an appropriation of funds for the current fiscal period. For the purpose of this subsection, the General Assembly has considered a purpose, position, or other expenditure when that purpose is included in a bill which fails a reading, or if the purpose is included in the version of a bill that passes one house, but the bill is enacted without the purpose.

(b) Notwithstanding any other provision of law, no fee shall be increased if the General Assembly has rejected an increase of that fee for the current fiscal period. For the purpose of this subsection, the General Assembly has rejected a fee increase when that fee increase is included in a bill which fails a reading, or if the fee increase is included in the version of a bill that passes one house, but the bill is enacted without the fee increase. (2006-66, s. 6.4; 2006-203, s. 3.)

§ 143C-6-5.5. Limitation on use of State funds for abortions.

No State funds may be used for the performance of abortions or to support the administration of any governmental health plan or government-offered insurance policy offering abortion, except that this prohibition shall not apply where (i) the life of the mother would be endangered if the unborn child were carried to term or (ii) the pregnancy is the result of a rape or incest. Nothing in this section shall be construed to limit medical care provided after a spontaneous miscarriage. (2011-145, s. 29.23(a).)

§ 143C-6-6. Positions included in the State Payroll.

(a) Before a State agency establishes a new position or changes the funding of an existing position, the agency shall submit the proposed action to the Director for approval. The Director shall review the proposed action to ensure that funds for the action are included in the amount appropriated to the agency. If the Director approves the action, the Director shall notify the agency and the Controller of the approval. The Controller shall not honor a voucher in payment of a payroll that includes a new position or a change in an existing position that has not been approved by the Director.

(b) Payments on behalf of employees for hospital-medical insurance, longevity payments, salary increments, and legislative salary increases, required employer salary-related contributions for retirement benefits, death benefits, the Disability Income Plan and social security for employees shall be paid from the General Fund or the Highway Fund, only to the extent of the proportionate part paid from the General Fund or Highway Fund, in support of the salary of the employee, and the remainder of the employer's contribution requirements shall be paid from the same source that supplies the remainder of the employee's salary.

(c) Subsection (a) of this section does not apply to The University of North Carolina. (2006-203, s. 3; 2007-484, s. 34.)

§ 143C-6-7. Compliance with Chapter and appropriations acts by State agencies.

(a) Compliance With Chapter and Appropriations Acts. - Except as otherwise provided by law, all expenditures of State funds by a State agency shall be made in compliance with the State budget as enacted by the General Assembly and certified by the Director. If the Director finds that a State agency has spent or encumbered State funds for an unauthorized purpose, the Director shall take appropriate administrative action to ensure that no further irregularities occur and shall report to the Attorney General any facts that pertain to an apparent violation of a penal statute or an apparent instance of malfeasance, misfeasance, or nonfeasance by a person.

(b) Repayment of Funds Spent for an Unauthorized Purpose. - In addition to the provisions of subsection (a) of this section, if the Director finds that a State agency violated this section, the Director shall withhold any future allocations for the unauthorized purpose and shall also withhold future allocations to the Department in an amount equal to the funds unlawfully spent. (2006-203, s. 3.)

§ 143C-6-8. State agencies may incur financial obligations only if authorized by the Director of the Budget and subject to the availability of appropriated funds.

(a) Limitation. - Unless otherwise authorized by the Director as provided by law, purchase orders, contracts, salary commitments, and any other financial obligations by State agencies shall be subject to the availability of appropriated funds or available funds that are not State funds as defined in this Chapter. Any employment contract or salary commitment that is paid in whole or in part with State funds shall also be subject to this limitation.

(b) Notice. - Any written purchase order, contract, salary commitment, or other financial obligation subject to this section shall include a clause that sets forth the limitation imposed by subsection (a) of this section. Where this section applies but there is no written document to which the limitation may be added, the entity that administers the State funds at issue shall notify the person or entity of the limitation. (2006-203, s. 3; 2012-142, s. 6.13(a).)

§ 143C-6-9. Use of lapsed salary savings.

Lapsed salary savings may be expended only for nonrecurring purposes or line items. (2006-203, s. 3.)

§ 143C-6-10. Flexible compensation plan.

Notwithstanding any other provision of law, the Director may establish a program of dependent care assistance and a flexible compensation plan for eligible officers and employees of State agencies as provided in G.S. 126-95. With the approval of the Director, savings in the employer's share of contributions under the Federal Insurance Contributions Act on account of the reduction in salary may also be used as provided by G.S. 126-95. (2007-117, s. 3(c).)

Part 2. Highway Appropriations.

§ 143C-6-11. Highway appropriation.

(a) General Provisions. - Appropriations made for transportation projects are subject to the provisions in this section. If the provisions in this section conflict with the budget acts, the budget acts prevail.

(b) Cash Flow Management of Transportation Projects. - Transportation Project funds shall be budgeted, expended, and accounted for on a "cash flow" basis. Pursuant to this end, transportation project contracts shall be planned and limited so payments due at any time will not exceed the cash available to pay them.

(c) Appropriations Are for Payments and Contract Commitments to Be Made in the Appropriation Fiscal Year. - The appropriations for transportation projects are for maximum payments estimated to be made during the appropriation fiscal year and for maximum contracting authority for future years. Transportation project contracts shall be scheduled so that the total contract payments and other expenditures charged to projects in the fiscal year for each transportation project appropriation item will not exceed the current appropriations provided by the General Assembly and unspent prior appropriations made by the General Assembly for the particular appropriation item.

(d) Payments Subject to Availability of Funds. - The annual appropriations for transportation projects shall be expended only to the extent that sufficient funds are available in the Highway Fund.

(e) Retainage Fully Funded. - The Department of Transportation shall fully fund retainage from transportation project contracts in the year in which the work is performed.

(f) Five Percent (5%) of the Cash Balance Required. - The Department of Transportation shall maintain an available cash balance at the end of each month equal to at least five percent (5%) of the unpaid balance of the total transportation project contract obligations. In the event this cash position is not maintained, no further transportation project contract commitments may be entered into until the cash balance has been regained. For the purposes of awarding contracts involving federal aid, any amount due from the federal government and the Highway Bond Fund as a result of unreimbursed expenditures may be considered as cash for the purposes of this provision.

(g) Anticipation of Revenues. - In awarding State transportation project contracts requiring payments beyond a biennium, the Director may anticipate revenues as authorized and certified by the General Assembly to continue contract payments for up to seventy-five percent (75%) of the revenues which are estimated for the first fiscal year of the succeeding biennium and which are not required for other budget items. Up to fifty percent (50%) of the revenues not required for other budget items may be anticipated for the second and subsequent fiscal years' contract payments. Up to forty percent (40%) of the revenues not required for other budget items may be anticipated for the first year of the second succeeding biennium and up to twenty percent (20%) of the revenues not required for other budget items may be anticipated for the second year of the second succeeding biennium.

(h) Amounts Encumbered. - Transportation project appropriations may be encumbered in the amount of allotments made to the Department of Transportation by the Director for the estimated payments for transportation project contract work to be performed in the appropriation fiscal year. The allotments shall be multiyear allotments and shall be based on estimated revenues and shall be subject to the maximum contract authority contained in subsection (c) above. Payment for transportation project work performed pursuant to contract in any fiscal year other than the current fiscal year is subject to appropriations by the General Assembly. Transportation project contracts shall contain a schedule of estimated completion progress, and any acceleration of this progress shall be subject to the approval of the Department of Transportation provided funds are available. The State reserves the right to terminate or suspend any transportation project contract, and any transportation project contract shall be so terminated or suspended if funds will not be available for payment of the work to be performed during that fiscal year pursuant to the contract. In the event of termination of any contract, the contractor shall be given a written notice of termination at least 60 days before completion of scheduled work for which funds are available. In the event of termination, the contractor shall be paid for the work already performed in accordance with the contract specifications.

(i) Provision Incorporated in Contracts. - The provisions of subsection (h) of this section shall be incorporated verbatim in all transportation project contracts.

(j) Existing Contracts Are Not Affected. - The provisions of this section shall not apply to transportation project contracts awarded by the Department of Transportation prior to July 15, 1980.

(k) The Department of Transportation shall do all of the following:

(1) Utilize cash flow financing to the extent possible to fund transportation projects with the goal of reducing the combined average daily cash balance of the Highway Fund and the Highway Trust Fund to an amount equal to the twelve percent (12%) of the combined estimate of the yearly receipts of the Funds. The target amount shall include an amount necessary to make all municipal-aid funding requirements of the Department.

(2) Establish necessary management controls to facilitate use of cash flow financing, such as establishment of a financial planning committee, development of a monthly financing report, establishment of appropriate fund cash level targets, review of revenue forecasting procedures, and reduction of accrued unbilled costs.

(3) Report annually, on October 1 of each year, to the Joint Legislative Transportation Oversight Committee on its cash management policies and results. (2006-203, s. 3.)

§§ 143C-6-12 through 143C-6-20: Reserved for future codification purposes.

Part 3. Non-State Entities Receiving State Funds.

§ 143C-6-21. Payments to nonprofits.

Except as otherwise provided by law, an annual appropriation of one hundred thousand dollars ($100,000) or less to or for the use of a nonprofit corporation may be made in a single annual payment, in the discretion of the Director of the Budget. An annual appropriation of more than one hundred thousand dollars ($100,000) to or for the use of a nonprofit corporation shall be made in quarterly or monthly payments, in the discretion of the Director of the Budget. (2006-203, s. 3; 2013-360, s. 6.12(o).)

§ 143C-6-22. Use of State funds by non-State entities.

(a) Disbursement and Use of State Funds. - Every non-State entity that receives, uses, or expends any State funds shall use or expend the funds only for the purposes for which they were appropriated by the General Assembly. State funds include federal funds that flow through the State Treasury.

(b) Compliance by Non-State Entities. - If the Director of the Budget finds that a non-State entity has spent or encumbered State funds for an unauthorized purpose, or fails to submit or falsifies the information required by G.S. 143C-6-23 or any other provision of law, the Director shall take appropriate administrative action to ensure that no further irregularities or violations of law occur and shall report to the Attorney General any facts that pertain to an apparent violation of a criminal law or an apparent instance of malfeasance, misfeasance, or nonfeasance in connection with the use of State funds. Appropriate administrative action may include suspending or withholding the disbursement of State funds and recovering State funds previously disbursed.

(c) Civil Actions. - Civil actions to recover State funds or to obtain other mandatory orders in the name of the State on relation of the Attorney General, or in the name of the Office of State Budget and Management, shall be filed in the General Court of Justice in Wake County. (2006-203, s. 3.)

§ 143C-6-23. State grant funds: administration; oversight and reporting requirements.

(a) Definitions. - The following definitions apply in this section:

(1) "Grant" and "grant funds" means State funds disbursed as a grant by a State agency; however, the terms do not include any payment made by the Medicaid program, the State Health Plan for Teachers and State Employees, or other similar medical programs.

(2) "Grantee" means a non-State entity that receives State funds as a grant from a State agency but does not include any non-State entity subject to the audit and other reporting requirements of the Local Government Commission.

(3) "Subgrantee" means a non-State entity that receives State funds as a grant from a grantee or from another subgrantee but does not include any non-State entity subject to the audit and other reporting requirements of the Local Government Commission.

(b) Conflict of Interest Policy. - Every grantee shall file with the State agency disbursing funds to the grantee a copy of that grantee's policy addressing conflicts of interest that may arise involving the grantee's management employees and the members of its board of directors or other governing body. The policy shall address situations in which any of these individuals may directly or indirectly benefit, except as the grantee's employees or members of its board or other governing body, from the grantee's disbursing of State funds, and shall include actions to be taken by the grantee or the individual, or both, to avoid conflicts of interest and the appearance of impropriety. The policy shall be filed before the disbursing State agency may disburse the grant funds.

(c) No Overdue Tax Debts. - Every grantee shall file with the State agency or department disbursing funds to the grantee a written statement completed by that grantee's board of directors or other governing body stating that the grantee does not have any overdue tax debts, as defined by G.S. 105-243.1, at the federal, State, or local level. The written statement shall be made under oath and shall be filed before the disbursing State agency or department may disburse the grant funds. A person who makes a false statement in violation of this subsection is guilty of a criminal offense punishable as provided by G.S. 143C-10-1.

(d) Office of State Budget Rules Must Require Uniform Administration of State Grants. - The Office of State Budget and Management shall adopt rules to ensure the uniform administration of State grants by all grantor State agencies and grantees or subgrantees. The Office of State Budget and Management shall consult with the Office of the State Auditor and the Attorney General in establishing the rules required by this subsection. The rules shall establish policies and procedures for disbursements of State grants and for State agency oversight, monitoring, and evaluation of grantees and subgrantees. The policies and procedures shall:

(1) Ensure that the purpose and reporting requirements of each grant are specified to the grantee.

(2) Ensure that grantees specify the purpose and reporting requirements for grants made to subgrantees.

(3) Ensure that State funds are spent in accordance with the purposes for which they were granted.

(4) Hold the grantees and subgrantees accountable for the legal and appropriate expenditure of grant funds.

(5) Provide for adequate oversight and monitoring to prevent the misuse of grant funds.

(6) Establish mandatory periodic reporting requirements for grantees and subgrantees, including methods of reporting, to provide financial and program performance information. The mandatory periodic reporting requirements shall require grantees and subgrantees to file with the State Auditor copies of reports and statements that are filed with State agencies pursuant to this subsection. Compliance with the mandatory periodic reporting requirements of this subdivision shall not require grantees and subgrantees to file with the State Auditor the information described in subsections (b) and (c) of this section.

(7) Require grantees and subgrantees to maintain reports, records, and other information to properly account for the expenditure of all grant funds and to make such reports, records, and other information available to the grantor State agency for oversight, monitoring, and evaluation purposes.

(8) Require grantees and subgrantees to ensure that work papers in the possession of their auditors are available to the State Auditor for the purposes set out in subsection (i) of this section.

(9) Require grantees to be responsible for managing and monitoring each project, program, or activity supported by grant funds and each subgrantee project, program, or activity supported by grant funds.

(10) Provide procedures for the suspension of further disbursements or use of grant funds for noncompliance with these rules or other inappropriate use of the funds.

(11) Provide procedures for use in appropriate circumstances for reinstatement of disbursements that have been suspended for noncompliance with these rules or other inappropriate use of grant funds.

(12) Provide procedures for the recovery and return to the grantor State agency of unexpended grant funds from a grantee or subgrantee if the grantee or subgrantee is unable to fulfill the purposes of the grant.

(e) Rules Are Subject to the Administrative Procedure Act. - Notwithstanding the provisions of G.S. 150B-2(8a)b. rules adopted pursuant to subsection (d) of this section are subject to the provisions of Chapter 150B of the General Statutes.

(f) Suspension and Recovery of Funds to Grant Recipients for Noncompliance. - The Office of State Budget and Management, after consultation with the administering State agency, shall have the power to suspend disbursement of grant funds to grantees or subgrantees, to prevent further use of grant funds already disbursed, and to recover grant funds already disbursed for noncompliance with rules adopted pursuant to subsection (d) of this section. If the grant funds are a pass-through of funds granted by an agency of the United States, then the Office of State Budget and Management must consult with the granting agency of the United States and the State agency that is the recipient of the pass-through funds prior to taking the actions authorized by this subsection.

(g) Audit Oversight. - The State Auditor has audit oversight, with respect to grant funds received by the grantee or subgrantee, pursuant to Article 5A of Chapter 147 of the General Statutes, of every grantee or subgrantee that receives, uses, or expends grant funds. A grantee or subgrantee must, upon request, furnish to the State Auditor for audit all books, records, and other information necessary for the State Auditor to account fully for the use and expenditure of grant funds received by the grantee or subgrantee. The grantee or subgrantee must furnish any additional financial or budgetary information requested by the State Auditor, including audit work papers in the possession of any auditor of a grantee or subgrantee directly related to the use and expenditure of grant funds.

(h)   Report on Grant Recipients That Failed to Comply. - Not later than May 1, 2007, and by May 1 of every succeeding year, the Office of State Budget and Management shall report to the Joint Legislative Commission on Governmental Operations and the Fiscal Research Division on all grantees or subgrantees that failed to comply with this section with respect to grant funds received in the prior fiscal year.

(i)   State Agencies to Submit Grant List to Auditor. - No later than October 1 of each year, each State agency shall submit a list to the State Auditor, in the format prescribed by the State Auditor, of every grantee to which the agency disbursed grant funds in the prior fiscal year. The list shall include the amount disbursed to each grantee and other information as required by the State Auditor to comply with the requirements of this section. (2006-203, s. 3; 2007-323, s. 28.22A(o); 2007-345, s. 12.)

Article 7.

Federal and Other Receipts.

§ 143C-7-1. Funds creating an obligation.

(a)   Report to Director. - A State agency, other than the judicial branch, that submits to the federal government or to any other party an application for funds that will be subject to this Chapter shall first provide to the Director a copy of the application along with any related information the Director may require. The judicial branch shall provide the Director with a copy of the application and any related information after making the application.

(b)   Contract Provision. - A State agency that receives funds pursuant to an application that must be reported to the Director under subsection (a) of this section shall include in any related contract or other grant instrument a clause specifically stating that the expenditure of money deposited in the State treasury is subject to acts of appropriation by the General Assembly. (2006-203, s. 3; 2007-393, s. 9.)

§ 143C-7-2. Federal Block Grants.

(a) Plans Submitted and Reviewed. - The Secretary of each State agency that receives and administers federal Block Grant funds shall prepare and submit the agency's Block Grant plans to the Director of the Budget. The Director of the Budget shall submit the Block Grant plans to the General Assembly as part of the Recommended State Budget submitted pursuant to G.S. 143C-3-5.

(b) Information To Be Included in Plans. - Each State agency shall submit a separate Block Grant plan for each Block Grant received and administered by the agency, and each plan shall include all of the following:

(1) A delineation of the proposed dollar amount by activity and by category, including dollar amounts to be used for administrative costs.

(2) A comparison of the proposed funding with two prior years' program budgets. (2006-203, s. 3; 2013-360, s. 6.12(p).)

Article 8.

Budgeting Capital Improvement Projects.

§ 143C-8-1. Legislative intent; purpose.

(a) Legislative Intent. - The General Assembly recognizes the need to establish a comprehensive process for capital improvement planning and budgeting that is fully integrated with State financial planning and debt management.

(b) Capital Improvement Planning and Budgeting Process. - The capital improvement planning and budgeting process shall include the following elements:

(1) An inventory of facilities owned by State agencies.

(2) Criteria used to evaluate capital improvement needs.

(3) A six-year capital improvement needs estimate.

(4) A six-year capital improvements plan.

(5) Recommendations for capital improvements set forth in the Recommended State Budget as specified in G.S. 143C-3-5.

(c) Office of State Budget and Management to Manage Planning Process. - The Office of State Budget and Management has responsibility for management of the capital improvement planning process. The Director of the Budget may assign to any State agency or institution such duties and responsibilities as may, in the Director's judgment, be necessary to the successful administration of the capital improvement planning process. (1997-443, s. 34.9; 2000-140, s. 93.1(a); 2001-424, s. 12.2(b); 2006-203, s. 3.)

§ 143C-8-2. Capital facilities inventory.

(a) The Department of Administration shall develop and maintain an automated inventory of all facilities owned by State agencies pursuant to G.S. 143-341(4). The inventory shall include the location, occupying agency, ownership, size, description, condition assessment, maintenance record, parking and employee facilities, and other information to determine maintenance needs and prepare life-cycle cost evaluations of each facility listed in the inventory. The Department of Administration shall update and publish the inventory at least once every three years. The Department shall also record in the inventory acquisitions of new facilities and significant changes in existing facilities as they occur.

(b) No later than October 1 of each even-numbered year, the Department of Administration shall provide a summary of the information maintained in the inventory described in subsection (a) of this section to the Fiscal Research

Division of the Legislative Services Commission. This summary shall include all of the following:

(1) A summary of the number, type, square footage or acreage, and condition of facilities allocated to or owned by each State agency.

(2) A summary of the geographical distribution of State facilities.

(3) An estimate of the percentage increase or decrease of square footage or acreage allocated to or owned by each State agency since the last report was submitted pursuant to this subsection.

(4) Any other information requested by the Fiscal Research Division. (1997-443, s. 34.9; 2006-203, s. 3; 2013-360, s. 6.12(q).)

§ 143C-8-3. Capital improvement needs criteria.

The Office of State Budget and Management shall develop a weighted list of factors that may be used to evaluate the need for capital improvement projects. The list shall include all of the following:

(1) Preservation, adequacy and use of existing facilities.

(2) Health and safety considerations.

(3) Operational efficiencies.

(4) Projected demand for governmental services. (1997-443, s. 34.9; 2000-140, s. 93.1(a); 2001-424, s. 12.2(b); 2006-203, s. 3.)

§ 143C-8-4. Agency capital improvement needs estimates.

(a) Needs Estimate Required. - On or before September 1 of each even-numbered year, each State agency shall submit to the Office of State Budget and Management and to the Division of Fiscal Research a six-year capital improvement needs estimate. This estimate shall describe the agency's anticipated capital needs for each year of the six-year planning period. Capital improvement needs estimates shall be shown in two parts.

(b) Repairs and Renovations Needs Estimate. - The first part of the capital improvement needs estimates shall include only requirements for repairs and renovations necessary to maintain the existing use of existing facilities. Each proposed repair and renovation expenditure shall be justified by reference to the Facilities Condition Assessment Program operated by the Office of State Construction.

(c) Real Property and New Construction or Facility Rehabilitation Needs Estimate. - The second part of the capital improvement needs estimates shall include only proposals for real property acquisition and projects involving construction of new facilities or rehabilitation of existing facilities to accommodate uses for which the existing facilities were not originally designed. Each project included in this part shall be justified by reference to the needs evaluation criteria established by the Office of State Budget and Management pursuant to G.S. 143C-8-3.

For capital projects of The University of North Carolina and its constituent institutions, the Office of State Budget and Management shall utilize the needs evaluation information approved by the Board of Governors of The University of North Carolina developed pursuant to G.S. 116-11(9). (1997-443, s. 34.9; 2000-140, s. 93.1(a); 2001-424, s. 12.2(b); 2006-203, s. 3.)

§ 143C-8-5. Six-year capital improvements plan.

(a) General. - The State capital improvement plan shall address the long-term capital improvement needs of all State government agencies and shall incorporate all capital projects, however financed, proposed to meet those needs, except that transportation infrastructure projects shall be excluded. On or before December 31 of each even-numbered year, the Director of the Budget shall prepare and transmit to the General Assembly a six-year capital improvement plan. When preparing the plan, the Director of the Budget shall consider the capital improvement needs estimates submitted by State agencies as required in G.S. 143C-8-4. The plan shall be prepared in two parts.

(b) Repair and Renovations Requirements. - The first part of the capital improvement plan shall set forth repair and renovations requirements that, in the judgment of the Director of the Budget, should be met within each year of the six-year planning period to protect and preserve existing capital improvement facilities. The plan shall identify individual projects in priority order by State agency and shall specify the means of financing.

(c) Real Property Acquisition, New Construction, or Facility Rehabilitations. - The second part of the capital improvement plan shall set forth an integrated schedule for real property acquisition, new construction, or rehabilitation of existing facilities that, in the judgment of the Director of the Budget, should be initiated within each year of the six-year planning period. The plan shall contain for each project (i) estimates of real property acquisition, and construction or rehabilitation costs (ii) a means of financing the project, and (iii) an estimated schedule for the completion of the project. Where the means of financing would involve direct or indirect debt service obligations, a schedule of those obligations shall be presented. (1997-443, s. 34.9; 2006-203, s. 3.)

§ 143C-8-6. Recommendations for capital improvements set forth in the Recommended State Budget.

(a) Budget Director's Recommendations. - The Director of the Budget shall recommend expenditures for repairs and renovations of existing facilities, and real property acquisition, new construction, or rehabilitation of existing facilities in the Recommended State Budget in accordance with G.S. 143C-3-5.

(b) Repairs and Renovations in the Recommended State Budget. - The Recommended State Budget shall contain for repairs and renovations of existing facilities: (i) the amount recommended for each State agency, (ii) a summary of the recommendations by project type, and (iii) the means of financing.

(c) Repairs and Renovations in the Budget Support Document. - The Budget Support Document shall contain for each repair and renovation project recommended in accordance with subsection (b) of this section: (i) a project description and justification, (ii) a detailed cost estimate, (iii) an estimated schedule for the completion of the project, and (iv) an explanation of the means of financing.

(d) Other Capital Projects in the Recommended State Budget. - The Recommended State Budget shall contain for each capital project involving real property acquisition, new construction, building area (sq. ft.) expansions, or the rehabilitation of existing facilities to accommodate new or expanded uses: (i) a project description and statement of need, (ii) an estimate of acquisition and construction or rehabilitation costs, and (iii) a means of financing the project.

(e) Other Capital Projects in the Budget Support Document. - The Budget Support Document shall contain for each capital project recommended in accordance with subsection (d) of this section: (i) a detailed project description and justification, (ii) a detailed estimate of acquisition, planning, design, site development, construction, contingency and other related costs, (iii) an estimated schedule of cash flow requirements over the life of the project, (iv) an estimated schedule for the completion of the project, (v) an estimate of maintenance and operating costs, including personnel, for the project, covering the first five years of operation, (vi) an estimate of revenues, if any, likely to be derived from the project, covering the first five years of operation, and (vii) an explanation of the means of financing. (2006-203, s. 3; 2007-117, s. 5(b); 2010-96, s. 17.)

§ 143C-8-7. When a State agency may begin a capital improvement project.

No State agency may expend funds for the construction or renovation of any capital improvement project except as needed to comply with this Article or otherwise authorized by the General Assembly. Funds that become available by gifts, excess patient receipts above those budgeted at the University of North Carolina Hospitals at Chapel Hill, federal or private grants, receipts becoming a part of special funds by act of the General Assembly, or any other funds available to a State agency or institution may be utilized for advanced planning through the working drawing phase of capital improvement projects, upon approval of the Director of the Budget. (2006-203, s. 3.)

§ 143C-8-8. When a State agency may increase the cost of a capital improvement project.

Upon the request of the administration of a State agency, the Director of the Budget may, when in the Director's opinion it is in the best interest of the State to do so, increase the cost of a capital improvement project. Provided, however, that if the Director of the Budget increases the cost of a project, the Director shall report that action to the Joint Legislative Commission on Governmental Operations at its next meeting. The increase may be funded from gifts, federal or private grants, special fund receipts, excess patient receipts above those budgeted at the University of North Carolina Hospitals at Chapel Hill, or direct capital improvement appropriations to that department or institution. (2006-203, s. 3.)

§ 143C-8-9. When a State agency may change the scope of a capital improvement project.

A State agency may increase the scope of a capital improvement project only if the General Assembly authorizes the increase. A State agency may decrease the scope of a capital improvement project if the Director authorizes the decrease. To obtain the Director's authorization for a decrease in the scope of a capital improvement project, a State agency shall submit its request to the Director in writing and shall state the reason for the request. (2006-203, s. 3.)

§ 143C-8-10. Project Reserve Account.

(a) Project Reserve Account. - There is established a Project Reserve Account. When a construction contract is entered for a capital improvement project for which the General Assembly has enacted an appropriation, the appropriation is encumbered for the project's costs of real property acquisition, planning, design, site development, construction, contingencies, and other related costs. If the amount appropriated for the project exceeds the amount encumbered, the excess shall be credited to the Project Reserve Account, unless otherwise required by law. The Director may authorize funds in the Account to be used for any of the following:

(1) An emergency repair and renovation project at a State facility.

(2) The award of a project contract when bids for the contract exceed the amount appropriated for it if the project was designed within the scope intended by the appropriation and if the Director finds that all means to award the contract within the appropriation were reasonably attempted.

(3) A reversion to the principal fund from which revenue was appropriated for a project when the amount encumbered for the project is less than the amount appropriated.

(b) Reporting Requirement. - Whenever the Director authorizes the use of funds from the Project Reserve Account, the Director shall report the action to the Joint Legislative Commission on Governmental Operations at its next meeting. (2006-203, s. 3; 2007-117, s. 6.)

§ 143C-8-11. Reversion of appropriation and lapse of project authorization.

(a) Reversion of Appropriation. - A State agency shall begin the planning of or the construction of an authorized capital improvement project during the fiscal year in which the funds are appropriated. If it does not, the Director may credit the appropriation to the Project Reserve Account, unless otherwise required by law. If the Director does not credit the appropriation to the Project Reserve Account, the appropriation shall revert to the principal fund from which it was appropriated. The Director may, for good cause, allow a State agency to take up to an additional 12 months to take the actions required by this subsection.

(b) Lapse of Project Authorization. - Authorizations for capital improvement projects shall lapse if any of the following occur: (i) the appropriation for a capital improvement project reverts, (ii) the construction of a project does not begin during the first two fiscal years in which funds are appropriated, or (iii) the Director redirects funds appropriated for a capital improvement project in accordance with G.S. 143C-6-2. The Director may, for good cause, allow a State agency to take up to an additional 12 months to begin construction of a project; however, if the Director approves an extension of time under this subsection and construction of the project has not begun by the end of the extension, the authorization for the project shall lapse. (2006-203, s. 3.)

§ 143C-8-12. University system capital improvement projects from sources that are not General Fund sources: approval of new project or change in scope of existing project.

Notwithstanding any other provision of this Chapter, the Board of Governors of The University of North Carolina may approve: (i) expenditures to plan a capital improvement project of The University of North Carolina the planning for which is to be funded entirely with non-General Fund money, (ii) expenditures for a capital improvement project of The University of North Carolina that is to be funded and operated entirely with non-General Fund money, or (iii) a change in the scope of any previously approved capital improvement project of The University of North Carolina provided that both the project and change in scope are funded entirely with non-General Fund money. The Board of Governors shall report any expenditure made pursuant to this section to the Office of State Budget and Management and to the Joint Legislative Commission on Governmental Operations. (2006-203, s. 3; 2011-145, s. 30.10(a).)

Article 9.

Special Funds and Fee Reports.

§ 143C-9-1. Medicaid Special Fund; transfers to Department of Health and Human Services.

(a) The Medicaid Special Fund is established as a nonreverting special fund in the Department of Health and Human Services. The Medicaid Special Fund shall consist of the federal Medicaid disproportionate share monies remaining after payments are made to hospitals. Annually, the Department shall transfer the disproportionate share gain, after payments are made to hospitals, to the Medicaid Special Fund. Funds deposited to the Medicaid Special Fund shall only be available for expenditure upon an act of appropriation of the General Assembly.

Political subdivisions may appropriate funds directly to the Department of Health and Human Services for Medicaid programs. Other public agencies and private sources may transfer funds to the Department for Medicaid programs. The Department may accept unconditional and unrestricted donations of such funds. Notwithstanding the provisions of this Article which might forbid such transfer or donation, the University of North Carolina Hospitals at Chapel Hill may transfer funds as provided by the previous sentence of this section.

(b) Contributed funds shall be subject to the Department of Health and Human Services administrative control and shall be allocated only as specifically provided in the Current Operations Appropriations Act, except such contributions shall not reduce State general revenue funding. At the end of any fiscal year, the unobligated balance of any such funds shall not revert to the

General Fund, but shall be reappropriated for these purposes in the next fiscal year. (2006-203, s. 3; 2007-117, s. 7.)

§ 143C-9-2. Trust Fund for Mental Health, Developmental Disabilities, and Substance Abuse Services and Bridge Funding Needs.

(a) The Trust Fund for Mental Health, Developmental Disabilities, and Substance Abuse Services and Bridge Funding Needs is established as an interest-bearing, nonreverting special trust fund in the Office of State Budget and Management. Moneys in the Trust Fund shall be held in trust and used solely to increase community-based services that meet the mental health, developmental disabilities, and substance abuse services needs of the State. The Trust Fund shall be used to supplement and not to supplant or replace existing State and local funding available to meet the mental health, developmental disabilities, and substance abuse services needs of the State.

The State Treasurer shall hold the Trust Fund separate and apart from all other moneys, funds, and accounts. The State Treasurer shall be the custodian of the Trust Fund and shall invest its assets in accordance with G.S. 147-69.2 and G.S. 147-69.3. Investment earnings credited to the assets of the Trust Fund shall become part of the Trust Fund. Any balance remaining in the Trust Fund at the end of any fiscal year shall be carried forward in the Trust Fund for the next succeeding fiscal year.

Moneys in the Trust Fund shall be expended only in accordance with subsection (b) of this section and in accordance with limitations and directions enacted by the General Assembly.

(b) Moneys in the Trust Fund for Mental Health, Developmental Disabilities, and Substance Abuse Services and Bridge Funding Needs shall be allocated to area programs to be used only to:

(1) Provide start-up funds and operating support for programs and services that provide more appropriate and cost-effective community treatment alternatives for individuals currently residing in the State's mental health, developmental disabilities, and substance abuse services institutions.

(2) Repealed by Session Laws 2007-323, s. 10.49(w1), effective July 1, 2007.

(3) Facilitate reform of the mental health, developmental disabilities, and substance abuse services system and expand and enhance treatment and prevention services in these program areas to remove waiting lists and provide appropriate and safe services for clients.

(4) Provide bridge funding to maintain appropriate client services during transitional periods as a result of facility closings, including departmental restructuring of services.

(5) Repealed by Session Laws 2007-323, s. 10.49(w1), effective July 1, 2007.

(c) Notwithstanding G.S. 143C-1-2, any nonrecurring savings in State appropriations realized from the closure of any State psychiatric hospitals that are in excess of the cost of operating and maintaining a new State psychiatric hospital shall not revert to the General Fund but shall be placed in the Trust Fund and shall be used for the purposes authorized in this section. Notwithstanding G.S. 143C-1-2, recurring savings realized from the closure of any State psychiatric hospitals shall not revert to the General Fund but shall be credited to the Department of Health and Human Services to be used only for the purposes of subsections (b)(1) and (b)(3) of this section.

(d) Beginning July 1, 2007, the Secretary of the Department of Health and Human Services shall report annually to the Fiscal Research Division on the expenditures made during the preceding fiscal year from the Trust Fund. The report shall identify each expenditure by recipient and purpose and shall indicate the authority under subsection (b) of this section for the expenditure. (2006-203, s. 3; 2007-323, s. 10.49(w1).)

§ 143C-9-3. Settlement Reserve Fund.

(a) The "Settlement Reserve Fund" is established in the General Fund to receive proceeds from tobacco litigation settlement agreements or final orders or judgments of a court in litigation between tobacco companies and the states. Funds credited to the Settlement Reserve Fund each fiscal year shall be included in General Fund availability as nontax revenue.

(b), (c) Repealed by Session Laws 2011-145, s. 6.11(i), effective July 1, 2011.

(d) Unless prohibited by federal law, federal funds provided to the State by block grant or otherwise as part of federal legislation implementing a settlement between United States tobacco companies and the states shall be credited to the Settlement Reserve Fund. Unless otherwise encumbered or distributed under a settlement agreement or final order or judgment of the court, funds paid to the State or a State agency pursuant to a tobacco litigation settlement agreement, or a final order or judgment of a court in litigation between tobacco companies and the states, shall be credited to the Settlement Reserve Fund. (2006-203, s. 3; 2011-145, s. 6.11(i); 2013-360, s. 6.4(e); 2013-363, s. 1.5.)

§ 143C-9-4. Biennial fee report.

The Office of State Budget and Management shall prepare a report biennially on the fees charged by each State department, bureau, division, board, commission, institution, and agency during the previous two fiscal years. The report shall include the statutory or regulatory authority for each fee, the amount of the fee, when the amount of the fee was last changed, the number of times the fee was collected during the prior fiscal year, and the total receipts from the fee during the prior fiscal year. (2006-203, s. 3; 2007-323, s. 6.3.)

§ 143C-9-5. Assignment to the State of rights to tobacco manufacturer escrow funds.

A tobacco product manufacturer that elects to place funds into escrow pursuant to G.S. 66-291(a)(2) may make an assignment of its interest in the funds to the benefit of the State. The assignment applies to all funds, and any earnings and appreciation, that are in the escrow account at the time of the assignment or are subsequently deposited into the escrow account and are not released under the provisions of subdivision (1) or (2) of G.S. 66-291(b) at any time on or before the expiration of 10 years from the date of assignment. The assignment is irrevocable and shall include any reversionary interest in the escrow account and the funds therein that would otherwise belong to the tobacco manufacturer, including the right to receive the escrowed funds pursuant to G.S. 66-291(b)(3).

An assignment of rights executed pursuant to this section shall be in writing and shall be signed by a duly authorized representative of the tobacco product manufacturer making the assignment. An assignment is effective upon delivery to the Attorney General and the financial institution where the escrow account is maintained. (2006-66, s. 6.19(d); 2006-221, s. 3A; 2006-259, ss. 40(d), 40.5.)

§ 143C-9-6. JDIG Reserve.

(a) The State Controller shall establish a reserve in the General Fund to be known as the JDIG Reserve. Funds from the JDIG Reserve shall not be transferred except in accordance with G.S. 143B-437.63.

(b) It is the intent of the General Assembly to appropriate funds annually to the JDIG Reserve established in this section in amounts sufficient to meet the anticipated cash requirements for each fiscal year of the Job Development Investment Grant Program established pursuant to G.S. 143B-437.52. (2006-66, s. 6.19(f); 2006-221, s. 3A; 2006-259, ss. 40(f), 40.5; 2013-360, s. 6.12(f).)

§ 143C-9-7. Indian Gaming Education Revenue Fund.

(a) The "Indian Gaming Education Revenue Fund" is established in the State Treasury. Funds shall be expended from the Indian Gaming Education Revenue Fund only by specific appropriation by the General Assembly.

(b) Upon appropriation by the General Assembly, funds received in the Indian Gaming Education Revenue Fund shall be allocated quarterly by the State Board of Education to local school administrative units, charter schools, and regional schools on the basis of allotted average daily membership. The funds allotted by the State Board of Education pursuant to this section shall be nonreverting. Funds received pursuant to this section by local school administrative units shall be expended for classroom teachers, teacher assistants, classroom materials or supplies, or textbooks. (2012-6, s. 1; 2013-360, s. 6.12(r).)

§ 143C-9-8. One North Carolina Fund Reserve.

(a) The State Controller shall establish a reserve in the General Fund to be known as the One North Carolina Fund Reserve. Funds from the One North Carolina Fund Reserve shall not be transferred except in accordance with G.S. 143B-437.75.

(b) It is the intent of the General Assembly to appropriate funds annually to the One North Carolina Fund Reserve established in this section in amounts sufficient to meet the anticipated cash requirements for each fiscal year of the One North Carolina Fund Program established pursuant to G.S. 143B-437.71. (2012-142, s. 13.6(f); 2013-360, s. 6.12(g).)

Article 10.

Penalties.

§ 143C-10-1. Offenses for violation of Chapter.

(a) Class 1 misdemeanor. - It is a Class 1 misdemeanor for a person to knowingly and willfully do any one or more of the following:

(1) Withdraw funds from the State treasury for any purpose not authorized by an act of appropriation.

(2) Approve any fraudulent, erroneous, or otherwise invalid claim or bill to be paid from an appropriation.

(3) Make a written statement, give a certificate, issue a report, or utter a document required by this Chapter, any portion of which is false.

(4) Fail or refuse to perform a duty imposed by this Chapter.

(b) Class A1 misdemeanor. - It is a Class A1 misdemeanor for a person to make a false statement in violation of G.S. 143C-6-23(c).

(c) Forfeiture of Office or Employment. - An appointed officer or employee of the State or an officer or employee of a political subdivision of the State, whether elected or appointed, forfeits his office or employment upon conviction of an offense under this section. An elected officer of the State is subject to impeachment for committing any of the offenses specified in this section. (2006-203, s. 3.)

§ 143C-10-2. Civil liability for violation of Chapter.

A person convicted of an offense under G.S. 143C-10-1 is liable in a civil action for any damages suffered by the State in consequence of the offense. (2006-203, s. 3.)

§ 143C-10-3. Suspension from office or impeachment for refusal to comply with Chapter.

(a)   State Officers or Employees of the Executive Branch. - The Governor may suspend from the performance of his or her duties any State officer or employee of the executive branch except an officer elected by the people, who persists, after notice and warning, in failing or refusing to comply with the provisions of this Chapter or any lawful administrative directive issued pursuant to this Chapter. Before acting to suspend, the Governor shall give the accused notice and an opportunity to be heard in his or her own defense. The Governor shall report the facts leading to suspension to the Attorney General who may initiate appropriate criminal or civil proceedings. The Governor may apply to the General Court of Justice for a restraining order and injunction if a suspended officer or employee persists in performing official acts.

(b)   Elected Officers. - A State officer elected by the people who knowingly and willfully fails or refuses to comply with any provision of this Chapter or any lawful administrative directive issued under this Chapter is subject to impeachment. (2006-203, s. 3; 2007-393, s. 10.)

Chapter 143D.

The State Governmental Accountability and Internal Control Act.

Article 1.

General Provisions.
§ 143D-1. Title.

This Chapter shall be known and may be cited as the "State Governmental Accountability and Internal Control Act." (2007-520, s. 1.)

§ 143D-2. Purpose.

The purpose of this Chapter is to ensure a strong and effective system of internal control within State government and to clearly indicate responsibilities related to that system of internal control. Therefore, it is the intent of the General Assembly in this Chapter to clearly establish responsibilities related to internal control within State government. (2007-520, s. 1.)

§ 143D-3. Definitions.

The following definitions apply in this Chapter:

(1)   Internal control. - An integral process, effected by an entity's governing body, management, and other personnel, designed to provide reasonable assurance regarding the achievement of objectives related to the effectiveness and efficiency of operations, reliability of financial reporting, and compliance with applicable laws and regulations.

(2)   Principal executive officer. - Executive head of a State agency.

(3)   Principal fiscal officer. - Chief fiscal officer of a State agency.

(4)   State agency. - Any department, institution, board, commission, committee, division, bureau, officer, official, or any other entity for which the State has oversight responsibility, including, but not limited to, any university, mental or specialty hospital, community college, or clerk of court. (2007-520, s. 1.)

§ 143D-4. : Reserved for future codification purposes.

§ 143D-5. : Reserved for future codification purposes.

Article 2.

Internal Control Responsibilities.

§ 143D-6. Standards setting responsibilities.

The State Controller, in consultation with the State Auditor, shall establish comprehensive standards, policies, and procedures to ensure a strong and effective system of internal control within State government. These standards, policies, and procedures shall be made readily available to all State agencies, and the State Controller shall make appropriate education efforts to inform relevant State agency staffs of the standards, policies, procedures, and internal control best practices. These efforts shall include the development of training courses, manuals, and other information sources to promulgate internal control standards, policies, procedures, and best practices throughout all State agencies. (2007-520, s. 1.)

§ 143D-7. Agency management responsibilities.

The management of each State agency bears full responsibility for establishing and maintaining a proper system of internal control within that agency. Each principal executive officer and each principal fiscal officer shall annually certify, in a manner prescribed by the State Controller, that the agency has in place a proper system of internal control. The State Controller shall develop policies and procedures to direct agencies in their evaluation.

The management of each State agency also bears the responsibility periodically to submit accurate and complete financial information to the State Controller for compilation into North Carolina State government's various financial reports and other related financial information disseminated to the public. With the submission of such periodic reports to the State Controller, each agency's principal executive officer and each agency's principal fiscal officer shall certify, in a manner prescribed by the State Controller, to the accuracy and completeness of the financial information submitted. (2007-520, s. 1.)

§ 143D-8. Internal control documentation.

Each State agency shall maintain documentation, as prescribed by the State Controller, of the system of internal control within that agency. All internal control documentation shall be available upon request for examination by the State Controller and the State Auditor. (2007-520, s. 1; 2008-187, s. 27.)

§ 143D-9: Reserved for future codification purposes.

§ 143D-10: Reserved for future codification purposes.

Article 3.

Accountability.

§ 143D-11. Violations.

The State Controller, in consultation with the State Auditor, shall establish a mechanism to allow for the reporting and investigation of violations of the provisions of this Chapter. This mechanism shall encourage all State employees to become familiar with the provisions of this Chapter and to report any known violations. (2007-520, s. 1.)

§ 143D-12. Penalties.

A willful or continued failure of an employee paid from State funds or employed by a State agency to adhere to the requirements of this Chapter is sufficient cause for disciplinary action, up to and including dismissal of the employee. (2007-520, s. 1.)

Chapter 144.

State Flag, Official Governmental Flags, Motto, and Colors.

§ 144-1. State flag.

The flag of North Carolina shall consist of a blue union, containing in the center thereof a white star with the letter "N" in gilt on the left and the letter "C" in gilt on the right of said star, the circle containing the same to be one third the width of said union. The fly of the flag shall consist of two equally proportioned bars, the upper bar to be red, the lower bar to be white; the length of the bars horizontally shall be equal to the perpendicular length of the union, and the total length of the flag shall be one half more than its width. Above the star in the center of the union there shall be a gilt scroll in semicircular form, containing in black letters this inscription: "May 20th 1775" and below the star there shall be a similar scroll containing in black letters the inscription: "April 12th 1776". (1885, c. 291; Rev., s. 5321; C.S., s. 7535; 1991, c. 361, s. 1.)

§ 144-2. State motto.

The words "esse quam videri" are hereby adopted as the motto of this State, and as such shall be engraved on the great seal of North Carolina and likewise at the foot of the coat of arms of the State as a part thereof. On the coat of arms, in addition to the motto, at the bottom, there shall be inscribed at the top the words, "May 20th, 1775." (1893, c. 145; Rev., s. 5320; C.S., s. 7536.)

§ 144-3. Flags to be displayed on public buildings and institutions.

The board of trustees or managers of the several State institutions and public buildings shall provide a North Carolina flag, of such dimensions and material as they may deem best, and the same shall be displayed from a staff upon the top of each and every such building, at all times except during inclement weather, and upon the death of any State officer or any prominent citizen the flag shall be put at half-staff until the burial of such person has taken place. (1907, c. 838, s. 2; C.S., s. 7537; 2009-570, s. 23.)

§ 144-4. Flags to be displayed at county courthouses.

The boards of county commissioners of the several counties in this State shall likewise authorize the procuring of a North Carolina flag, to be displayed either on a staff upon the top or draped behind the judge's stand, in each and every courthouse in the State, and the State flag shall be displayed at each and every term of court held, and on such other public occasions as the commissioners may deem proper. (1907, c. 838, s. 3; C.S., s. 7538.)

§ 144-5. Flags to conform to law.

No State flag shall be allowed in or over any building here mentioned unless such flag conforms to the description of the State flag contained in this chapter. (1907, c. 838, s. 4; C.S., s. 7539.)

§ 144-6. State colors.

Red and blue, of shades as adopted and appearing in the North Carolina State flag and the American flag, shall be, and hereby are, declared to be the official State colors for the State of North Carolina.

The use of such official State colors on ribbons attached to State documents with the great seal and/or seals of State departments is permissive and discretionary but not directory. (1945, c. 878.)

§ 144-7. Display of official governmental flags; public restrictions.

(a) A county, city, consolidated city-county, or unified government shall not prohibit an official governmental flag from being flown or displayed if the official governmental flag is flown or displayed:

(1) In accordance with the patriotic customs set forth in 4 U.S.C. §§ 5-10, as amended; and

(2) Upon private or public property with the consent of either the owner of the property or of any person having lawful control of the property.

(b) Notwithstanding subsection (a) of this section, for the purpose of protecting the public health, safety, and welfare, reasonable restrictions on flag size, number of flags, location, and height of flagpoles are not prohibited, provided that such restrictions shall not discriminate against any official governmental flag in any manner.

(c) For purposes of this section, an "official governmental flag" shall mean any of the following:

(1) The flag of the United States of America.

(2) The flag of nations recognized by the United States of America.

(3) The flag of the State of North Carolina.

(4) The flag of any state or territory of the United States.

(5) The flag of a political subdivision of any state or territory of the United States. (2005-360, s. 1.)

§ 144-8. State salute to the North Carolina flag.

The phrase "I salute the flag of North Carolina and pledge to the Old North State love, loyalty, and faith." is adopted as the official salute to the North Carolina flag. (2007-36, s. 1.)

§ 144-9. Retirement of State flag.

An official flag of the State that is no longer a fitting emblem for display because it is worn, tattered, or otherwise damaged may be respectfully retired by fire. (2010-189, s. 1.)

Chapter 145.

State Symbols and Other Official Adoptions.

§ 145-1. State flower.

The dogwood is hereby adopted as the official flower of the State of North Carolina. (1941, c. 289.)

§ 145-2. State bird.

The cardinal is hereby declared to be the official State bird of North Carolina. (1943, c. 595.)

§ 145-3. State tree.

The pine is hereby adopted as the official State tree of the State of North Carolina. (1963, c. 41.)

§ 145-4. State shell.

The Scotch bonnet is hereby adopted as the official State shell of the State of North Carolina. (1965, c. 681.)

§ 145-5. State mammal.

The gray squirrel (Sciurus carolinensis) is hereby adopted as the official State mammal of the State of North Carolina. (1969, c. 1207.)

§ 145-6. State saltwater fish.

The channel bass (red drum) is hereby adopted as the official State saltwater fish of the State of North Carolina. (1971, c. 274.)

§ 145-7. State insect.

The honeybee is hereby adopted as the official State insect of the State of North Carolina. (1973, c. 55.)

§ 145-8. State stone.

The emerald is hereby adopted as the official State precious stone of the State of North Carolina. (1973, c. 136, s. 1.)

§ 145-9. State reptile.

The turtle is adopted as the official State reptile of the State of North Carolina, and the eastern box turtle is designated as the emblem representing the turtles inhabiting North Carolina. (1979, c. 154, s. 1.)

§ 145-10. State rock.

Granite is adopted as the official State rock of the State of North Carolina. (1979, c. 906, s. 1.)

§ 145-10.1. State beverage.

Milk is hereby adopted as the official State beverage of the State of North Carolina. (1987, c. 347.)

§ 145-11. State historical boat.

The Shad Boat is adopted as the official State historical boat of the State of North Carolina. (1987, c. 366.)

§ 145-12. State language.

(a) Purpose. English is the common language of the people of the United States of America and the State of North Carolina. This section is intended to preserve, protect and strengthen the English language, and not to supersede any of the rights guaranteed to the people by the Constitution of the United States or the Constitution of North Carolina.

(b)   English as the Official Language of North Carolina. English is the official language of the State of North Carolina.

(c)   Expired. (1987, c. 480, c. 877, s. 1.1.)

§ 145-13. The State dog.

The Plott Hound is adopted as the official dog of the State of North Carolina. (1989, c. 773, s. 1.)

§ 145-14. The State Military Academy.

Oak Ridge Military Academy, in Oak Ridge, North Carolina, as long as it remains a military academy is adopted as the official military academy of the State of North Carolina. (1991, c. 728, s. 1.)

§ 145-15. State tartan.

The Carolina Tartan is adopted as the official tartan of the State of North Carolina. (1991, c. 85, s. 1.)

§ 145-16. State Watermelon Festivals.

(a)   The Hertford County Watermelon Festival is adopted as the official Northeastern North Carolina Watermelon Festival. The Hertford County Watermelon Festival shall be observed annually during the last four days of the first week in August.

(b) The Fair Bluff Watermelon Festival in Columbus County is adopted as the official Southeastern North Carolina Watermelon Festival. The Fair Bluff Watermelon Festival shall be observed annually during mid-July.

(c) Nothing in this act shall be construed to obligate the General Assembly to appropriate funds to implement the provisions of this act.

(d) Nothing in this act shall be construed to obligate Hertford County or Columbus County to expend funds for the purposes of this act. (1993, s. 212, s. 1.)

§ 145-17. State vegetable.

The sweet potato is adopted as the official vegetable of the State of North Carolina. (1995, c. 521, s. 3.)

§ 145-18. State fruit and State berries.

(a) The official fruit of the State of North Carolina is the Scuppernong grape (Vitis genus).

(b) The official red berry of the State is the strawberry (Fragaria genus).

(c) The official blue berry of the State is the blueberry (Vaccinium genus). (2001-488, s. 1.)

§ 145-19. State International Festival.

Folkmoot USA is adopted as the official international festival of the State of North Carolina. (2003-315, s. 1.)

§ 145-20. State wildflower.

The Carolina Lily (Lilium michauxii) is adopted as the official wildflower of the State of North Carolina. (2003-426, s. 1.)

§ 145-21. State Aviation Hall of Fame and Museum and State Museum of Aviation.

The Asheboro Municipal Airport is designated as the official location of the North Carolina Aviation Hall of Fame and the North Carolina Aviation Museum. The Wilmington International Airport is designated as the official location of the North Carolina Museum of Aviation. (2003-363, s. 1.)

§ 145-22. State carnivorous plant.

The Venus flytrap (Dionaea muscipula) is adopted as the official carnivorous plant of the State of North Carolina. (2005-74, s. 1.)

§ 145-23. State birthplace of traditional pottery.

The Seagrove area, including portions of Randolph, Chatham, Lee, Moore, and Montgomery Counties, is designated as the official location of the birthplace of North Carolina traditional pottery. (2005-78, s. 1; 2006-264, s. 70.)

§ 145-24. Official State dances.

(a)   Clogging is adopted as the official folk dance of North Carolina.

(b)   Shagging is adopted as the official popular dance of North Carolina. (2005-218, s. 1.)

§ 145-25. State Christmas tree.

The Fraser fir (Abies fraseri) is adopted as the official Christmas tree of the State of North Carolina. (2005-387, s. 1.)

§ 145-26. State freshwater trout.

The Southern Appalachian strain of brook trout (Salvelinus fontinalis) is adopted as the official freshwater trout of the State of North Carolina. (2005-387, s. 2.)

§ 145-27. State Collard Festival.

The Ayden Collard Festival is adopted as the official collard festival of the State of North Carolina. (2007-28, s. 1.)

§ 145-28. State food festival.

The Lexington Barbecue Festival is adopted as the official food festival of the Piedmont Triad Region of the State of North Carolina. (2007-533, s. 1.)

§ 145-29. State community theater.

The Thalian Association in Wilmington, North Carolina, is adopted as the official community theater of North Carolina. (2007-68, s. 1.)

§ 145-30. State potato festival.

The Albemarle Potato Festival is adopted as the official Irish potato festival of the State of North Carolina. (2009-24, s. 1.)

§ 145-31. State horse.

The Colonial Spanish Mustang is adopted as the official horse of the State of North Carolina. (2010-6, s. 1.)

§ 145-32. Honor and Remember Flag.

The Honor and Remember Flag created by Honor and Remember, Inc., is adopted as a symbol to honor and recognize members of the Armed Forces of the United States who have died in the line of duty. (2010-191, s. 4; 2011-183, s. 106.)

§ 145-33. State Shad Festival; Blue Monday Shad Fry.

(a) The Grifton Shad Festival is adopted as the official Shad Festival of the State of North Carolina.

(b) The East Arcadia Blue Monday Shad Fry is adopted as the official Blue Monday Shad Fry of the State of North Carolina. (2011-36, s. 1; 2013-282, s. 1.)

§ 145-34. State herring festival.

The Herring Festival held in the Town of Jamesville is adopted as the official herring festival of the State of North Carolina. (2011-59, s. 1.)

§ 145-35. State mineral.

Gold (Aurum) is adopted as the official State mineral of the State of North Carolina. (2011-233, s. 1.)

§ 145-36. State sport.

Stock car racing is adopted as the official sport of North Carolina. (2011-187, s. 1.)

§ 145-37. State Shrimp Festival.

The Sneads Ferry Shrimp Festival is adopted as the official shrimp festival of the State of North Carolina. (2011-65, s. 1.)

§ 145-38. State butterfly.

The Eastern tiger swallowtail (Papilio glaucus) is adopted as the official State butterfly of the State of North Carolina. (2012-29, s. 1.)

§ 145-39. State spring and fall livermush festivals.

(a) The Shelby Livermush Festival is adopted as the official fall livermush festival of the State of North Carolina.

(b) The Marion Livermush Festival is adopted as the official spring livermush festival of the State of North Carolina. (2012-29, s. 1.)

§ 145-40. State mullet festival.

The Swansboro Mullet Festival is adopted as the official mullet festival of the State of North Carolina. (2012-29, s. 1.)

§ 145-41. State fossil.

The fossilized teeth of the megalodon shark is adopted as the official fossil of the State of North Carolina. (2013-189, s. 1.)

§ 145-42. State frog.

The pine barrens tree frog (Hyla andersonii) is adopted as the official frog of the State of North Carolina. (2013-189, s. 1.)

§ 145-43. State salamander.

The marbled salamander (Ambystoma opacum) is adopted as the official salamander of the State of North Carolina. (2013-189, s. 1.)

§ 145-44. State marsupial.

The Virginia opossum (Didelphis virginiana) is adopted as the official marsupial of the State of North Carolina. (2013-189, s. 1.)

§ 145-45. State folk art.

The whirligigs created by Vollis Simpson are adopted as the official folk art of the State of North Carolina. (2013-189, s. 1.)

§ 145-46. State art medium.

Clay is adopted as the official art medium of the State of North Carolina. (2013-189, s. 1.)

§ 145-47. State peanut festival.

The Dublin Peanut Festival, held the third Saturday of September of every year, is adopted as the official peanut festival of the State of North Carolina. (2013-313, s. 1.)

Chapter 146.

State Lands.

SUBCHAPTER I. UNALLOCATED STATE LANDS.

Article 1.

General Provisions.

§ 146-1. Intent of Subchapter.

(a) It is the purpose and intent of this Subchapter to vest in the Department of Administration, subject to rules and regulations adopted by the Governor and approved by the Council of State as hereinafter provided, responsibility for the management, control and disposition of all vacant and unappropriated lands, swamplands, lands acquired by the State by virtue of being sold for taxes, and submerged lands, title to which is vested in the State or in any State agency, to be exercised subject to the provisions of this Subchapter.

(b) Further, it is the intent of this Subchapter to establish within the Department, a method for obtaining easements for State-owned lands covered by navigable waters that includes compensation, recognizes the common law rights of riparian or littoral property owners, and balances those rights with the State's obligation to protect public trust rights for all of its citizens. The North Carolina General Assembly finds that the State is unable to provide the necessary access for its citizens to exercise public trust rights and, therefore, recognizes the role that publicly and privately owned piers, docks, wharves, marinas, and other structures located in or over State-owned lands covered by navigable waters generally serve in furthering public trust purposes including:

(1) Providing citizens with access and ability to exercise public trust boating, fishing, and swimming activities;

(2) Enhancing the value of appurtenant upland property values with the resulting increased collection of ad valorem taxes;

(3) Enhancing tourism which is essential to the economy of the State and, in particular, to the coastal counties; and

(4) Increasing local participation in boating and fishing activities with the resulting increase in taxes paid for fuel, fishing tackle, boat equipment, and imported boats and motors which taxes contribute to the sound economy of the State, and some of which are paid into the federal Wallop-Breaux Fund for redistribution to the State for water resource enhancements and water access improvements.

(c) Nothing in this Subchapter shall apply to a privately owned lake or any hydroelectric reservoir licensed by the Federal Energy Regulatory Commission.

(d) Nothing in this Subchapter shall be construed to limit or expand the full exercise of common law riparian or littoral rights. (1959, c. 683, s. 1; 1995, c. 529, s. 1.)

§ 146-2. Department of Administration given control of certain State lands; general powers.

The power to manage, control, and dispose of the vacant and unappropriated lands, swamplands, lands acquired by the State by virtue of being sold for taxes, and submerged lands is hereby vested in the Department of Administration, subject to rules and regulations adopted by the Governor and approved by the Council of State, and subject to the provisions of this Subchapter. The Department of Administration shall have the following general powers and duties with respect to those lands:

(1) To take such measures as it deems necessary to establish, protect, preserve, and enhance the interest of the State in those lands, and to call upon the Attorney General for legal assistance in performing this duty.

(2) Subject to the approval of the Governor and Council of State, to adopt such rules and regulations at it may deem necessary to carry out its duties under the provisions of this Subchapter. (1959, c. 683, s. 1.)

Article 2.

Dispositions.

§ 146-3. What lands may be sold.

Any State lands may be disposed of by the State in the manner prescribed in this Chapter, with the following exceptions:

(1) No submerged lands may be conveyed in fee, but easements therein may be granted, as provided in this Subchapter.

(2) No natural lake belonging to the State or to any State agency on January 1, 1959, and having an area of 50 acres or more, may be in any manner disposed of, but all such lakes shall be retained by the State for the use and benefit of all the people of the State and administered as provided for other recreational areas owned by the State. (1854-5, c. 21; R.C., c. 42, s. 1; Code, s. 2751; Rev., s. 1693; 1911, c. 8; C.S., ss. 7540, 7544; 1929, c. 165; G.S., ss. 146-1, 146-7, 146-12; 1959, c. 683, s. 1.)

§ 146-4. Sales of certain lands; procedure; deeds; disposition of proceeds.

The Department of Administration may sell the vacant and unappropriated lands, swamplands, and lands acquired by the State by virtue of being sold for taxes, at public or private sale, at such times, upon such consideration, in such portions, and upon such terms as are deemed proper by the Department and approved by the Governor and Council of State. Every deed conveying any part of those lands in fee shall be executed in the manner required by G.S. 146-74 through 146-78, and shall be approved by the Governor and Council of State as therein required. The net proceeds of all such sales of those lands shall be paid into the State Literary Fund. Whenever negotiations are begun by the Department for the purpose of selling swampland or the timber thereon, the Department shall promptly notify the State Board of Education of that fact. If the Board deems the proposed sale inadvisable, it may so inform the Governor and Council of State, who may give due consideration to the representations of the Board in determining whether to approve or disapprove the proposed transaction. (R.C., c. 66, s. 12; 1872-3, c. 194, s. 2; Code, ss. 2514, 2515, 2529; 1889, c. 243, s. 4; Rev., s. 4049; C.S., s. 7621; G.S., s. 146-94; 1959, c. 683, s. 1.)

§ 146-5. Reservation to the State.

In any sale of the vacant and unappropriated lands or swamplands by the State, the following powers may be expressly reserved to the State, to be exercised according to law:

(1)   The State may make any reasonable and expedient regulations respecting the repair of the canals which have been cut by the State, or the enlargement of such canals.

(2)   The State may impose taxes on the lands benefited by those canals for their repair, and they shall not be closed.

(3)   The navigation of the canals shall be free to all persons, subject to a right in the State to impose tolls.

(4)   All landowners on the canals may drain into them, subject only to such general regulations as now are or hereafter may be made by law in such cases.

(5)   The roads along the banks of the canals shall be public roads. (1872-3, c. 118; Code, s. 2534; Rev., s. 4050; C.S., s. 7622; G.S., s. 146-95; 1959, c. 683, s. 1.)

§ 146-6. Title to land raised from navigable water.

(a)   If any land is, by any process of nature or as a result of the erection of any pier, jetty or breakwater, raised above the high watermark of any navigable water, title thereto shall vest in the owner of that land which, immediately prior to the raising of the land in question, directly adjoined the navigable water. The tract, title to which is thus vested in a riparian owner, shall include only the front of his formerly riparian tract and shall be confined within extensions of his property lines, which extensions shall be perpendicular to the channel, or main watercourses.

(b)   If any land is, by act of man, raised above the high watermark of any navigable water by filling, except such filling be to reclaim lands theretofore lost to the owner by natural causes or as otherwise provided under the proviso of subsection (d), title thereto shall vest in the State and the land so raised shall become a part of the vacant and unappropriated lands of the State, unless the commission of the act which caused the raising of the land in question shall have been previously approved in the manner provided in subsection (c) of this section. Title to land so raised, however, does not vest in the State if the land was raised within the bounds of a conveyance made by the State Board of Education, which included regularly flooded estuarine marshlands or lands beneath navigable waters, or if the land was raised under permits issued to private individuals pursuant to G.S. 113-229, G.S. 113A-100 through 113A-128, or both.

(c) If any owner of land adjoining any navigable water desires to fill in the area immediately in front of his land, he may apply to the Department of Administration for an easement to make such fill. The applicant shall deliver to each owner of riparian property adjoining that of the applicant, a copy of the application filed with the Department of Administration, and each such person shall have 30 days from the date of such service to file with the Department of Administration written objections to the granting of the proposed easement. If the Department of Administration finds that the purpose of the proposed fill is to reclaim lands theretofore lost to the owner by natural causes, no easement to fill shall be required. In such a case the Department shall give the applicant written permission to proceed with the project. If the purpose of the proposed fill is not to reclaim lands lost by natural causes and the Department finds that the proposed fill will not impede navigation or otherwise interfere with the use of the navigable water by the public or injure any adjoining riparian owner, it shall issue to such applicant an easement to fill and shall fix the consideration to be paid for the easement, subject to the approval of the Governor and Council of State in each instance. The granting by the State of the written permission or easement so to fill shall be deemed conclusive evidence and proof that the applicant has complied with all requisite conditions precedent to the issuance of such written permission or easement, and his right shall not thereafter be subject to challenge by reason of any alleged omission on his part. None of the provisions of this section shall relieve any riparian owner of the requirements imposed by the applicable laws and regulations of the United States. Upon completion of such filling, the Governor and Council of State may, upon request, direct the execution of a quitclaim deed therefor to the owner to whom the easement was granted, conveying the land so raised, upon such terms as are deemed proper by the Department and approved by the Governor and Council of State.

(d) If an island is, by any process of nature or by act of man, formed in any navigable water, title to such island shall vest in the State and the island shall become a part of the vacant and unappropriated lands of the State. Provided, however, that if in any process of dredging, by either the State or federal government, for the purpose of deepening any harbor or inland waterway, or clearing out or creating the same, a deposit of the excavated material is made upon the lands of any owner, and title to which at the time is not vested in either the State or federal government, or any other person, whether such excavation be deposited with or without the approval of the owner or owners of such lands, all such additions to lands shall accrue to the use and benefit of the owner or owners of the land or lands on which such deposit shall have been made, and such owner or owners shall be deemed vested in fee simple with the title to the same.

(e) The Governor and Council of State may, upon proof satisfactory to them that any land has been raised above the high watermark of any navigable water by any process of nature or by the erection of any pier, jetty or breakwater, and that this, or any other provision of this section vests title in the riparian owner thereof, whenever it may be necessary to do so in order to establish clear title to such land in the riparian owner, direct execution of a quitclaim deed thereto, conveying to such owner all of the State's right, title, and interest in such raised land.

(f) Notwithstanding the other provisions of this section, the title to land in or immediately along the Atlantic Ocean raised above the mean high water mark by publicly financed projects which involve hydraulic dredging or other deposition of spoil materials or sand vests in the State. Title to such lands raised through projects that received no public funding vests in the adjacent littoral proprietor. All such raised lands shall remain open to the free use and enjoyment of the people of the State, consistent with the public trust rights in ocean beaches, which rights are part of the common heritage of the people of this State. (1959, c. 683, s. 1; 1979, c. 414; 1985, c. 276.)

§ 146-6.1. Repealed by Session Laws 1977, c. 366.

§ 146-7. Sale of timber rights; procedure; instruments conveying rights; disposition of proceeds.

The Department of Administration may sell timber rights in the vacant and unappropriated lands, swamplands, and lands acquired by the State by virtue of being sold for taxes, at public or private sale, at such times, upon such consideration, in such portions, and upon such terms as are deemed proper by the Department and approved by the Governor and Council of State. Every instrument conveying timber rights shall be executed in the manner required of deeds by G.S. 146-74 through 146-78, and shall be approved by the Governor and Council of State as therein required, or by the agency designated by the Governor and Council of State to approve conveyances of such rights. The net proceeds of all sales of timber from those lands shall be paid into the State Literary Fund. (1959, c. 683, s. 1.)

§ 146-8. Disposition of mineral deposits in State lands under water.

The State, acting at the request of the Department of Environment and Natural Resources, is fully authorized and empowered to sell, lease, or otherwise dispose of any and all mineral deposits belonging to the State which may be found in the bottoms of any sounds, rivers, creeks, or other waters of the State. The State, acting at the request of the Department of Environment and Natural Resources, is authorized and empowered to convey or lease to such person or persons as it may, in its discretion, determine, the right to take, dig, and remove from such bottoms such mineral deposits found therein belonging to the State as may be sold, leased, or otherwise disposed of to them by the State. The State, acting at the request of the Department of Environment and Natural Resources, is authorized to grant to any person, firm, or corporation, within designated boundaries for definite periods of time, the right to such mineral deposits, or to sell, lease, or otherwise dispose of same upon such other terms and conditions as may be deemed wise and expedient by the State and to the best interest of the State. Before any such sale, lease, or contract is made, it shall be approved by the Department of Administration and by the Governor and Council of State.

Any sale, lease, or other disposition of such mineral deposits shall be made subject to all rights of navigation and subject to such other terms and conditions as may be imposed by the State.

The net proceeds derived from the sale, lease, or other disposition of such mineral deposits shall be paid into the treasury of the State, but the same shall be used exclusively by the Department of Environment and Natural Resources in paying the costs of administration of this section and for the development and conservation of the natural resources of the State, including any advertising program which may be adopted for such purpose, all of which shall be subject to the approval of the Governor, acting by and with the advice of the Council of State. (1937, c. 285; C.S., s. 113-26; 1959, c. 683, s. 1; 1973, c. 1262, s. 86; 1977, c. 771, s. 4; 1989, c. 727, s. 218; 1997-443, s. 11A.119(a).)

§ 146-9. Disposition of mineral deposits in State lands not under water.

The Department of Administration may sell, lease, or otherwise dispose of mineral rights or deposits in the vacant and unappropriated lands, swamplands, and lands acquired by the State by virtue of being sold for taxes, not lying beneath the waters of the State, at such times, upon such consideration, in such portions, and upon such terms as are deemed proper by the Department and approved by the Governor and Council of State. Every instrument conveying such rights shall be executed in the manner required of deeds by G.S. 146-74 through 146-78, and shall be approved by the Governor and Council of State as therein provided, or by the agency designated by the Governor and Council of State to approve conveyances of such rights. The net proceeds of dispositions of all such mineral rights or deposits shall be paid into the State Literary Fund. (1959, c. 683, s. 1.)

§ 146-10. Leases.

The Department of Administration may lease or rent the vacant and unappropriated lands, swamplands, and lands acquired by the State by virtue of being sold for taxes, at such times, upon such consideration, in such portions, and upon such terms as it may deem proper. Every lease or rental of such lands by the Department shall be approved by the Governor and Council of State, or by the agency designated by the Governor and Council of State to approve such leases and rentals. (1959, c. 683, s. 1.)

§ 146-11. Easements, rights-of-way, etc.

The Department of Administration may grant easements, rights-of-way, dumping rights and other interests in State lands, for the purpose of

(1)   Cooperating with the federal government,

(2) Utilizing the natural resources of the State, or

(3) Otherwise serving the public interest.

The Department shall fix the terms and consideration upon which such rights may be granted. Every instrument conveying such interests shall be executed in the manner required of deeds by G.S. 146-74 through 146-78, and shall be approved by the Governor and Council of State as therein provided, or by the agency designated by the Governor and Council of State to approve conveyances of such interests. (1959, c. 683, s. 1.)

§ 146-12. Easements in lands covered by water.

(a) The Department of Administration may grant, to adjoining riparian or littoral owners, easements in lands covered by navigable waters or by the waters of any lake owned by the State for such purposes and upon such conditions as it may deem proper, with the approval of the Governor and Council of State. The Department may, with the approval of the Governor and Council of State, revoke any such easement upon the violation by the grantee or his assigns of the conditions upon which it was granted.

Every such easement shall include only the front of the tract owned by the riparian or littoral owner to whom the easement is granted, shall extend no further than the deep water, and shall in no respect obstruct or impair navigation.

When any such easement is granted in front of the lands of any incorporated town, the governing body of the town shall regulate the line on deep water to which wharves may be built.

(b) Easements Not Requiring Approval by the Governor or Council of State. - In accordance with the provisions in subsections (c) through (m) of this section, the Department of Administration shall grant easements to adjoining riparian or littoral owners in State-owned lands covered by navigable waters without the approval of the Governor and the Council of State for:

(1) Existing structures permitted under Article 7 of Chapter 113A or structures existing prior to the effective date of the permitting requirements of Article 7 of Chapter 113A of the General Statutes.

(2) New structures permitted under Article 7 of Chapter 113A of the General Statutes after the effective date of this section.

(c) Voluntary Easement Applications for Existing Structures. - Riparian or littoral property owners of existing structures may voluntarily obtain an easement under subsection (b) of this section in accordance with the procedures set forth in this section. For purposes of this section, the term "existing structures" means all presently existing piers, docks, marinas, wharves, and other structures located over or upon State-owned lands covered by navigable waters. Applications for voluntary easements shall be received by the State Property Office no later than October 1, 2001.

(d) Notification of Availability of Voluntary Easements. - The State Property Office shall provide public notice of the availability of voluntary easements by placing an advertisement in one newspaper of general circulation in each of the coastal counties identified under G.S. 113A-103(2) at least once every six months. The final notice shall be placed no later than September 1, 2001.

(e) Mandatory Easement Applications for New Structures. - Riparian or littoral property owners of new structures shall obtain an easement under subsection (b) of this section in accordance with the procedures set forth in this section.

(f) Easement Application. - An application by a riparian or littoral owner of a new or existing structure for an easement under subsection (b) of this section shall include all of the following and shall:

(1) Be made in writing to the State Property Office and include the full name and address of the easement applicant.

(2) Include a plat depicting the footprint and total square footage of all structures located in or over State-owned lands covered by navigable waters. The footprint shall include the total square footage of the area of State-owned lands covered by navigable waters that are enclosed on three or more sides by any structure.

(3) Include a copy of any "CAMA" permit required for structures under Article 7 of Chapter 113A of the General Statutes.

(4)   Include a copy of the deed or other instrument through which the applicant establishes ownership of the adjacent riparian or littoral property.

(5)   Specify the use or uses associated with the structure to be covered by the easement.

(6)   Include the appropriate easement purchase payment.

(g)   Easement Terms. - Any easement granted under subsection (b) of this section shall be in a form suitable for recordation and shall be executed by either the Director or Deputy Director of the State Property Office. The State-owned lands covered by navigable waters included within the easement shall be limited to the footprint of the structure. The terms of each easement shall provide that the easement:

(1)   Is appurtenant to specifically described, adjacent riparian or littoral property and runs with the land.

(2)   Specifies that the holder of the easement shall not exclude or prevent the public from exercising public trust rights, including commercial and recreational fishing, shellfishing, seine netting, pound netting, and other fishing rights.

(3)   Specifies that the holder of the easement obtains no additional rights to interfere with the approval, issuance, or renewal of shellfish or water column leases or to interfere with the use or cultivation of existing shellfish leases, water column leases, or shellfish franchises.

(4)   Specifies that any rights conveyed to the holder of the easement are not inconsistent with the rights conferred by previous conveyances made by the State for the same property.

(5)   Is valid for a term of 50 years from the date of issuance.

(6)   Is eligible for one renewal term of 50 years.

(7)   Is granted in the public interest for good and valuable consideration received by the State.

(8)   Specifies by metes and bounds description or attached plat the footprint of the structure for which the easement is issued.

(9) Describes the uses of the structure for which the easement is being granted, which may include:

a. Providing reasonable access for all vessels traditionally used in the main watercourse area to deep water or, where present, to a specified navigational channel;

b. Mooring vessels at or adjacent to the structure;

c. Enhancing or improving the value of the adjacent riparian or littoral property; and

d. All other reasonable, nonexclusive public trust uses as specified in the easement application, to the extent not otherwise limited by provisions of this Subchapter or any other law.

(10) Specifies that rights granted include the right to repair, rebuild, or restore existing structures consistent with Article 7 of Chapter 113A of the General Statutes.

(11) Specifies that the exercise of any rights under the easement shall be contingent upon obtaining all required permits.

(h) Easement Purchase Payment. - The easement purchase payment for easements issued under subsection (b) of this section shall be computed on the basis of one thousand dollars ($1,000) per acre of footprint coverage prorated in increments of two hundred fifty dollars ($250.00) rounded up to the nearest quarter acre. The minimum payment shall be five hundred dollars ($500.00) if any payment is owed after the riparian credit is applied. In recognition of common law riparian and littoral rights and a declared public policy concern that easements provided under this section be available to all citizens, a credit shall be given against any easement purchase payment in an amount equal to the number of linear feet of shoreline multiplied by a factor of 54 feet. No linear feet of shoreline may be used in computing the credit if that area of shoreline has been the basis of a previous credit. For purposes of determining the linear feet of shoreline owned, an application submitted by a corporation or other entity whose members include riparian or littoral lot owners, which owners have the right to use the structure for which the easement is sought, and whose lots are restricted from construction thereon of other structures for similar use, shall be considered an application whose easement purchase payment shall be determined by using the entirety of such use restricted shoreline for purposes of determining the applicable riparian credit. Shoreline utilization shall be considered "use restricted" if riparian or littoral structures are prohibited by either permit condition or by restrictive covenant or similar, enforceable private restriction.

(i) Easement Issuance. - Within 75 days of receipt of a completed application under subsection (f) of this section, the Director or Deputy Director of the State Property Office shall issue the requested easement in a form sufficient for recording in the register of deeds of the county or counties in which any part of the structure is located. The act of easement issuance under subsection (b) of this section shall be exempt from the provisions in Chapter 150B of the General Statutes. Failure to issue the requested easement within 75 days of receipt of a completed application and any applicable easement purchase payments shall be treated as issuance of the requested easement and shall entitle the applicant to execution and issuance of the easement.

(j) Easement Renewal. - Upon written request from the current easement holder, easements shall be renewed for one additional term of 50 years. Renewal easements shall be subject to the terms, conditions, and purchase payments applicable to initial easements at the time of renewal. Written notification of expiring easements shall be provided by the State Property Office at least 180 days prior to expiration of the initial easement term. Letter applications for renewal easements shall be submitted within 180 days of the notice of expiration by the State Property Office.

(k) Easement Modification. - Any expansion of the footprint of an existing structure shall require an easement or modification of any existing easement. The application for a modification of an easement shall be as provided in subsection (f) of this section. The easement purchase payment shall be based only on the footprint of the expansion after applying the riparian credit. The minimum easement purchase payment shall be five hundred dollars ($500.00) if any payment is owed after the riparian credit is applied. Easement holders may voluntarily apply for modification of an easement to correct any material errors or omissions. No easement purchase payment shall be required for the modification of an existing use that does not expand the footprint of the existing structure. No refunds shall be provided for any modification that reduces the footprint.

(l) Easement Transfers. - An easement granted under subsection (b) of this section shall be transferred to a subsequent owner of the adjacent riparian or littoral property upon written notification to the State Property Office. The notification shall be given within 12 months of the transfer of title to the adjacent riparian or littoral property and shall be accompanied by the instrument of transfer and an easement purchase payment as follows:

(1) During the first 25 years of the easement term, the easement purchase payment shall be the same as the initial payment; and

(2) During the second 25 years of the easement term, the easement purchase payment shall be twice the amount of the initial payment.

(m) Easement Revocation. - Easements issued under subsection (b) of this section may be revoked in accordance with the provisions of G.S. 146-12(a). Any revocation shall entitle the easement holder to seek administrative review in accordance with the provisions of Article 3 of Chapter 150B of the General Statutes.

(n) Exemptions. - The following types of structures shall not require an easement under this section:

(1) Piers, docks, or similar structures for the exclusive use of the owner or occupant of the adjacent riparian or littoral property, which generate no revenue directly related to the structure and which accommodate no more than ten vessels;

(2) Structures constructed by any public utility that provide or assist in the provision of utility service;

(3) Structures constructed or owned by the State of North Carolina, or any political subdivision, agency, or department of the State, for the duration that the structures are owned by the entity; or

(4) Structures on submerged lands or lands covered by navigable waters not owned by or for the benefit of the public that have been created by dredging or excavating lands. (1854-5, c. 21; R.C., c. 42, s. 1; Code, s. 2751; 1889, c. 555; 1891, c. 532; 1893, cc. 4, 17, 349; 1901, c. 364; Rev., s. 1696; C.S., s. 7543; G.S., s. 146-6; 1959, c. 683, s. 1; 1995, c. 529, s. 2; 1998-217, s. 35(a), (b).)

§ 146-13. Erection of piers on State lakes restricted.

No person, firm, or corporation shall erect upon the floor of, or in or upon, the waters of any State lake, any dock, pier, pavilion, boathouse, bathhouse, or other structure, without first having secured a permit to do so from the Department of Administration, or from the agency designated by the Department to issue such permits. Each permit shall set forth in required detail the size, cost, and nature of such structure; and any person, firm, or corporation erecting any such structure without a proper permit or not in accordance with the specifications of such permit shall be guilty of a Class 3 misdemeanor. The State may immediately proceed to remove such unlawful structure through due process of law, or may abate or remove the same as a nuisance after five days' notice. (1933, c. 516, s. 3; G.S., s. 146-10; 1959, c. 683, s. 1; 1993, c. 539, s. 1051; 1994, Ex. Sess., c. 24, s. 14(c).)

§ 146-14. Proceeds of dispositions of certain State lands.

The net proceeds of all sales, leases, rentals, or other dispositions of the vacant and unappropriated lands, swamplands, and lands acquired by the State by virtue of being sold for taxes, and all interests and rights therein, shall be paid into the State Literary Fund, except as otherwise provided in this Chapter. (1959, c. 683, s. 1.)

§ 146-14.1. Natural Resources Easement Fund.

The Natural Resources Easement Fund is established as a nonreverting fund within the Department of Administration. All easement purchase payment monies collected by the Secretary shall be deposited in the Fund. The Fund may be used for direct costs of administering the program. Fifty percent (50%) of the net proceeds in the Fund shall be transferred annually to the Marine Fisheries Commission, and fifty percent (50%) of the net proceeds in the Fund shall be transferred annually to the Wildlife Resources Commission, to be used by both Commissions for the sole purpose of enhancing public trust resources and increasing the public's access to and use of public trust resources, including, but not limited to, meeting the State's cost share obligations for federal Wallop-Breaux Fund projects, enhancing water resources and expanding the number of public boat ramps and other means of public waters access within the counties designated under G.S. 113A-103(2), and other public trust access purposes. (1995, c. 529, s. 3.)

§ 146-15. Definition of net proceeds.

For the purposes of this Subchapter, the term "net proceeds" means the gross amount received from the sale, lease, rental, or other disposition of any State lands, less

(1) Such expenses incurred incident to that sale, lease, rental, or other disposition as may be allowed under rules and regulations adopted by the Governor and approved by the Council of State; and

(2) Repealed by Session Laws 1993, c. 553, s. 52.

(3) A service charge to be paid into the State Land Fund.

The amount or rate of such service charge shall be fixed by rules and regulations adopted by the Governor and approved by the Council of State, but as to any particular sale, lease, rental, or other disposition, it shall not exceed ten percent (10%) of the gross amount received from such sale, lease, rental, or other disposition. Notwithstanding any other provision of this Subchapter, no service charge shall be paid into the State Land Fund from proceeds derived from the sale of land or products of land owned or held for the use of the Wildlife Resources Commission, or purchased or acquired with funds of the Wildlife Resources Commission. (1959, c. 683, s. 1; 1993, c. 553, s. 52.)

Article 3.

Discovery and Reclamation.

§ 146-16. Department of Administration to supervise.

The Department of Administration shall be responsible for discovering, inventorying, surveying, and reclaiming the vacant and unappropriated lands, swamplands, and lands acquired by the State by virtue of being sold for taxes, and shall take all measures necessary to that end. All expenses incurred in the performance of these activities shall be paid from the State Land Fund, unless otherwise provided by the General Assembly. (1959, c. 683, s. 1.)

§ 146-17. Mapping and discovery agreements.

The Department of Administration, acting on behalf of the State, for the purpose of discovering State lands, may, with the approval of the Governor and Council of State, enter into agreements with counties, municipalities, persons, firms, and corporations providing for the discovery of State land by the systematic mapping of the counties of the State and by other appropriate means. All expenses incurred by the Department incident to such mapping and discovery agreements shall be paid from the State Land Fund, unless otherwise provided by the General Assembly. (1959, c. 683, s. 1.)

§ 146-17.1. Rewards; reclamation of certain State lands; wrongful removal of timber from State lands.

(a) The Department of Administration, acting on behalf of the State, for the purpose of discovering State lands, may, with the approval of the Governor and Council of State, pay any person, firm or corporation who shall provide information that leads to the successful reclamation of any swamplands or vacant and unappropriated lands of the State, a reward equal to one percent (1%) of the appraised value of the reclaimed land, or one thousand dollars ($1,000), whichever sum is less. All expenses incurred by the Department pursuant to this subsection shall be paid from the State Land Fund, unless otherwise provided by the General Assembly.

(b) The Department of Administration, acting on behalf of the State, may, with the approval of the Governor and Council of State, pay any person, firm or corporation who shall provide information that leads to a successful monetary recovery by the State from any person, firm or corporation who wrongfully cuts or removes timber from State lands, a reward equal to one percent (1%) of the amount of said monetary recovery, or one thousand dollars ($1,000), whichever sum is less. All expenses incurred by the Department pursuant to this subsection shall be paid from said monetary recovery, unless otherwise provided by the General Assembly.

(c) No State employee or official, or other public employee or official, shall be eligible for a reward pursuant to subsections (a) or (b) of this section for providing any information obtained in the normal course of his or her official duties. (1979, c. 742, s. 1.)

Article 4.

Miscellaneous Provisions.

§ 146-18. Recreational use of State lakes regulated.

All recreation, except hunting and fishing, in, upon, or above any or all of the State lakes referred to in this Subchapter may be regulated in the public interest by the State agency having administrative authority over these areas. (1933, c. 516, s. 1; G.S., s. 146-8; 1959, c. 683, s. 1.)

§ 146-19. Fishing license fees for nonresidents of counties in which State lakes are situated.

The Wildlife Resources Commission, through its authorized agent or agents, is hereby authorized to require of nonresidents of the county within which a State lake is situated a daily or weekly permit in lieu of the regular "resident State license" for fishing with hook and line or rod and reel within said lake in accordance with the regulations of the Commission relating to said lake. Except for the provisions of this section, the laws and regulations dealing with the issuance of fishing permits by said Commission must be complied with. (1933, c. 516, s. 4; G.S., s. 146-11; 1959, c. 683, s. 1.)

§ 146-20. Forfeiture for failure to register deeds.

All the grants and deeds for swamplands made prior to November 1, 1883, must have been proved and registered, in the county where the lands are situate, within 12 months from November 1, 1883, and every such grant or deed, not being so registered within that time, shall be void, and the title of the proprietor in such lands shall revert to the State; but the provisions of this section shall be applicable only to the swamplands which have been surveyed or taken possession of by, or are vested in, the State or its agencies. (R.S., c. 67, s. 10; R.C., c. 66, s. 10; Code, ss. 2513, 3866; Rev., s. 4046; C.S., s. 7623; G.S., s. 146-96; 1959, c. 683, s. 1.)

§ 146-20.1. Conveyance of certain marshlands validated; public trust rights reserved.

(a) Validation. - All conveyances of swamplands, including regularly flooded estuarine marshlands, that have previously been made by the Literary Fund, the North Carolina Literary Board, or the State Board of Education are declared valid, and the person to whom the conveyance was made or his successor in title is declared to have title to the marshland.

(b) Reservation. - Areas of regularly flooded estuarine marshlands within conveyances validated by subsection (a) remain subject to all public trust rights. (1985, c. 278, s. 1.)

SUBCHAPTER II. ALLOCATED STATE LANDS.

Article 5.

General Provisions.

§ 146-21. Intent of Subchapter.

It is the purpose and intent of this Subchapter to provide for and regulate the acquisition, disposition, and management of all State lands other than the vacant and unappropriated lands, swamplands, lands acquired by the State by virtue of being sold for taxes, and submerged lands. (1959, c. 683, s. 1.)

Article 6.

Acquisitions.

§ 146-22. All acquisitions to be made by Department of Administration.

(a) Every acquisition of land on behalf of the State or any State agency, whether by purchase, condemnation, lease, or rental, shall be made by the Department of Administration and approved by the Governor and Council of State.

(b) If the proposed acquisition is a purchase or gift of land with an appraised value of at least twenty-five thousand dollars ($25,000), and the acquisition is for other than a transportation purpose, the acquisition may only be made after written notice to the Joint Legislative Commission on Governmental Operations, to the board of commissioners and the county manager, if any, of the county in which the land is located, and to the governing body and the city manager, if any, of the municipality in which the land is located if the land is located within a municipality. The notice shall be given to the chairs of the Commission and of the county and municipal governing boards at least 30 days prior to the acquisition, and the chairs shall forward a copy of the notice to the members of their respective bodies within three days of their receipt of the notice. The board of commissioners, individual commissioners, the governing body of the municipality, and individual members of that body may provide written comments on the acquisition to the Department of Administration; the Department shall forward the comments to the Governor and the Council of State.

In determining whether the appraised value is at least twenty-five thousand dollars ($25,000), the value of the property in fee simple shall be used.

The State may not purchase land as a tenant-in-common without consultation with the Joint Legislative Commission on Governmental Operations if the appraised value of the property in fee simple is at least twenty-five thousand dollars ($25,000).

(c) Acquisitions on behalf of the University of North Carolina Health Care System shall be made in accordance with G.S. 116-37(i), acquisitions on behalf of the University of North Carolina Hospitals at Chapel Hill shall be made in accordance with G.S. 116-37(a)(4), acquisitions on behalf of the clinical patient care programs of the School of Medicine of The University of North Carolina at Chapel Hill shall be made in accordance with G.S. 116-37(a)(4), and acquisitions on behalf of the Medical Faculty Practice Plan of the East Carolina University School of Medicine shall be made in accordance with G.S. 116-40.6(d). (1957, c. 584, s. 6; G.S., s. 146-103; 1959, c. 683, s. 1; 1983 (Reg. Sess., 1984), c. 1116, s. 97; 1998-212, s. 11.8(d); 2005-39, s. 1; 2007-322, s. 11; 2007-396, s. 1.)

§ 146-22.1. Acquisition of property.

In order to carry out the duties of the Department of Administration as set forth in Chapters 143 and 146 of the General Statutes, the Department of Administration is authorized and empowered to acquire by purchase, gift, condemnation or otherwise:

(1) Lands necessary for the construction and operation of State buildings and other governmental facilities.

(2) Lands necessary for construction and operation of parking facilities.

(3) An area in the City of Raleigh bounded by Edenton Street, Person Street, Peace Street, the right-of-way of the main line of Seaboard Coast Line Railway and North McDowell Street for the expansion of State governmental facilities, the public interest in, public use of, and the necessity for the acquisition of said area, being hereby declared as a matter of legislative determination.

(4) Lands necessary for the location, expansion, operation and improvement of hospital and mental health facilities and similar institutions maintained by the State of North Carolina.

(5) Lands necessary for public parks and forestry purposes.

(6) Lands involving historical sites, together with such adjacent lands as may be necessary for their preservation, maintenance and operation.

(7) Lands necessary for the location, expansion and improvement of any educational, penal or correctional institution.

(8) Lands necessary to provide public access to the waters within the State.

(9) Lands necessary for agricultural, experimental and research facilities.

(10) Utility and access easement, rights-of-way, estates for terms of years or fee simple title to lands necessary or convenient to the operation of state-owned facilities.

(11) Lands necessary for the development and preservation of the estuarine areas of the State.

(12) Lands necessary for the development of waterways within the State.

(13) Lands necessary for acquisition of all or part of an area of environmental concern, as requested pursuant to G.S. 113A-123.

(14) Lands necessary for the construction of hazardous waste facilities as defined in G.S. 130A-290, inactive hazardous substance or waste disposal sites as defined in G.S. 130A-310, Superfund sites as described in G.S. 130A-310.22, and lands necessary for the construction of low-level radioactive waste facilities as defined in G.S. 104E-5. (1969, c. 1091, s. 1; 1973, c. 1284, s. 2; 1981, c. 704, s. 23; 1989, c. 286, s. 11.)

§ 146-22.2. Appraisal of property to be acquired by State.

(a) Where an appraisal of real estate or an interest in real estate is required by law to be made before acquisition of the property by the State or an agency of the State, the appraisal shall be made by a real estate appraiser licensed or certified by the State under Article 5 of Chapter 93A of the General Statutes.

(b) (See notes) The provisions of subsection (a) of this section shall not apply to appraisals of real estate or an interest in real estate made by personnel within the Department of Transportation when the appraisal is anticipated to be less than ten thousand dollars ($10,000). In the event that the real estate or interest in real estate is in fact appraised at ten thousand dollars ($10,000) or more, the Department of Transportation must comply with the provisions of subsection (a) of this section. (1989 (Reg. Sess., 1990), c. 827, s. 12; 1991, c. 94, s. 1; 1993, c. 519, s. 1; 1993 (Reg. Sess., 1994), c. 691, s. 1.)

§ 146-22.3. Acquisition of land to be used to restore, enhance, preserve, or create wetlands.

(a) Payment. - A State agency that acquires land by purchase for the purpose of restoring, enhancing, preserving, or creating wetlands as required by a permit or an authorization issued by the United States Army Corps of Engineers under 33 U.S.C. § 1344 must pay to the county in which the land is located, as reimbursement, a sum equal to the estimated amount of ad valorem taxes that would have accrued to the county for the next 20 years had the land not been acquired by the State agency.

(b) Exception. - This section does not apply when the land purchased by the State agency and the wetlands permitted to be lost are located in the same county. In other circumstances, the governing body of the county and the State agency may enter into a written agreement to waive payment.

(c) Amount. - The estimated amount of ad valorem taxes that would have accrued for the next 20 years is the total assessed value of the acquired land excluded from the county's tax base multiplied by the tax rate set by the county board of commissioners in its most recent budget ordinance adopted under Chapter 159 of the General Statutes, and then multiplied by 20.

(d) Application. - This section applies only to land acquired in counties designated as a development tier one area under G.S. 143B-437.08. (2004-188, s. 4; 2006-252, s. 2.14.)

§ 146-22.4. Acquisition of wetlands from private mitigation banking companies.

(a) Payment for Taxes. - A State agency that acquires wetlands from a private mitigation banking company must pay a sum in lieu of ad valorem taxes to the county where the wetlands are located. The sum is equal to the estimated amount of ad valorem taxes that would have accrued for the next 20 years as computed in G.S. 146-22.3(c).

(b) Requirement for Acquisition. - A State agency may require, as a condition of accepting a donation of wetlands by a private mitigation banking company, that the company make adequate provisions for the long-term maintenance and management of the wetlands. These provisions may include reimbursement to the agency for payment of a sum in lieu of ad valorem taxes.

(c) Application. - This section applies only to land acquired in counties designated as a development tier one area under G.S. 143B-437.08. (2004-188, s. 5; 2006-252, s. 2.15.)

§ 146-22.5. Reimbursement of payment in lieu of future ad valorem taxes.

(a) If a State agency acquires land under G.S. 146-22.3 or G.S. 146-22.4 and later uses this land to mitigate wetlands permitted to be lost in the same county, then the county shall reimburse the State agency. The reimbursement shall equal the estimated amount of ad valorem taxes paid for the land in accordance with G.S. 146-22.3 minus ten percent (10%) of this amount multiplied by the number of years the State agency held the land before the wetlands were lost.

(b) Application. - This section applies only to land acquired in counties designated as a development tier one area under G.S. 143B-437.08. (2004-188, s. 6; 2005-435, s. 44; 2006-252, s. 2.16.)

§ 146-23. Agency must file statement of needs; Department must investigate.

Any State agency desiring to acquire land, whether by purchase, condemnation, lease, or rental, shall file with the Department of Administration an application setting forth its needs, and shall furnish such additional information as the Department may request relating thereto. Upon receipt of such application, the Department of Administration shall promptly investigate all aspects of the requested acquisition, including the existence of actual need for the requested property on the part of the requesting agency; the availability of land already owned by the State or by any State agency which might meet the requirements of the requesting agency; the availability, value, and status of title of other land, whether for purchase, condemnation, lease, or rental, which might meet the requirements of the requesting agency; and the availability of funds to pay for land if purchased, condemned, leased, or rented. The Department of Administration may make acquisitions at the request of the Governor and Council of State upon compliance with the investigation herein required. (1957, c. 584, s. 6; G.S., s. 146-104; 1959, c. 683, s. 1; 1969, c. 1091, s. 2.)

§ 146-23.1. Buildings having historic, architectural or cultural significance.

In order to promote the use of buildings having historic, architectural or cultural significance, the Department of Administration shall inform the North Carolina Historical Commission of all geographical areas in the State within which the State is actively seeking to lease space for the accommodation of State agencies. Within 60 days of the receipt of such information, the North Carolina Historical Commission shall identify for the Department of Administration all buildings within such geographical areas that (i) are known to be of historic, architectural or cultural significance (including but not limited to buildings listed or eligible to be listed on the National Register established pursuant to 16 U.S.C. 470(a)), and (ii) which may be suitable, whether or not in need of repair, alteration or addition, for acquisition or lease to meet the public building and space needs of State agencies. In addition, the North Carolina Historical Commission shall furnish the Department of Administration such additional information on the physical condition, usable space, and the nature and approximate costs of necessary historic rehabilitation as the department may request in order for the department to determine whether the acquisition or lease of space in such buildings is feasible and prudent.

In acquiring lease space pursuant to G.S. 146-25.1, the Department of Administration shall give preference to lease proposals involving buildings identified by the North Carolina Historical Commission as having historic, architectural or cultural significance. Provided, however, that such preference shall be given only when the Department of Administration, after investigation as provided in this Article, determines that such proposal is feasible, prudent and in the best interest of the State, as compared with available alternatives, such determination to include the State's policy to preserve historic buildings. (1977, c. 998, s. 1.)

§ 146-23.2. Purchase of buildings constructed or renovated to a certain energy-efficiency standard.

(a)   A State agency shall not acquire by purchase any building unless the building was designed and constructed to at least the same standards for energy efficiency and water use that the design and construction of a comparable State building was required to meet at the time the building under consideration for purchase was constructed. Further, a State agency shall not acquire by purchase any building that had a major renovation unless the major renovation of the building was designed and constructed to at least the same standards for energy efficiency and water use that the design and construction of a major renovation of a comparable State building was required to meet at the time the building under consideration for purchase was renovated.

(b)   This section does not apply to the purchase of a building having historic, architectural, or cultural significance under Part 4 of Article 2 of Chapter 143B of the General Statutes. This section does not apply to buildings that are acquired by devise or gift. (2008-203, s. 3.)

§ 146-24. Procedure for purchase or condemnation.

(a) If, after investigation, the Department determines that it is in the best interest of the State that land be acquired, the Department shall proceed to negotiate with the owners of the desired land for its purchase.

(b) If the purchase price and other terms are agreed upon, the Department shall then submit to the Governor and Council of State the proposed purchase, together with a copy of the deed, for their approval or disapproval. If the Governor and Council of State approve the proposed purchase, the Department shall pay for the land and accept delivery of a deed thereto. All conveyances of purchased real property shall be made to "the State of North Carolina," and no such conveyance shall be made to a particular agency, or to the State for the use or benefit of a particular agency.

(c) If negotiations for the purchase of the land are unsuccessful, or if the State cannot obtain a good and sufficient title thereto by purchase from the owners, then the Department of Administration may request permission of the Governor and Council of State to exercise the right of eminent domain and acquire any such land by condemnation in the same manner as is provided for the Board of Transportation by Article 9 of Chapter 136 of the General Statutes. Upon approval by the Governor and Council of State, the Department may proceed to exercise the right of eminent domain. Approval by no other State agency shall be required as a prerequisite to the exercise of the power of eminent domain by the Department. Provided that when the procedures of Article 9 of Chapter 136 are employed by the Department, any person named in or served with a complaint and declaration of taking shall have 120 days from the date of service thereof within which to file answer. (1957, c. 584, s. 6; G.S., s. 146-105; 1959, c. 683, s. 1; 1967, c. 512, s. 1; 1973, c. 507, s. 5; 1981, c. 245, s. 1.)

§ 146-24.1. The power of eminent domain.

In carrying out the duties and purposes set forth in Chapters 143 and 146 of the General Statutes, the Department of Administration is vested with the power of eminent domain and shall have the right and power to acquire such lands, easements, rights-of-way or estates for years by condemnation in the manner prescribed by G.S. 146-24 of the General Statutes. The power of eminent domain herein granted is supplemental to and in addition to the power of eminent domain which may be now or hereafter vested in any State agency as defined by G.S. 146-64 and the Department of Administration may exercise on behalf of such agency the power vested in said agency or the power vested in the Department of Administration herein; and the Department of Administration may follow the procedure set forth in G.S. 146-24 or the procedure of such agency, at the option of the Department of Administration. Where such acquisition is made at the request of an agency, such agency shall make a determination of the necessity therefor; where such acquisition is on behalf of the State or at the request of the Department of Administration, such findings shall be made by the Director of Administration. Provided, however, that all such acquisitions shall have the approval of the Governor and Council of State as provided in G.S. 146-24.

This section shall not apply to public projects and condemnations for which specific statutory condemnation authority and procedures are otherwise provided. (1969, c. 1091, ss. 3, 4.)

§ 146-25. Leases and rentals.

If, after investigation, the Department of Administration determines that it is in the best interest of the State that land be leased or rented for the use of the State or of any State agency, the Department shall proceed to negotiate with the owners for the lease or rental of such property. All lease and rental agreements entered into by the Department shall be promptly submitted to the Governor and Council of State for approval or disapproval. (1957, c. 584, s. 6; G.S., s. 146-106; 1959, c. 683, s. 1.)

§ 146-25.1. Proposals to be secured for leases.

(a) If pursuant to G.S. 146-25, the Department of Administration determines that it is in the best interest of the State to lease or rent land and the rental is estimated to exceed twenty-five thousand dollars ($25,000) per year or the term will exceed three years, the Department shall require the State agency desiring to rent land to prepare and submit for its approval a set of specifications for its needs. Upon approval of specifications, the Department shall prepare a public advertisement. The State agency shall place such advertisement in a newspaper of general circulation in the county for proposals from prospective lessors of said land and shall make such other distribution thereof as the Department directs. The advertisement shall be run for at least five consecutive days, and shall provide that proposals shall be received for at least seven days from the date of the last advertisement in the State Property Office of the Department. The provisions of this section do not apply to property owned by governmental agencies and leased to other governmental agencies.

(b) The Department may negotiate with the prospective lessors for leasing of the needed land, taking into account not only the rental offered, but the type of land, the location, its suitability for the purposes, services offered by the lessor, and all other relevant factors. In the event either no proposal or no acceptable proposal is received after advertising in accordance with subsection (a) of this section, the Department may negotiate in the open market for leasing of the needed land.

(c) The Department of Administration shall present the proposed transaction to the Council of State for its consideration as provided by this Article. In the event the lowest rental proposed is not presented to the Council of State, that body may require a statement of justification, and may examine all proposals. (1973, c. 1448; 1975, c. 523; 1977, c. 485; 1979, c. 43, s. 1; 1983 (Reg. Sess., 1984), c. 1116, s. 97; 1999-252, s. 1.)

§ 146-26. Donations and devises to State.

No devise or donation of land or any interest therein to the State or to any State agency shall be effective to vest title to the land or any interest therein in the State or in any State agency until the devise or donation is accepted by the Governor and Council of State. If the land is devised or donated to the State or to any State agency as an historic property, then title shall not vest until the Historical Commission reports to the Joint Legislative Commission on Governmental Operations as provided in G.S. 121-9. Upon acceptance by the Governor and Council of State, title to the said land or interest therein shall immediately vest as of the time title would have vested but for the above requirement of reporting to the Joint Legislative Commission on Governmental Operations if an historic property and acceptance by the Governor and Council of State. (1957, c. 584, s. 6; G.S., s. 146-107; 1959, c. 683, s. 1; 1996, 2nd Ex. Sess., c. 18, s. 7.7(b).)

§ 146-26.1. Relocation assistance.

In the acquisition of any real property by the Department of Administration for a public use, the Department of Administration shall be vested with the authority as set forth in Article 2 of Chapter 133 of the General Statutes. (1971, c. 540; 1973, c. 507, s. 5; 1977, c. 464, s. 34; 1993, c. 553, s. 52.1.)

Article 7.

Dispositions.

§ 146-27. The role of the Department of Administration in sales, leases, and rentals.

(a) General. - Every sale, lease, rental, or gift of land owned by the State or by any State agency shall be made by the Department of Administration and approved by the Governor and Council of State. A lease or rental of land owned by the State may not exceed a period of 99 years. The Department of Administration may initiate proceedings for sales, leases, rentals, and gifts of land owned by the State or by any State agency.

(b) Large Disposition. - If a proposed disposition is a sale or gift of land with an appraised value of at least twenty-five thousand dollars ($25,000), the sale or gift shall not be made until after consultation with the Joint Legislative Commission on Governmental Operations.

(c) Expired effective September 1, 2007. (1957, c. 584, s. 6; G.S., s. 146-108; 1959, c. 683, s. 1; 1977, c. 425, ss. 1, 2; 1987, c. 738, s. 47(b); 1993, c. 561, s. 32(a); 1998-159, s. 5; 2005-276, s. 6.25(a).)

§ 146-28. Agency must file application with Department; Department must investigate.

Any State agency desiring to sell, lease, or rent any land owned by the State or by any State agency shall file with the Department of Administration an application setting forth the facts relating to the proposed transaction, and shall furnish the Department with such additional information as the Department may request relating thereto. Upon receipt of such application, the Department of Administration shall promptly investigate all aspects of the proposed transaction, including particularly present and future State need for the land proposed to be conveyed, leased, or rented. (1957, c. 584, s. 6; G.S., s. 146-109; 1959, c. 683, s. 1.)

§ 146-29. Procedure for sale, lease, or rental.

If, after investigation, the Department of Administration determines that it is in the best interest of the State that land be sold, leased, or rented, the Department shall proceed with its sale, lease, or rental, as the case may be, in accordance with rules adopted by the Governor and approved by the Council of State. If an agreement of sale, lease, or rental is reached, the proposed transaction shall then be submitted to the Governor and Council of State for their approval or disapproval. Every conveyance in fee of land owned by the State or by any State agency shall be made and executed in the manner prescribed in G.S. 146-74 through 146-78. (1957, c. 584, s. 6; G.S., s. 146-110; 1959, c. 683, s. 1.)

§ 146-29.1. Lease or sale of real property for less than fair market value.

(a) Real property owned by the State or any State agency may not be sold, leased, or rented at less than fair market value to any private entity that operates, or is established to operate for profit.

(b) Real property owned by the State or by any State agency may be sold, leased, or rented at less than fair market value to a public entity. "Public entity" means a county, municipal corporation, local board of education, community college, special district or other political subdivision of the State and the United States or any of its agencies. Any such sale, lease, or rental shall be reported at least 30 days prior to the sale, lease, or rental to the Joint Legislative Commission on Governmental Operations and the Fiscal Research Division of the Legislative Services Office, with the details of such transaction.

(c) Real property owned by the State or by any State agency may be sold, leased, or rented at less than market value to a private, nonprofit corporation, association, organization or society if the Department of Administration determines both of the following:

(1) The transaction is in consideration of public service rendered or to be rendered by the nonprofit.

(2) The property will be used in connection with the nonprofit's tax-exempt purpose and not in connection with its unrelated trade or business, as defined in section 513 of the Code. For the purposes of this subdivision, the term "Code" has the same meaning as in G.S. 105-228.90.

The transaction shall be reported in detail at least 30 days prior to the sale, lease, or rental to the Joint Legislative Commission on Governmental Operations and the Fiscal Research Division of the Legislative Services Office. The fact that any sale of property under this subsection shall not be subject to a reversionary interest in the State shall be expressly made known to the Joint Legislative Commission on Government Operations, and the Governor and Council of State, prior to the transaction being authorized.

(d) Any sale, lease, or rental of real property made in conformity with the provisions of this section is not a violation of G.S. 66-58(a).

(e) All sales, leases, or rentals, prior to July 15, 1986, of real property owned by the State or any State agency are not invalid because of a conflict with G.S. 66-58(a) or with a prior version of this section, but any renewal of any such lease or rental agreement on or after July 15, 1986, shall conform to the requirements of this section.

(f) If the fair market value of State-owned real property exceeds one million dollars ($1,000,000), a gift of any interest in the property or a sale, lease, or rental of any interest in the property for below fair market value shall not be effective until the later of the following:

(1) If a bill that specifically disapproves the transaction is introduced in either house of the General Assembly before the 31st legislative day of the next regular session of the General Assembly that begins at least 25 days after the date that the agreement making the transfer is entered into, the earlier of (i) the day that an unfavorable final action is taken on the bill or (ii) the day that the General Assembly adjourns without ratifying the bill.

(2) The 31st legislative day of the session of the General Assembly described in subdivision (1) of this section, if a bill disapproving the transaction is not introduced before that day.

(f1) For the purpose of subsection (f) of this section:

(1) "Next regular session" means:

a. For odd-numbered years its initial convening.

b. For even-numbered years the first reconvening of the regular session as provided in the joint resolution setting the date for reconvening.

(2) "Adjourns" means:

a. For odd-numbered years the date the General Assembly adjourns by joint resolution for a period of more than 30 days.

b. For even-numbered years the date of sine die adjournment.

(f2) If the transaction is approved under subsection (f) of this section, but the agreement provides a later effective date, then it takes effect on the date specified in the agreement.

(f3) Nothing in subsection (f) of this section restricts the General Assembly from enacting a law specifically approving the transaction.

(g) If the General Assembly ratifies a disapproving bill, the disapproved transaction shall not be effective unless it is vetoed by the Governor and the veto is not overridden, and in such case the transaction is effective upon sine die adjournment of that regular session.

The terms of any agreement to transfer an interest in real property under this section are deemed to incorporate the provisions of subsections (f) through (f2) of this section, and any transaction that does not comply with these subsections is void. (1985, c. 479, s. 172(a); 1985 (Reg. Sess., 1986), c. 1014, s. 188(a); 1993, c. 561, s. 32(c); 1999-252, s. 2; 2013-360, s. 36.8(a).)

§ 146-29.2. Lease or interest in real property for communication purposes.

(a) The following definitions apply in this section:

(1) Antenna. - Communications equipment that transmits, receives, or transmits and receives electromagnetic radio signals used in the provision of all types of wireless communications services.

(2) Buildings. - Structures owned or leased by the State on which equipment may be placed or attached.

(3) Collocation. - The placement or installation of wireless facilities on existing structures, including electrical transmission towers, water towers, buildings, and other structures capable of structurally supporting the attachment of wireless facilities in compliance with applicable building and line safety codes.

(4) Equipment. - Antennas, transmitters, receivers, cables, wires, transformers, power supplies, electric and communication lines necessary for the provision of television broadcast signals, radio wave signals, wireless data or wireless telecommunication services to a discrete geographic area, and all other apparatuses and appurtenances, including shelters, cabinets, buildings, platforms, and ice bridges used to house or otherwise protect equipment.

(5) Ground area. - The area of real property surrounding the base of towers on which the equipment and appurtenances necessary for the operation and stability of the towers, including guy wires and security fencing, are constructed or installed.

(6) Provider. - Any person that is engaged in the transmission, reception, or dissemination of television broadcast signals, radio wave signals, or electromagnetic radio signals used in the provision of wireless communications service, or the provisioning of wireless infrastructure.

(7) Tower. - New or existing structures, such as a monopole, lattice tower, guyed tower, fire observation tower or water tower that are designed to support or are capable of supporting equipment used in the transmission or receipt of television broadcast signals, radio wave signals, or electromagnetic radio signals used in the provision of wireless communication service.

(b) The State may lease real property, or may grant an easement or license with an interest in real property for the following communication purposes:

(1) Constructing, installing, and operating towers and equipment on State land.

(2) Installing and operating equipment on towers, buildings, or ground area owned or leased by the State.

(c) If otherwise feasible and determined by the Department of Administration to be in the best interest of the State:

(1) New towers constructed on State land shall be designed for collocation. This requirement shall not apply to towers constructed on State land by the State or any of its agencies or by a "public entity" as that term is defined in G.S. 146-29.1(b).

(2) The State shall encourage the collocation of equipment on existing towers and buildings owned by the State.

(3) The State shall sublease for collocation purposes space on any tower or ground area leased by the State, if allowed under the terms of the lease.

(4) The State shall, to the extent practicable, adopt standard terms and conditions for applications to lease, easements, or other conveyances of an interest in real property for communication purposes.

(d) Pursuant to G.S. 143-341(4)f., the Governor, acting with the approval of the Council of State, may adopt rules authorizing the Department of Administration to enter into or approve classes of leases, easements, or licenses with an interest in real property for the purposes set forth in this section. The rules may allow for execution of leases or other instruments by the Department of Administration rather than execution of the instruments in the manner prescribed in G.S. 146-74 through G.S. 146-78.

(e) Land in the State Parks System, as defined in G.S. 113-449.9, may only be leased or conveyed for the purposes of this section upon the approval of the Secretary of the Department of Environment and Natural Resources. Lease or conveyance of land in the State Parks System for the purposes of this section shall comply with the requirements of Articles 2 and 2C of Chapter 113 of the General Statutes. When selecting a location for a communications tower or antenna in the State Parks System, the State shall choose a location that minimizes the visual impact on the surrounding landscape. No land acquired or developed using funds from the Federal Land and Water Conservation Fund shall be leased or conveyed for the purposes of this section.

(f) City and county ordinances apply to communications towers and antennas authorized under this section. (1998-158, s. 3; 2013-185, s. 3.)

§ 146-30. Application of net proceeds.

(a) (Effective until January 1, 2016) The net proceeds of any disposition made in accordance with this Subchapter shall be handled in accordance with the following priority: First, in accordance with the provisions of any trust or other instrument of title whereby title to such real property was heretofore acquired or is hereafter acquired; second, as provided by any other act of the General Assembly; third, as follows:

(1) If the appraised value of the land exceeds six million dollars ($6,000,000), the net proceeds shall be deposited with the State Treasurer to support the General Fund.

(2) If the appraised value of the land does not exceed six million dollars ($6,000,000), the net proceeds shall be deposited as follows:

a. Twenty-five percent (25%) to the State agency to which the property was allocated. These funds may be used for any purpose authorized by law and are hereby appropriated.

b. Twenty-five percent (25%) to the State Treasurer to support the General Fund.

c. Fifty (50%) to the State Treasurer to be deposited in the Teachers' and State Employees' Retirement System of North Carolina. These funds are hereby appropriated.

However, no State lands or contract shall be divided for the purpose of evading the appraised value of the provisions of this Subchapter.

(a) (Effective January 1, 2016) The net proceeds of any disposition made in accordance with this Subchapter shall be handled in accordance with the following priority: First, in accordance with the provisions of any trust or other instrument of title whereby title to such real property was heretofore acquired or is hereafter acquired; second, as provided by any other act of the General Assembly; third, the net proceeds shall be deposited with the State Treasurer. Provided, however, nothing herein shall be construed as prohibiting the disposition of any State lands by exchange for other lands, but if the appraised value in fee simple of any property involved in the exchange is at least twenty-five thousand dollars ($25,000), then such exchange may not be made without consultation with the Joint Legislative Commission on Governmental Operations.

(a1) (Expires January 1, 2016) Nothing in this section shall be construed to prohibit the disposition of any State lands by exchange for other lands, but if the appraised value in fee simple of any property involved in the exchange is at least twenty-five thousand dollars ($25,000), then such exchange may not be made without consultation with the Joint Legislative Commission on Governmental Operations.

(b) For the purposes of this Subchapter, the term "net proceeds" means the gross amount received from the sale, lease, rental, or other disposition of any State lands, less

(1) Such expenses incurred incident to that sale, lease, rental, or other disposition as may be allowed under rules and regulations adopted by the Governor and approved by the Council of State; and

(2) Repealed by Session Laws 1993, c. 553, s. 52.2.

(3) A service charge to be paid into the State Land Fund.

(b1) Notwithstanding the other provisions of this section, no service charge into the State Land Fund shall be deducted from or levied against the proceeds of any disposition by lease, rental, or easement of State lands that are designated as part of the Centennial Campus as defined by G.S. 116-198.33(4), that are designated as part of the Horace Williams Campus as defined by G.S. 116-198.33(4a), or that are designated as part of a Millennial Campus as defined by G.S. 116-198.33(4b). All net proceeds of those dispositions are governed by G.S. 116-36.5.

(b2) Notwithstanding the other provisions of this section, no service charge into the State Land Fund shall be deducted from or levied against the proceeds of any disposition by lease, rental, or easement of State lands purchased and owned by the North Carolina State Highway Patrol, Department of Public Safety, as part of the Voice Interoperability Plan for Emergency Responders (VIPER) project being managed by the North Carolina State Highway Patrol, Department of Public Safety. All net proceeds of these dispositions shall be deposited into an account created in the Department of Public Safety to be used only for the purpose of constructing, maintaining, or supporting the VIPER network.

(c) The amount or rate of such service charge shall be fixed by rules and regulations adopted by the Governor and approved by the Council of State, but as to any particular sale, lease, rental, or other disposition, it shall not exceed ten percent (10%) of the gross amount received from such sale, lease, rental, or other disposition. Notwithstanding any other provision of this Subchapter, the net proceeds derived from the sale of land or products of land owned by or under the supervision and control of the Wildlife Resources Commission, or acquired or purchased with funds of that Commission, shall be paid into the Wildlife Resources Fund. Provided, however, the net proceeds derived from the sale of land or timber from land owned by or under the supervision and control of the Department of Agriculture and Consumer Services shall be deposited with the State Treasurer in a capital improvement account to the credit of the Department of Agriculture and Consumer Services, to be used for such specific capital improvement projects or other purposes as are provided by transfer of funds from those accounts in the Capital Improvement Appropriations Act. Provided further, the net proceeds derived from the sale of park land owned by or under the supervision and control of the Department of Environment and Natural Resources shall be deposited with the State Treasurer in a capital improvement account to the credit of the Department of Administration to be used for the purpose of park land acquisition as provided by transfer of funds from those accounts in the Capital Improvement Appropriations Act. In the Capital Improvement Appropriations Act, line items for purchase of park and agricultural lands will be established for use by the Departments of Administration and Agriculture. The use of such funds for any specific capital improvement project or land acquisition is subject to approval by the Director of the Budget. No other use may be made of funds in these line items without approval by the General Assembly except for incidental expenses related to the project or land acquisition. Additionally with the approval of the Director of the Budget, either Department may request funds from the Contingency and Emergency Fund when the necessity of prompt purchase of available land can be demonstrated and funds in the capital improvement accounts are insufficient. Provided further, the net proceeds derived from the sale of any portion of the land owned by the State in or around the Butner Reservation on or after July 1,

1980, shall be deposited with the State Treasurer in a capital improvement account to the credit of the Department of Health and Human Services to make capital improvements on or to property owned by the State in the Butner Reservation subject to approval by the Office of State Budget and Management, and may be used to build industrial access roads to industries located or to be located on the Butner Reservation, to construct new city streets in the Butner Reservation, extend water and sewer service on the Butner Reservation, repair storm drains on the Butner Reservation, and for other capital uses on the Reservation as determined by the Secretary. Provided further, notwithstanding any other provision of this Subchapter, the proceeds derived from the lease dispositions of land or facilities owned or under the supervision and control of East Carolina University's Division of Health Sciences for the delivery of health care services shall be deposited in clinical accounts at East Carolina University to be used to improve access to patient care. (1959, c. 683, s. 1; 1975, 2nd Sess., c. 983, s. 30; 1977, c. 771, s. 4; c. 1012; 1979, c. 608, s. 1; 1981, c. 859, s. 23.4; c. 1127, s. 33; 1981 (Reg. Sess., 1982), c. 1282, s. 24; 1983, c. 717, ss. 86, 86.1, 86.2, 87; c. 761, s. 166; 1983 (Reg. Sess., 1984), c. 1034, s. 164; c. 1116, s. 97(d); 1989, c. 727, s. 218(155); c. 799, s. 26; 1993, c. 321, s. 260.1; c. 553, s. 52.2; 1997-261, s. 109; 1997-443, s. 11A.119(a); 1998-159, s. 4; 1999-234, s. 8; 2000-140, s. 93.1(a); 2000-177, s. 9; 2001-424, s. 12.2(b); 2007-269, s. 12; 2009-376, s. 15; 2011-145, s. 19.1(g); 2011-373, ss. 1, 2; 2012-194, s. 67.)

Article 8.

Miscellaneous Provisions.

§ 146-31. Right of appeal to Governor and Council of State.

The requesting agency, in the event of disagreement with a decision of the Department of Administration regarding the acquisition or disposition of land pursuant to the provisions of this Subchapter, shall have the right of appeal to the Governor and Council of State. (1957, c. 584, s. 6; G.S., s. 146-113; 1959, c. 683, s. 1.)

§ 146-32. Exemptions as to leases, etc.

The Governor, acting with the approval of the Council of State, may adopt rules and regulations:

(1) Exempting from any or all of the requirements of this Subchapter such classes of lease, rental, easement, and right-of-way transactions as he deems advisable; and

(2) Authorizing any State agency to enter into and/or approve those classes of transactions exempted by such rules and regulations from the requirements of this Chapter.

(3) No rule or regulation adopted under this section may exempt from the provisions of G.S. 146-25.1 any class of lease or rental which has a duration of more than 21 days, unless the class of lease or rental:

a. Is a lease or rental necessitated by a fire, flood, or other disaster that forces the agency seeking the new lease or rental to cease use of real property;

b. Is a lease or rental necessitated because an agency had intended to move to new or renovated real property that was not completed when planned, but a lease or rental exempted under this subparagraph may not be for a period of more than six months; or

c. Is a lease or rental which requires a unique location or a location that adjoins or is in close proximity to an existing rental location. (1959, c. 683, s. 1; 1983 (Reg. Sess., 1984), c. 1116, s. 97; 1985, c. 479, s. 173; 1999-252, s. 3; 1999-456, s. 38.)

§ 146-33. State agencies to locate and mark boundaries of lands.

Every State agency shall locate and identify, and shall mark and keep marked, the boundaries of all lands allocated to that agency or under its control. The Department of Administration shall locate and identify, and mark and keep marked, the boundaries of all State lands not allocated to or under the control of any other State agency. The chief administrative officer of every State agency is authorized to contract with the Division of Adult Correction of the Department of Public Safety for the furnishing, upon such conditions as may be agreed upon from time to time between the Division of Adult Correction of the Department of Public Safety and the chief administrative officer of that agency, of prison labor for use where feasible in the performance of these duties. (1957, c. 584, s. 2; G.S., s. 143-145.1; 1959, c. 683, s. 1; 1967, c. 996, s. 13; 2011-145, s. 19.1(h); 2012-83, s. 57.)

§ 146-34. Agencies may establish agreed boundaries.

Every State agency may establish agreed boundaries between lands allocated to it or under its control, and the lands of any other owner, subject to the approval of the Governor and Council of State. The Department of Administration is authorized to establish agreed boundaries between State lands not allocated to or under the control of any other State agency and the lands of any other owner, subject to the approval of the Governor and Council of State. The Attorney General shall represent the State in all proceedings to establish boundaries which cannot be established by agreement. (1957, c. 584, s. 3; G.S., s. 143-145.2; 1959, c. 683, s. 1.)

§ 146-35. Severance approval delegation.

The Governor, acting with the approval of the Council of State, may adopt rules and regulations delegating to any other State agency the authority to approve the severance of buildings and standing timber from State lands. Upon such approval of severance, the buildings or timber affected shall be, for the purposes of this Chapter, treated as personal property. (1959, c. 683, s. 1.)

§ 146-36. Acquisitions for and conveyances to federal government.

The Governor and Council of State may, whenever they find that it is in the best interest of the State to do so, enter into any contract or other agreement which will be sufficient to comply with federal laws or regulations, binding the State to acquire for and to convey to the United States government land or any interest in land, and to do such other acts and things as may be necessary for such compliance.

The Governor and Council of State may authorize any conveyance to the United States government to be made upon nominal consideration whenever they deem it to be in the best interest of the State to do so. (1959, c. 683, s. 1.)

SUBCHAPTER III. ENTRIES AND GRANTS.

Article 9.

General Provisions.

§ 146-37. Intent of Subchapter.

It is the purpose and intent of this Subchapter to protect vested rights, titles, and interests acquired under the laws governing entries and grants as they read immediately prior to June 2, 1959. (1959, c. 683, s. 1.)

§ 146-38. Pending entries.

All entries which have been filed with entry-takers within one year prior to June 2, 1959, or filed more than one year prior to June 2, 1959, but still pending due to the filing of protest to the entry, shall be processed pursuant to the provisions of Chapter 146 of the General Statutes as it read immediately prior to June 2, 1959. Every such entry shall be paid for within one year from the date of entry, unless a protest be filed to the entry, in which event it shall be paid for within one year after final judgment on the protest; and all entries not thus paid for shall become null and void, and shall not be subject to renewal. It shall be the duty of both the enterer and protestant to conclude, within 12 months from June 2, 1959, all actions wherein a protest has been filed, and such cases shall be given preference on the dockets of the courts of the State. Any action not so concluded shall be deemed a lapse as to enterer and protestant. It is not the intent of this proviso to void any previous grant of the State of North Carolina, or to divest any vested right, but to terminate all rights accrued on account of an entry wherein no grant has been made. Provided that the resident judge of the superior court or the judge holding the superior courts of the district where the land lies, may, for good cause shown, extend the time within which an action in which a protest has been filed is required by this section to be concluded; but no single extension shall exceed one year in duration. A copy of this section shall be mailed by the Secretary of State to all parties to actions wherein protests have been filed as may be determined by records available in his office, and to all clerks of the superior court of the State. (1959, c. 683, s. 1.)

§ 146-39. Void grants; not color of title.

Every entry made and every grant issued for any lands not authorized by G.S. 146-1 through 146-77, as those sections read immediately prior to June 2, 1959, to be entered or granted shall be void.

Every grant of land issued since March 6, 1893, in pursuance of the statutes regulating entries and grants, shall, if such land or any portion thereof has been heretofore granted by this State, so far as relates to any such land heretofore granted, be absolutely void for all purposes whatever, shall confer no rights upon the grantee therein or those claiming under such grantee, and shall in no case and under no circumstances constitute any color of title to any person. (R.C., c. 42, s. 2; Code, s. 2755; 1893, c. 490; Rev., s. 1699; C.S., s. 7545; G.S., s. 146-13; 1959, c. 683, s. 1.)

Article 10.

Surveys.

§ 146-40. Record of surveys to be kept.

The county commissioners of the several counties of the State shall provide a suitable book or books for recording of surveys of entries of land, to be known as Record of Surveys, to be kept in the office of register of deeds as other records are kept. Such record shall have an alphabetical and numerical index, the numerical index to run consecutively. It shall be the duty of every county surveyor or his deputy surveyor who makes a survey to record in such book a perfect and complete record of all surveys of lands made upon any warrant issued upon any entry, and date and sign same as of the date such survey was made. (1905, c. 242; Rev., s. 1722; C.S., s. 7570; G.S., s. 146-39; 1959, c. 683, s. 1.)

§ 146-41. Former surveys recorded.

Where any ex-surveyor of a county is alive and has correct minutes or notes of surveys of land on entries made by him during his term of office, it shall be lawful for him to record and index such survey in the Record of Surveys, and the county commissioners shall pay for such services ten cents (10¢) for each survey so recorded and indexed. (1905, c. 242, s. 2; Rev., s. 1725; C.S., s. 7571; G.S., s. 146-40; 1959, c. 683, s. 1.)

§ 146-42. What record must show; received as evidence.

All surveys so recorded in such book shall show the number of the tract of land, the name of the party entering, and the name of the assignee if there be any assignee; and shall be duly indexed, both alphabetically and numerically, in such record in the name of the party making the entry and in the name of the assignee if there be any assignee. Such record of any surveyor or deputy surveyor when so made shall be read in evidence in any action or proceeding in any court: Provided that if such record differs from the original certificates of survey heretofore made or on file in the office of the Secretary of State, such original or certified copy of the certificate in the Secretary of State's office shall control. (1905, c. 242, ss. 2, 3, 6; Rev., s. 1723; C.S., s. 7572; G.S., s. 146-41; 1959, c. 683, s. 1.)

Article 11.

Grants.

§ 146-43. Cutting timber on land before obtaining a grant.

If any person shall make an entry of any lands, and before perfecting title to same shall enter upon such lands and cut therefrom any wood, trees, or timber, he shall be guilty of a Class 1 misdemeanor. Any person found guilty under the provisions of this section shall further pay to the State double the value of the wood, trees, or timber taken from the land, and it shall be the duty of the solicitor of the district in which the land lies to sue for the same. (1903, c. 272, s. 4; Rev., s. 3741; C.S., s. 7582; G.S., s. 146-51; 1959, c. 683, s. 1; 1993, c. 539, s. 1052; 1994, Ex. Sess., c. 24, s. 14(c).)

§ 146-44. Card index system for grants.

The Secretary of State shall install in his office a card index system for grants, and every warrant, plot, and survey that can be found shall be encased in separate envelopes. Each card and envelope shall show substantially the following:

_____ County
_____ Acres

Name
_____

Grant No._____ Issued
_____

Grant Book _____ Page
_____

Entry No. _____ Entered
_____

File No.
_____

Location
_____

Remarks
_____

Such grant books as are old and falling to pieces shall be recopied, and whenever any part of the record of a grant is partly gone or destroyed the Secretary of State shall restore same, if he can do so with accuracy from the description in the plot and survey upon which the grant was issued and original record made. (1909, c. 505, ss. 1, 2, 3; C.S., s. 7584; G.S., s. 146-53; 1959, c. 683, s. 1.)

§ 146-45. Grant of Moore's Creek Battlefield authorized.

In conjunction with an act of Congress relating to the establishment of the Moore's Creek National Military Park (June 2, 1926, c. 448, s. 2, 44 Stat. 684; U. S. Code, Title 16, ss. 422-422(d)), the Governor of the State of North Carolina is hereby authorized to execute to the United States government a deed vesting the title to Moore's Creek Battlefield, Pender County, in said United States government on behalf of the State of North Carolina, to preserve the same as an historical battlefield: Provided that the consent of the State of North Carolina to such acquisition by the United States is upon the express condition that the State of North Carolina shall so far retain a concurrent jurisdiction with the United States over such battlefield as that all civil and criminal processes issued from the courts of the State of North Carolina may be executed thereon in like manner as if this authority had not been given: Provided further, that the title to said battlefield so conveyed to the United States shall revert to the State of North Carolina unless said land is used for the purpose for which it is ceded. (1925, c. 40; 1927, c. 56; G.S., s. 146-54; 1959, c. 683, s. 1.)

Article 12.

Correction of Grants.

§ 146-46. When grants may issue.

In any case where, under the provisions of this Subchapter, the Secretary of State is authorized to issue a grant or a duplicate grant to correct an error in a prior grant, the grant of correction shall be authenticated by the Governor, countersigned by the Secretary of State, and recorded in the office of the Secretary of State. The date of the entry and the number of the survey from the certificate of survey upon which the grant is founded shall be inserted in every such grant, and a copy of the plot shall be attached to the grant. (1777, c. 114, s. 10, P.R.; 1783, c. 185, s. 14, P.R.; 1796, c. 455, P.R.; 1799, c. 525, s. 2, P.R.; R.C., c. 42, ss. 12, 22; Code, ss. 2769, 2779; 1889, c. 522; Rev., ss. 1729, 1734, 1735; C.S., s. 7578; G.S., s. 146-47; 1959, c. 683, s. 1.)

§ 146-47. Change of county line before grant issued or registered.

All grants issued on entries for lands which were entered in one county, and before the issuing of the grants therefor or the registration of the grants, by the change of former county lines or the establishment of new lines, the lands so entered were placed in a county or in counties different from that in which they were situated, and the grants were registered in the county where the entries were made, shall be good and valid, and the registration of the grant shall have the same force and effect as if they had been registered in the county where the lands were situated. All persons claiming under and by such grants may have them, or a certified copy of the same, from the office of the Secretary of State, or from the office of the register of deeds when they had been erroneously registered, recorded in the office of the register of deeds of the county or counties where the lands lie, and such registration shall have the same force and effect as if the grants had been duly registered in such county or counties. (1897, c. 37; Rev., s. 1736; C.S., s. 7585; G.S., s. 146-55; 1959, c. 683, s. 1.)

§ 146-48. Entries in wrong county.

Whereas many citizens of the State, on making entries of lands near the lines of the county wherein they reside, either for want of proper knowledge of the land laws of the State or not knowing the county lines, have frequently made entries and extended their surveys on such entries into other counties than those wherein they were made, and obtained grants on the same; and whereas doubts have existed with respect to the validity of the titles to lands situated as aforesaid, so far as they extend into other counties than those where the entries were made; for remedy whereof it is hereby declared that all grants issued on entries made for lands situated as aforesaid shall be good and valid against any entries thereafter made or grants issued thereon. (1805, c. 675, P.R.; 1834, c. 17; R.C., c. 42, s. 27; Code, s. 2784; Rev., s. 1737; C.S., s. 7586; G.S., s. 146-56; 1959, c. 683, s. 1.)

§ 146-49. Errors in surveys of plots corrected.

Whenever there may be an error by the surveyor in plotting or making out the certificate for the Secretary's office, or whenever the Secretary shall make a mistake in making out the courses agreeable to such returns, or misname the claimant, or make other mistake, so that such claimant shall be injured thereby, the claimant may prefer a petition to the superior court of the county in which the land lies, setting forth the injury which he might sustain in consequence of such error or mistake, with all the matters and things relative thereto. The court may hear testimony respecting the truth of the allegations set forth in the petition; and if it shall appear by the testimony, from the return of the surveyor or the error of the Secretary, that the patentee is liable to be injured thereby, the court shall direct the clerk to certify the facts to the Secretary of State, who shall file the same in his office, and correct the error in the patent, and likewise in the records of his office. The costs of such suit shall be paid by the petitioner, except when any person may have made himself a party to prevent the prayer of the petitioner being granted, in which case the costs shall be paid as the court may decree. The benefits granted by this section to the patentees of land shall be extended in all cases to persons claiming by, from, or under their grants, by descent, devise, or purchase. When any error is ordered to be rectified, and the same has been carried through from the grant into mesne conveyances, the court shall direct a copy of the order to be recorded in the register's book of the county: Provided no such petition shall be brought but within three years after the date of the patent; and if brought after that time, the court shall dismiss the same, and all proceedings had thereon shall be null and of no effect: Provided further, nothing herein shall affect the rights or interest of any person claiming under a patent issued between the period of the date of the grant alleged to be erroneous and the time of filing the petition, unless such person shall have had due notice of the filing of the petition, by service of a copy thereof, and an opportunity of defending his rights before the court according to the course of the common law. (1790, c. 326, P.R.; 1798, c. 504, P.R.; 1804, c. 655, P.R.; 1814, c. 876, P.R.; R.C., c. 42, s. 28; Code, s. 2785; Rev., s. 1738; C.S., s. 7587; G.S., s. 146-57; 1959, c. 683, s. 1.)

§ 146-50. Resurvey of lands to correct grants.

Persons who have entered vacant lands shall not be defeated in their just claims by mistakes or errors in the surveys and plots furnished by surveyors. In every case where the purchase money has been paid into the State treasury within the time prescribed by law after entry, and the survey or plot furnished shall be found to be defective or erroneous, the party having thus made entry and paid the purchase price may obtain another warrant of survey from the register of deeds of the county where the land lies, and have his entry surveyed as is directed by existing laws. On presenting a certificate of survey and two fair plots thereof to the Secretary of State within six months after the payment of the purchase money, the party making such entry and paying such purchase price shall be entitled to receive, and it shall be the duty of the Secretary of State to issue to him, the proper grant for the lands so entered. (1901, c. 734; Rev., s. 1739; C.S., s. 7588; G.S., s. 146-58; 1959, c. 683, s. 1.)

§ 146-51. Lost seal replaced.

In all cases where the seal annexed to a grant is lost or destroyed, the Governor may, on the certificate of the Secretary of State that the grant was fairly obtained, cause the seal of the State to be affixed thereto. (1807, c. 727, P.R.; R.C., c. 42, s. 24; Code, s. 2781; Rev., s. 1740; C.S., s. 7589; G.S., s. 146-59; 1959, c. 683, s. 1.)

§ 146-52. Errors in grants corrected.

If in issuing any grant the number of the grant or the name of the grantee or any material words or figures suggested by the context have been omitted or not correctly written or given, or the description in the body of the grant does not correspond with the plot and description in the surveyor's certificate attached to the grant, or if in recording the grant in his office the Secretary of State has heretofore made or may hereafter make any mistake or omission by which any part of any grant has not been correctly recorded, the Secretary of State shall, upon the application of any party interested and the payment to him of his lawful fees, correct the original grant by inserting in the proper place the words, figures, or names omitted or not correctly given or suggested by the context; or if the description in the grant does not correspond with the surveyor's plot or certificate, the Secretary of State shall make the former correspond with the latter as the true facts may require. In case the party interested shall prefer it, the Secretary of State shall issue a duplicate of the original grant, including therein the corrections made; and in those cases in which grants have not been correctly recorded, he shall make the proper corrections upon his records, or by rerecording, as he may prefer; and any grant corrected as aforesaid may be recorded in any county of the State as other grants are recorded, and have relation to the time of the entry and date of the grant as in other cases. (1889, c. 460; Rev., s. 1741; C.S., s. 7590; G.S., s. 146-60; 1959, c. 683, s. 1.)

§ 146-53. Irregular entries validated.

Wherever persons have, prior to January 1, 1883, irregularly entered lands and have paid the fees required by law to the Secretary of State, and have obtained grants for such lands duly executed, the title to the lands shall not be affected by reason of such irregular entries; and the grants are hereby declared to be as valid as if such entries had been properly made. (1868-9, c. 100, s. 4; c. 173, s. 6; 1874-5, c. 48; Code, s. 2761; Rev., s. 1743; C.S., s. 7591; G.S., s. 146-61; 1959, c. 683, s. 1.)

§ 146-54. Grant signed by deputy Secretary of State validated.

Where State grants have heretofore been issued and the name of the Secretary of State has been affixed thereto by his deputy or chief clerk, or by anyone purporting to act in such capacity, such grants are hereby declared valid; but nothing herein contained shall interfere with vested rights. (1905, c. 512; Rev., s. 1744; C.S., s. 7592; G.S., s. 146-62; 1959, c. 683, s. 1.)

§ 146-55. Registration of grants.

Every person obtaining a grant shall, within two years after such grant is perfected, cause the same to be registered in the county where the land lies; and any person may cause to be there registered any certified copy of a grant from the office of the Secretary of State, which shall have the same effect as if the original had been registered. (1783, c. 185, s. 14, P.R.; 1796, c. 455, P.R.; 1799, c. 525, s. 2, P.R.; R.S., c. 42, s. 24; R.C., c. 42, s. 22; Code, s. 2779; Rev., s. 1729; C.S., s. 7579; G.S., s. 146-48; 1959, c. 683, s. 1.)

§ 146-56. Time for registering grants extended.

All grants from the State of North Carolina of lands and interests in land heretofore made, which were required or allowed to be registered within a time specified by law, or in the grants themselves, may be registered in the counties in which the lands lie respectively at any time within six years from January 1, 1918, notwithstanding the fact that such specified time has already expired, and all such grants heretofore registered after the expiration of such specified time shall be taken and treated as if they had been registered within such specified time: Provided that nothing herein contained shall be held or have the effect to divest any rights, titles, or equities in or to the land covered by such grants, or any of them, acquired by any person from the State of North Carolina by or through any entry or grant made or issued since such grants were respectively issued, or those claiming through or under such subsequent entry or grant. (1893, c. 40; 1901, c. 175; 1905, c. 6; Rev., s. 1747; 1907, c. 805; 1909, c. 167; 1911, c. 182; Ex. Sess. 1913, cc. 27, 45; 1915, c. 170; 1917, c. 84; C.S., s. 7593; Ex. Sess. 1920, c. 78; 1921, c. 153; G.S., s. 146-63; 1959, c. 683, s. 1.)

§ 146-57. Time for registering grants and other instruments extended.

The time is hereby extended until September 1, 1926, for the proving and registering of all deeds of gift, grants from the State, or other instruments of writing heretofore executed and which are permitted or required by law to be registered, and which were or are required to be proved and registered within a limited time from the date of their execution; and all such instruments which have heretofore been or may be probated and registered before the expiration of the period herein limited shall be held and deemed, from and after the date of such registration, to have been probated and registered in due time, if proved in due form, and registration thereof be in other respects valid: Provided that nothing in this section shall be held or deemed to validate or attempt to validate or give effect to any informal instrument; and provided further that this section shall not affect pending litigation: Provided further that nothing herein contained shall be held deemed to place any limitation upon the time allowed for the registration of any instrument where no such limit is now fixed by law. (Ex. Sess. 1924, c. 20; G.S., s. 146-64; 1959, c. 683, s. 1.)

§ 146-58. Time for registering grants further extended.

The time for the registration of grants issued by the State of North Carolina is hereby extended for a period of two years from January 1, 1925: Provided that nothing herein contained shall be held or have the effect to divest any rights, titles, or equities in or to the land covered by such grants, or any of them, acquired by any person from the State of North Carolina by or through any entry or grant made or issued since such grants were respectively issued, or those claiming through or under such subsequent entry or grant. (1925, c. 97; G.S., s. 146-65; 1959, c. 683, s. 1.)

§ 146-59. Time for registering grants or copies extended.

The time for the registration of grants issued by the State of North Carolina, or copies of such grants duly certified by the Secretary of State under his official seal, be and the same hereby is extended for a period of two years from January 1, 1927, and such grants or copies thereof duly certified as above set forth may be registered within such time as fully as the original might have been registered at any time heretofore: Provided that nothing herein contained shall be held or have the effect to divest any rights, titles, or equities in or to the land covered by such grants or any of them, acquired by any person from the State of North Carolina by or through any entry or grant made or issued since such grants were respectively issued, or those claiming through or under such subsequent entry or grant. (1927, c. 140; G.S., s. 146-66; 1959, c. 683, s. 1.)

§ 146-60. Further extension of time for registering grants or copies for two years from January 1, 1947.

The time for the registration of grants issued by the State of North Carolina, or copies of such grants duly certified by the Secretary of State under his official seal, be and the same hereby is extended for a period of two years from January 1, 1947, next ensuing, and such grants or copies thereof duly certified as above set forth may be registered within such time as fully as the original might have been registered at any time heretofore: Provided that nothing herein contained shall be held or have the effect to divest any rights, titles, or equities in or to the land covered by such grants or any of them acquired by any person from the State of North Carolina by or through any entry or grant made or issued since such grants were respectively issued, or those claiming through or under such subsequent entry or grant. (1947, c. 99; G.S., s. 146-66.1; 1959, c. 683, s. 1.)

§ 146-60.1. Further extension of time for registering grants or copies for four years from January 1, 1977.

The time for the registration of grants issued by the State of North Carolina, or copies of such grants duly certified by the Secretary of State under his official seal, be and the same hereby is extended for a period of four years from January 1, 1977, and such grants or copies thereof duly certified as above set forth may be registered within such time as fully as the original might have been registered at any time heretofore: Provided that nothing herein contained shall be held or have the effect to divest any rights, titles, or equities in or to the land covered by such grants or any of them acquired by any person from the State of North Carolina by or through any entry or grant made or issued since such grants were respectively issued, or those claiming through or under such subsequent entry or grant. (1977, c. 701.)

Article 13.

Grants Vacated.

§ 146-61. Civil action to vacate grant.

When any person claiming title to lands under a grant or patent from the King of Great Britain, any of the lords proprietors of North Carolina, or from the State of North Carolina, shall consider himself aggrieved by any grant or patent issued or made since July 4, 1776, to any other person, against law or obtained by false suggestions, surprise, or fraud, the person aggrieved may bring a civil action in the superior court for the county in which such land may be, together with an authenticated copy of such grant or patent, briefly stating the grounds whereon such patent should be repealed and vacated, whereupon the grantee, patentee, or the person, owner, or claimant under such grant or patent, shall be required to show cause why the same shall not be repealed and vacated. (R.C., c. 42, s. 29; Code, s. 2786; Rev., s. 1748; C.S., s. 7594; G.S., s. 146-67; 1959, c. 683, s. 1.)

§ 146-62. Judgment recorded in Secretary of State's office.

If, upon verdict or demurrer, the court believe that the patent or grant was made against law or obtained by fraud, surprise, or upon untrue suggestions, it may vacate the same; and a copy of such judgment, after being recorded at large, shall be filed by the petitioner in the Secretary of State's office, where it shall be recorded in a book kept for that purpose; and the Secretary shall note in the margin of the original record of the grant the entry of the judgment, with a reference to the record in his office. (R.C., c. 42, s. 30; Code, s. 2787; Rev., s. 1749; C.S., s. 7595; G.S., s. 146-68; 1959, c. 683, s. 1.)

§ 146-63. Action by State to vacate grants.

An action may be brought by the Attorney General in the name of the State for the purpose of vacating or annulling letters patent granted by the State, in the following cases:

(1) When he has reason to believe that such letters patent were obtained by means of some fraudulent suggestion or concealment of a material fact, made by the person to whom the same were issued or made, or with his consent or knowledge; or

(2) When he has reason to believe that such letters patent were issued through mistake, or in ignorance of a material fact; or

(3) When he has reason to believe that the patentee, or those claiming under him, have done or omitted an act in violation of the terms and conditions on which the letters patent were granted, or have by any other means forfeited the interest acquired under the same. (C. C. P., s. 367; Code, s. 2788; Rev., s. 1750; C.S., s. 7596; G.S., s. 146-69; 1959, c. 683, s. 1.)

SUBCHAPTER IV. MISCELLANEOUS.

Article 14.

General Provisions.

§ 146-64. Definitions.

As used in this Chapter:

(1) "Acquired lands" means all State lands, title to which has been acquired by the State or by any State agency by purchase, devise, gift, condemnation, or adverse possession.

(2) "Escheated lands" means all State lands, title to which has been acquired by escheat.

(3) "Land" means real property, buildings, space in buildings, timber rights, mineral rights, rights-of-way, easements, options, and all other rights, estates, and interests in real property.

(4) "Navigable waters" means all waters which are navigable in fact.

(5) "State agency" includes every agency, institution, board, commission, bureau, council, department, division, officer, and employee of the State, but does not include counties, municipal corporations, political subdivisions of the State, county or city boards of education, or other local public bodies. The term "State agency" does not include any private corporation created by act of the General Assembly. In case of doubt as to whether a particular agency, corporation, or institution is a State agency for the purposes of this Chapter, the Attorney General, upon request of the Governor and Council of State, shall make a determination of the issue. Upon a finding by the Attorney General that an agency, corporation, or institution is not a State agency for the purpose of this Chapter, the Governor and Council of State may execute a deed or other appropriate instrument releasing and quitclaiming all title and interest of the State in the lands of that agency, corporation, or institution.

(6) "State lands" means all land and interests therein, title to which is vested in the State of North Carolina, or in any State agency, or in the State to the use of any agency, and specifically includes all vacant and unappropriated lands, swamplands, submerged lands, lands acquired by the State by virtue of being sold for taxes, escheated lands, and acquired lands.

(7) "Submerged lands" means State lands which lie beneath

a. Any navigable waters within the boundaries of this State, or

b. The Atlantic Ocean to a distance of three geographical miles seaward from the coastline of this State.

(8) "Swamplands" means lands too wet for cultivation except by drainage, and includes

a. All State lands which have been or are known as "swamp" or "marsh" lands, "pocosin bay," "briary bay" or "savanna," and which are a part of one swamp exceeding 2,000 acres in area, or which are a part of one swamp 2,000 acres or less in area which has been surveyed by the State; and

b. All State lands which are covered by the waters of any state-owned lake or pond.

(9) "Vacant and unappropriated lands" means all State lands title to which is vested in the State as sovereign, and land acquired by the State by virtue of being sold for taxes, except swamplands.

(10) For purposes of this Subchapter, "deep water" means the depth reasonably necessary to provide and allow reasonable access for all vessels traditionally used in the main watercourse area as of the time of the initial easement application. (1854-5, c. 21; R.C., c. 42, s. 1; Code, s. 2751; 1891, c. 302; Rev., ss. 1693, 1695; C.S., ss. 7540, 7542; G.S., ss. 146-1, 146-4; 1959, c. 683, s. 1; 1969, c. 1164; 1995, c. 529, s. 4; 2009-484, s. 10.)

§ 146-65. Exemptions from Chapter.

This Chapter does not apply to any of the following:

(1) The acquisition of highway rights-of-way, borrow pits, or other interests or estates in land acquired for the same or similar purposes, or to the disposition thereof, by the Board of Transportation or the North Carolina Turnpike Authority.

(2) The North Carolina State Ports Authority in exercising its powers under G.S. 136-260 through G.S. 136-275. (1957, c. 584, s. 6; G.S., s. 146-112; 1959, c. 683, s. 1; 1973, c. 507, s. 5; 1993, c. 553, s. 52.3; 2008-225, s. 10; 2011-145, s. 14.6(i).)

§ 146-66. Voidability of transactions contrary to Chapter.

Any sale, lease, rental, or other disposition of State lands or of any interest or right therein, made or entered into contrary to the provisions of this Chapter, shall be voidable in the discretion of the Governor and Council of State. (1957, c. 584, s. 6; G.S., s. 146-111; 1959, c. 683, s. 1.)

§ 146-67. Governor to employ persons.

The Governor may employ persons to perform such services as may be necessary to carry out the provisions of this Chapter, and he shall fix the compensation to be paid for such services. All expenditures for such services shall be paid from the State Land Fund on order of the Director of the Budget, or the officer designated by him to issue such orders. (1959, c. 683, s. 1.)

§ 146-68. Statutes of limitation.

The provisions of G.S. 1-35, 1-36, and 1-37 are made applicable to this Chapter. (1959, c. 683, s. 1.)

§ 146-69. Service on State in land actions.

In all actions and special proceedings brought by or against the State or any State agency with respect to State land or any interest therein, service of process upon the Secretary of Administration, with delivery to him of copies for the Attorney General and for the administrative head of each State agency known by the party in whose behalf service is made to have an interest in the land which is the subject of the action or proceeding, shall constitute service upon the State for all purposes. (1959, c. 683, s. 1; 1975, c. 879, s. 46.)

§ 146-70. Institution of land actions by the State.

Every action or special proceeding in behalf of the State or any State agency with respect to State lands or any interest therein, or with respect to land being condemned by the State, shall be brought by the Attorney General in the name of the State, upon the complaint of the Secretary of Administration. (1959, c. 683, s. 1; 1975, c. 879, s. 46.)

Article 15.

State Land Fund.

§ 146-71. State Land Fund created.

The State Land Fund, which is hereby created, shall consist of the moneys required by this Chapter to be paid into that fund, together with such amounts as the General Assembly may appropriate thereto. (1959, c. 683, s. 1.)

§ 146-72. Purpose.

The State Land Fund may, in accordance with rules and regulations adopted by the Governor and approved by the Council of State, be used for the following purposes:

(1) To pay any expenses incurred in carrying out the duties and responsibilities created by the provisions of this Chapter.

(2) For the acquisition of land, when appropriation is made for that purpose by the General Assembly. (1959, c. 683, s. 1.)

§ 146-73. Administration.

The State Land Fund shall be administered by the Department of Administration, in accordance with rules and regulations adopted by the Governor and approved by the Council of State. All expenditures from the fund shall be made upon order of the Director of the Budget, or of the officer designated by him to issue such orders. (1959, c. 683, s. 1.)

Article 16.

Form of Conveyances.

§ 146-74. Approval of conveyances.

Every proposed conveyance in fee, including conveyances by gift, of State lands shall be submitted to the Governor and Council of State for their approval. If the proposed conveyance is of State lands with an appraised value of at least twenty-five thousand dollars ($25,000), and it is for other than a transportation purpose, the Council of State shall consult with the Joint Legislative

Commission on Governmental Operations before making a final decision on the proposed conveyance. Upon approval of the proposed conveyance in fee by the Governor and Council of State, a deed for the land being conveyed shall be executed in the manner prescribed in this Article. (1957, c. 584, s. 7; G.S., ss. 143-147; 1959, c. 683, s. 1; 1983 (Reg. Sess., 1984), c. 1116, s. 97; 1993, c. 561, s. 32(b).)

§ 146-75. Execution; signature; attestation; seal.

Each such conveyance in fee shall be in the usual form of deeds of conveyance of real property and shall be executed in the name of the State of North Carolina, signed in the name of the State by the Governor, and attested by the Secretary of State; and the great seal of the State of North Carolina shall be affixed thereto. (1929, c. 143, s. 2; G.S., s. 143-148; 1959, c. 683, s. 1.)

§ 146-76. Exclusive method of conveying State lands.

The manner and method of conveying State lands herein set out shall be the exclusive and only method of conveying State lands in fee. Any conveyance thereof by any other person or executed in any other manner or by any other method shall not be effective to convey the interest or estate of the State in such land. (1929, c. 143, s. 4; G.S., s. 143-150; 1959, c. 683, s. 1.)

§ 146-77. Admission to registration in counties.

Each such conveyance shall be admitted to registration in the several counties of the State upon the probate required by law for deeds of corporations. (1929, c. 143, s. 3; G.S., s. 143-149; 1959, c. 683, s. 1.)

§ 146-78. Validation of conveyances of state-owned lands.

All conveyances heretofore made by the Governor, attested by the Secretary of State, and authorized by the Council of State, in the manner provided by G.S.

146-74 and 146-75 of any lands, the title to which was vested in the State for the use of any State institution, department, or agency, or vested in the State for any other purpose, are hereby ratified and validated. (1917, c. 129; C.S., s. 7524; 1951, c. 18; 1957, c. 584, s. 7; G.S., s. 143-146; 1959, c. 683, s. 1.)

Article 17.

Title in State.

§ 146-79. Title presumed in the State; tax titles.

In all controversies and suits for any land to which the State or any State agency or its assigns shall be a party, the title to such lands shall be taken and deemed to be in the State or the State agency or its assigns until the other party shall show that he has a good and valid title to such lands in himself.

In all controversies touching the title or the right of possession of any lands claimed by the State or by any State agency under any sale for taxes at any time heretofore made or which hereafter may be made, the deed of conveyance made by the sheriff or other officer or person making such sale, or who may have been authorized to execute such deed, shall be presumptive evidence that the lands therein mentioned were, at the time the lien for such taxes attached and at the time of the sale, the property of the person therein designated as the delinquent owner; that such lands were subject to taxation; that the taxes were duly levied and assessed; that the lands were duly listed; that the taxes were due and unpaid; that the manner in which the listing, assessment, levy, and sale were conducted was in all respects as the law directed; that all the prerequisites of the law were duly complied with by all officers or persons who had or whose duty it was to have had any part or action in any transaction relating to or affecting the title conveyed or purported to be conveyed by the deed, from the listing and valuation of the property up to the execution of the deed, both inclusive; and that all things whatsoever required by law to make a good and valid sale and vest the title in the purchaser were done, and that all recitals in such deed contained are true as to each and every of the matters so recited.

In all controversies and suits involving the title to real property claimed and held under and by virtue of a deed made substantially as above, the person claiming title adverse to the title conveyed by such deed shall be required to prove, in order to defeat such title, either that the real property was not subject to taxation for the year or years named in the deed, that the taxes had been paid before the sale, that the property had been redeemed from the sale according to the provisions of law, and that such redemption was had or made for the use or benefit of persons having the right of redemption under the laws of this State, or that there had been an entire omission to list or assess the property or to levy the taxes or to sell the property; but no person shall be permitted to question the title acquired under such sale and deed without first showing that he or the person under whom he claims title had title to the property at the time of the sale, and that all taxes due upon the property have been paid by such person or the person under whom he claims title. (1842-3, c. 36, s. 3; R.C., c. 66, s. 24; Code, s. 2527; 1889, c. 243; Rev., s. 4047; C.S., s. 7617; G.S., s. 146-90; 1959, c. 683, s. 1.)

§ 146-80. Statute of limitations.

No statute of limitations shall affect the title or mar the action of the State, or of any State agency, or of its assigns, unless the same would protect the person holding and claiming adversely against the State. Neither the State nor any State agency, nor its assigns, shall commence any action for the recovery of damages for timber cut and removed from lands owned by the State or by any State agency or for any other act of trespass committed on such lands, more than 10 years after the occurrence of such cutting, removal, or other act of trespass. The provisions of this section shall not have the effect of reviving any cause of action which was, at the date of ratification of this Chapter, barred by any applicable statute of limitations. (1842, c. 36, s. 5; R.C., c. 66, s. 25; Code, s. 2528; Rev., s. 4048; 1917, c. 287; C.S., s. 7618; G.S., s. 146-91; 1959, c. 683, s. 1.)

§ 146-81. Title to lands sold for taxes.

The title to all land acquired by the State by virtue of being sold for taxes is hereby vested in the State of North Carolina. (1917, c. 209; C.S., s. 7615; G.S., s. 146-88; 1959, c. 683, s. 1.)

§ 146-82. Protection of interest in lands sold for taxes.

Whenever any lands in which the State of North Carolina or any State agency has an interest, by way of mortgage or otherwise, are advertised to be sold for any taxes or special assessment, or under any lien, the Department of Administration is authorized, if in its judgment it is necessary to protect the interest of the State, to appear at any sale of such lands and to buy the same as any other person would. For the purpose of paying therefor, the Director of the Budget is authorized to draw upon the State Land Fund. (1917, c. 246; C.S., s. 7616; G.S., s. 146-89; 1959, c. 683, s. 1.)

Article 18.

Miscellaneous.

§ 146-83. Vested rights protected.

No provision of this Chapter shall be applied or construed to the detriment of vested rights, interests, or estates of any private individual, firm, or corporation, acquired prior to June 2, 1959. (1959, c. 683, s. 1.)

Chapter 147.

State Officers.

Article 1.

Classification and General Provisions.

§ 147-1. Public State officials classified.

The public officers of the State are legislative, executive, and judicial. But this classification shall not be construed as defining the legal powers of either class. (1868-9, c. 270, ss. 1, 2; Code, s. 3317; Rev., s. 5323; C.S., s. 7624.)

§ 147-2. Legislative officers.

The legislative officers are:

(1) Fifty Senators;

(2) One hundred and twenty members of the House of Representatives;

(3) A Speaker of the House of Representatives;

(4) A clerk and assistants in each house;

(5) A Sergeant-at-arms and assistants in each house;

(6) As many subordinates in each house as may be deemed necessary. (1868-9, c. 270, s. 3; Code, s. 3318; Rev., s. 5324; C.S., s. 7625; 1995, c. 379, s. 13.)

§ 147-3. Executive officers.

(a) Executive officers are either:

(1) Civil;

(2) Military.

(b) Civil executive officers are:

(1) General, or for the whole State;

(2) Special, or for special duties in different parts of the State;

(3) Local, or for a particular part of the State.

(c) The general civil executive officers of this State are as follows:

(1) A Governor;

(2) A Lieutenant Governor;

(3) Private secretary for the Governor;

(4) A Secretary of State;

(5) An Auditor;

(6) A Treasurer;

(7) An Attorney General;

(8) A Superintendent of Public Instruction;

(9) The members of the Governor's Council;

(10) A Commissioner of Agriculture;

(11) A Commissioner of Labor;

(12) A Commissioner of Insurance. (1868-9, c. 270, ss. 24, 25, 26; Code, s. 3319; 1899, c. 54, ss. 3, 4; c. 373; 1901, c. 479, s. 4; Rev., s. 5325; C.S., s. 7626; 1931, c. 312, s. 5; 1943, c. 170.)

§ 147-4. Executive officers - election; term; induction into office.

The executive department shall consist of a Governor, a Lieutenant Governor, a Secretary of State, an Auditor, a Treasurer, a Superintendent of Public Instruction, an Attorney General, a Commissioner of Agriculture, a Commissioner of Insurance, and a Commissioner of Labor, who shall be elected for a term of four years, by the qualified electors of the State, at the same time and places, and in the same manner, as members of the General Assembly are elected. Their term of office shall commence on the first day of January next after their election and continue until their successors are elected and qualified. The persons having the highest number of votes, respectively, shall be declared duly elected, but if two or more be equal and highest in votes for the same office, then one of them shall be chosen by joint ballot of both houses of the General Assembly. Contested elections shall be determined by a joint ballot of both houses of the General Assembly in such manner as shall be prescribed by law. (Const., art. 3, ss. 1, 3; 1897, c. 1, ss. 1, 2, 3; Rev., s. 5326; C.S., s. 7627; 1931, c. 312, s. 5; 1953, c. 2; 1981, c. 504, s. 7; 1985, c. 563, s. 12.)

§ 147-5. Executive officers - report to Governor; reports transmitted to General Assembly.

It shall be the duty of the officers of the executive department to submit their respective reports to the Governor to be transmitted by him with his message to the General Assembly. (1813, c. 60, s. 2, P.R.; Rev., s. 5373; C.S., s. 7628.)

Article 2.

Expenses of State Officers and State Departments.

§ 147-6. Expenses paid by warrants; statements filed.

All salaries, purchases of equipment and expenses authorized by law to be paid out of the various funds herebefore mentioned shall be paid by warrant drawn on the State Treasurer. The officer of State or head of any department thereof shall file an itemized statement of the salaries, bills for purchase of equipment and other expenses of his department, and warrants shall be drawn on the State Treasurer for the payment of all salaries, purchases of equipment, and expenses as authorized by law, to be paid by the said officer of State or head of any department thereof, as evidenced by statements so approved and filed. The State Treasurer is hereby authorized and directed to pay said warrants. (1919, c. 117, s. 2; C.S., s. 7630; 1983, c. 913, s. 44.)

§ 147-7. Traveling expenses on State's business.

When, to efficiently and properly carry into effect and execute any of the duties imposed by his appointment or by the provision of any statute of this State, and provide for the expenses thereof, it is required that any officer of the State or any employee of any department thereof shall travel from place to place, such traveling and other expenses as shall be required shall be approved by said officer or head of the department whose employee incurs such expenses. (1919, c. 117, s. 3; C.S., s. 7631.)

§ 147-8. Mileage allowance to officers or employees using public or private automobiles.

Where it is provided by any law affecting the State of North Carolina, or any subdivision thereof, whereby any employee or officer of the same is allowed to charge mileage for the use of any motor vehicle when owned by the State or any subdivision thereof or by any such employee or officer of the State or any subdivision thereof, when in the discharge of any duties imposed upon him by reason of his employment or office, the same is hereby repealed to the extent that said charge shall be limited to the actual miles traveled by said motor vehicle and no mileage charge shall be allowed for but one occupant of any motor vehicle so used, and provided further that no such mileage charge shall exceed seven cents (7¢) per mile. (1931, c. 382, s. 1; 1953, c. 675, s. 20.)

§ 147-9. Unlawful to pay more than allowance.

It shall be unlawful for any officer, auditor, bookkeeper, clerk or other employee of the State of North Carolina or any subdivision thereof to knowingly approve any claim or charge on the part of any person for mileage by reason of the use of any motor vehicle owned by the State or any subdivision thereof or by any person and used in the pursuit of his employment or office in excess of seven cents (7¢) per mile as set out in G.S. 147-8 and any officer, auditor, bookkeeper, clerk or other employee violating the provisions of this section shall be guilty of a Class 1 misdemeanor. (1931, c. 382, s. 2; 1953, c. 675, s. 21; 1993, c. 539, s. 1053; 1994, Ex. Sess., c. 24, s. 14(c).)

§ 147-9.1. Municipalities and counties exempt.

Nothing in this Article shall be deemed to be applicable to counties or municipalities or to limit or restrict the amount of any automobile mileage allowance, or automobile expense allowance, or any other travel expense allowance or payment which may be paid by a county or municipality or by any board, commission, or other agency of any county or municipality. (1967, c. 941; 1969, c. 180, s. 2.)

Article 2A.

Annuities and Deferred Compensation for Teachers and State Employees.

§ 147-9.2. Definitions.

The following words when used in this Article shall have the meanings ascribed to them in this section except when the context clearly indicates a different meaning:

(1) "Board" shall mean the Board of Trustees of the North Carolina Public Employee Deferred Compensation Plan established pursuant to Chapter 433 of the 1971 Session Laws and G.S. 143B-426.24.

(1a) "Chief executive officer" shall mean the person or group of persons responsible for the administration of any employer, or an agent of such chief executive officer duly authorized to enter into the contracts with teachers or State employees referred to in G.S. 147-9.3 and 147-9.4.

(2) "Employee" shall mean a permanent employee of the State of North Carolina, or of any of its departments or agencies, or of any of its wholly owned institutions and instrumentalities.

(3) "Employer" shall mean (i) the State of North Carolina, its departments and agencies, and its wholly owned institutions and instrumentalities or (ii) a local board of education.

(4) "Plan" shall mean the North Carolina Public Employee Deferred Compensation Plan.

(5) "Teacher" shall have the meaning provided in G.S. 135-1(25). (1971, c. 433, s. 1; 1983, c. 559, s. 2; 1991, c. 389, s. 1.)

§ 147-9.3. Annuity contracts; salary deductions.

Notwithstanding the provisions of G.S. 143B-426.40A and notwithstanding any provision of law relating to salaries or salary schedules of State employees, if the employee be one described in section 403(b)(1)(A)(i) or (ii) of the United States Internal Revenue Code, the chief executive officer of such employee, on behalf of the employer, may enter into an annual contract with the employee which provides for a reduction in salary below the total established compensation or salary schedule for a term of one year. The chief executive officer shall use the funds derived from the reduction in the salary of the employee to purchase a nonforfeitable annuity or retirement income contract for the benefit of said employee. An employee who has agreed to a salary reduction for this purpose shall not have the right to receive the amount of salary reduction in cash or in any other way except the annuity or retirement income contract. Funds used for the purchase of an annuity or retirement income contract shall not be in lieu of any amount earned by the employee before his election for a salary reduction has become effective. The agreement for salary reduction referred to herein shall be effective under the necessary regulations and procedures adopted by the chief executive officer and on forms prescribed by him. Notwithstanding any other provision of law, the amount by which the salary of an employee is reduced pursuant to this section shall not be excluded, but shall be included, in computing and making payroll deductions for social security and retirement system purposes, if any, and in computing and providing matching funds for retirement system purposes, if any. (1971, c. 433, s. 2; 1991, c. 389, s. 1; 2006-66, s. 6.19(a); 2006-203, s. 112; 2006-221, s. 3A; 2006-259, s. 40(a).)

§ 147-9.4. Deferred Compensation Plan.

Notwithstanding the provisions of G.S. 143B-426.40A and notwithstanding any provision of law relating to salaries or salary schedules of teachers or State employees, the chief executive officer of an employer, on behalf of the employer, may from time to time enter into a contract with a teacher or employee under which the teacher or employee irrevocably elects to defer receipt of a portion of his scheduled salary in the future, but only if, as a result of such contract, the income so deferred is deferred pursuant to the Plan provided for in G.S. 143B-426.24 or pursuant to some other plan established before January 1, 1983, and is not constructively received by the teacher or employee in the year in which it was earned, for State and federal income tax purposes. In addition, the income so deferred shall be invested in the manner provided in the applicable Plan; however, the teacher or employee may revoke his election to participate and may amend the amount of compensation to be deferred by signing and filing with the Board a written revocation or amendment on a form and in the manner approved by the Board. Any such revocation or amendment shall be effective prospectively only and shall cause no change in the allocation of amounts invested prior to the filing date of such revocation or amendment.

A teacher or employee who has agreed to the deferral of income pursuant to the Plan shall have the right to receive the income so deferred only in accordance with the provisions of the Plan. Funds so deferred shall not be in lieu of any amount earned by the teacher or employee before his election to defer compensation became effective. The agreement to defer income referred to herein shall be effective under such necessary regulations and procedures as are adopted by the Board, and on forms prepared or approved by it. A teacher or employee who agrees to defer income as provided in this section may authorize payroll deductions for deferral of the income. An employer shall make payroll deduction available for a teacher or employee who authorizes payroll deduction. Notwithstanding any other provisions of law, the amount by which the salary of a teacher or employee is deferred pursuant to the Plan shall not be excluded, but shall be included, in computing and making payroll deductions for social security and retirement system purposes, if any, and in computing and providing matching funds for retirement system purposes, if any.

Except for the applications of the provisions of G.S. 110-136, and in connection with a court-ordered equitable distribution under G.S. 50-20, the right of a teacher or employee, who elects to defer income pursuant to the North Carolina Public Employee Deferred Compensation Plan under G.S. 143B-426.24, to benefits that have vested under the Plan, is nonforfeitable. These benefits are exempt from levy, sale, and garnishment, except as provided by this section. (1971, c. 433, s. 3; 1983, c. 559, s. 3; 1985, c. 660, s. 4; 1989, c. 792, s. 2.10; 1991, c. 389, s. 1; 2006-66, s. 6.19(a); 2006-203, s. 113; 2006-221, s. 3A; 2006-259, s. 40(a).)

Article 3.

The Governor.

§ 147-10. Governor to reside in Raleigh; mansion and accessories.

The Governor shall reside in the City of Raleigh during his continuance in office. A convenient and commodious furnished dwelling house, supplied with necessary lights, fuel, and water, shall be provided for his accommodation; and an automobile and driver shall be provided and maintained for the use of the executive mansion. (1868-69, c. 270, ss. 32, 33; Code, ss. 3325, 3326; 1885, c. 244; Rev., s. 5327; 1919, c. 307; C.S., s. 7635.)

§ 147-11. Salary and expense allowance of Governor; allowance to person designated to represent Governor's office.

(a) The salary of the Governor shall be one hundred forty-one thousand two hundred sixty-five dollars ($141,265) annually, payable monthly.

(b) He shall be paid annually the sum of eleven thousand five hundred dollars ($11,500) as an expense allowance in attending to the business for the State and for expenses out of the State and in the State in representing the interest of the State and people, incident to the duties of his office, the said allowance to be paid monthly.

(c) In addition to the foregoing allowance, the actual expenses of the Governor while traveling outside the State on business incident to his office shall be paid by a warrant drawn on the State Treasurer. Whenever a person who is not a State official or employee is designated by the Governor to represent the Governor's office, such person shall be paid actual travel expenses incurred in the performance of such duty; provided that the payment of such travel expense shall conform to the provisions of the biennial appropriation act in effect at the time the payment is made. (1879, c. 240; Code, s. 3720; 1901, c. 8; Rev., s. 2736; 1907, c. 1009; 1911, c. 89; 1917, cc. 11, 235; 1919, c. 320; C.S., s. 3858; 1929, c. 276, s. 1; 1947, c. 994; 1953, c. 1, s. 1; 1961, c. 1157; 1963, c. 1178, s. 1; 1965, c. 1091, s. 1; 1971, c. 1083, s. 1; 1973, c. 600; 1977, 2nd Sess., c. 1136, s. 39; c. 1249, s. 5; 1979, 2nd Sess., c. 1137, s. 31; 1981, c. 1127, s. 7; 1983, c. 761, ss. 194, 195; c. 913, s. 45; 1983 (Reg. Sess., 1984), c. 1034, s. 217; 1985, c. 479, s. 215; 1985 (Reg. Sess., 1986), c. 1014, s. 20; 1987, c. 738, s. 11; 1987 (Reg. Sess., 1988), c. 1086, ss. 6, 172; 1989, c. 752, ss. 23(a), (b), 167; 1991 (Reg. Sess., 1992), c. 900, ss. 32(a), (b), 182; 1993, c. 321, s. 48; 1993 (Reg. Sess., 1994), c. 769, s. 7.1; 1995, c. 507, s. 7.1(a); 1996, 2nd Ex. Sess., c. 18, s. 28(a); 1997-443, s. 33(a); 1998-153, s. 3(a); 1999-237, s. 28(a); 2000-67, s. 26(a); 2004-124, s. 31.1(b); 2005-276, s. 29.1(a); 2006-66, s. 22.1(a); 2007-323, s. 28.1(a); 2008-107, s. 26.1(a); 2012-142, s. 25.01(b).)

§ 147-11.1. Succession to office of Governor; Acting Governor.

(a) Lieutenant Governor. -

(1) The Lieutenant Governor-elect shall become Governor upon the failure of the Governor-elect to qualify. The Lieutenant Governor shall become Governor upon the death, resignation, or removal from office of the Governor. The further order of succession to the office of Governor shall be prescribed by law. A successor shall serve for the remainder of the term of the Governor whom he succeeds and until a new Governor is elected and qualified.

(2) During the absence of the Governor from the State, or during the physical or mental incapacity of the Governor to perform the duties of his office, the Lieutenant Governor shall be Acting Governor. The further order of succession as Acting Governor shall be prescribed by law.

(b) President of Senate, Speaker of the House and Other Officers. -

(1) If, by reason of failure to qualify, death, resignation, or removal from office, there is neither a Governor nor a Lieutenant Governor to discharge the powers and duties of the office of Governor, then the President of the Senate shall, upon his resignation as President of the Senate and as Senator, become Governor.

(2) If, at the time when under subdivision (1) of this subsection the President of the Senate is to become Governor, there is no President of the Senate, or the President of the Senate fails to qualify as Governor, then the Speaker of the House of Representatives shall, upon his resignation as Speaker and as Representative, become Governor.

(3) If, at the time when under subdivision (2) of this subsection the Speaker of the House of Representatives is to become Governor, there is no Speaker of the House of Representatives, or the Speaker of the House of Representatives fails to qualify as Governor, then that officer of the State of North Carolina who is highest on the following list, and who is not under disability to serve as Governor, shall, upon his resignation of the office which places him in the order of succession, become Governor: Secretary of State, Auditor, Treasurer, Superintendent of Public Instruction, Attorney General, Commissioner of Agriculture, Commissioner of Labor, and Commissioner of Insurance.

(c) Acting Governor Generally. -

(1) If, by reason of absence from the State or physical or mental incapacity, there is neither a Governor nor a Lieutenant Governor qualified to discharge the

powers and duties of the office of Governor, then the President of the Senate shall become Acting Governor.

(2)   If, at the time when under subdivision (1) of this subsection the President of the Senate is to become Acting Governor, there is no President of the Senate, or the President of the Senate fails to qualify as Acting Governor, then the Speaker of the House of Representatives shall become Acting Governor.

(3)   If, at the time when under subdivision (2) of this subsection the Speaker of the House of Representatives is to become Acting Governor, there is no Speaker of the House of Representatives, or the Speaker of the House of Representatives fails to qualify as Acting Governor, then that officer of the State of North Carolina who is highest on the following list, and who is not under disability to serve as Acting Governor, shall become Acting Governor: Secretary of State, Auditor, Treasurer, Superintendent of Public Instruction, Attorney General, Commissioner of Agriculture, Commissioner of Labor, and Commissioner of Insurance.

(d)   Governor Serving under Subsection (c). - An individual serving as Acting Governor under subsection (c) of this section shall continue to act for the remainder of the term of the Governor whom he succeeds and until a new Governor is elected and qualified, except that:

(1)   If his tenure as Acting Governor is founded in whole or in part upon the absence of both the Governor and Lieutenant Governor from the State, then he shall act only until the Governor or Lieutenant Governor returns to the State; and

(2)   If his tenure as Acting Governor is founded in whole or in part upon the physical or mental incapacity of the Governor or Lieutenant Governor, then he shall act only until the removal of the incapacity of the Governor or Lieutenant Governor.

(e)   Officers to Which Subsections (b), (c) and (d) Applicable. - Subsections (b), (c), and (d) of this section shall apply only to such officers as are eligible to the office of Governor under the Constitution of North Carolina, and only to officers who are not under impeachment by the House of Representatives at the time they are to become Governor or Acting Governor.

(f) Compensation of Acting Governor. - During the period that any individual serves as Acting Governor under subsection (c) of this section, his compensation shall be at the rate then provided by law in the case of the Governor. (1961, c. 992, s. 1.)

§ 147-12. Powers and duties of Governor.

(a) In addition to the powers and duties prescribed by the Constitution, the Governor has the powers and duties prescribed in this and the following sections:

(1) To supervise the official conduct of all executive and ministerial officers; and when the Governor deems it advisable to visit all State institutions for the purpose of inquiring into the management and needs of the same.

(2) To see that all offices are filled, and the duties thereof performed, or in default thereof apply such remedy as the law allows, and if the remedy is imperfect, acquaint the General Assembly therewith.

(3) To make the appointments and fill the vacancies not otherwise provided for in all departments.

In every case where the Governor is authorized by statute to make an appointment to fill a State office, the Governor may also appoint to fill any vacancy occurring in that office, and the person the Governor appoints shall serve for the unexpired term of the office and until the person's successor is appointed and qualified.

In every case where the Governor is authorized by statute to appoint to fill a vacancy in an office in the executive branch of State government, the Governor may appoint an acting officer to serve

a. During the physical or mental incapacity of the regular holder of the office to discharge the duties of the office,

b. During the continued absence of the regular holder of the office, or

c. During a vacancy in an office and pending the selection and qualification, in the manner prescribed by statute, of a person to serve for the unexpired term.

An acting officer appointed in accordance with this subsection may perform any act and exercise any power which a regularly appointed holder of such office could lawfully perform and exercise. All powers granted to an acting officer under this subsection shall expire immediately

a. Upon the termination of the incapacity of the officer in whose stead the person acts,

b. Upon the return of the officer in whose stead the person acts, or

c. Upon the selection and qualification, in the manner prescribed by statute, of a person to serve for the unexpired term.

The Governor may determine (after such inquiry as the Governor deems appropriate) that any of the officers referred to in this paragraph is physically or mentally incapable of performing the duties of the office. The Governor may also determine that such incapacity has terminated.

The compensation of an acting officer appointed pursuant to the provisions of this subdivision shall be fixed by the Governor.

(3a) To make appointments to fill vacancies in offices subject to appointment by the General Assembly as provided in G.S. 120-122.

(3b) Whenever a statute calls for the Governor to appoint one person from each congressional district to a board or commission, and at the time of enactment of that statute, the gubernatorial appointments do not cover all of the congressional districts, then the Governor, in filling vacancies on that board or commission as they occur, shall make appointments to satisfy that requirement, but shall not be required to remove any person from office to satisfy the requirement.

(3c) Notwithstanding any other provision of law, whenever a statute calls for the Governor to appoint a person to an office subject to confirmation by the General Assembly, the Governor shall notify the President of the Senate and the Speaker of the House of Representatives by May 15 of the year in which the appointment is to be made of the name of the person the Governor is submitting to the General Assembly for confirmation.

(3d)   Notwithstanding any other provision of law, whenever a statute calls for the Governor to appoint a person to an office subject to confirmation by the Senate, the Governor shall notify the President of the Senate by May 15 of the year in which the appointment is to be made of the name of the person the Governor is submitting to the General Assembly for confirmation.

(4)   To be the sole official organ between the government of this State and other states, or the government of the United States.

(5)   To have the custody of the great seal of the State.

(6)   If the Governor is apprised by the affidavits of two responsible citizens of the State that there is imminent danger that the statute of this State forbidding prizefighting is about to be violated, the Governor shall use, as far as necessary, the civil and military power of the State to prevent it, and to have the offenders arrested and bound to keep the peace.

(7)   Repealed by Session Laws 1997-443, s. 32.30(j), effective July 1, 1999.

(8)   In carrying out ex officio duties, to designate the Governor's personal representative to attend meetings and to act in the Governor's behalf as the Governor directs.

(9)   To appoint such personal staff as the Governor deems necessary to carry out effectively the responsibilities of the Governor's office.

(10)   To contract in behalf of the State with the government of the United States to the extent allowed by the laws of North Carolina for the purpose of securing the benefits available to this State under the Federal Highway Safety Act of 1966. To that end, the Governor shall coordinate the activities of any and all departments and agencies of this State and its subdivisions relating thereto.

(11)   Upon being furnished information from law-enforcement officers that public roads or highways or other public vehicular areas, as defined in G.S. 20-4.01, are being blocked by privately owned and operated vehicles or by any other means, thereby impeding the free flow of goods and merchandise in North Carolina, if such information warrants, to declare that a state of emergency exists in the affected area, and to order that the Highway Patrol and/or National

Guard remove the offending vehicles or other causes of the blockade from the emergency area.

(12) To name and locate State government buildings, monuments, memorials, and improvements, as provided by G.S. 143B-373(1).

(13) To oversee and approve all memoranda of understanding and agreements between the State and foreign governments, as defined in G.S. 66-280(c), and international organizations. Any memoranda of understanding or agreements under this subsection to be signed on behalf of the State must first be approved by the Governor after review by the Attorney General, and after execution filed with the Secretary of State in accordance with G.S. 66-280.

(14) To negotiate and enter into Class III Tribal-State gaming compacts, and amendments thereto, on behalf of the State consistent with State law and the Indian Gaming Regulatory Act, Public Law 100-497, as necessary to allow a federally recognized Indian tribe to operate gaming activities in this State as permitted under federal law. The Governor shall report any gaming compact, or amendment thereto, to the Joint Legislative Commission on Governmental Operations.

(b) The Department of Transportation, the Division of Adult Correction of the Department of Public Safety, the State Highway Patrol, the Wildlife Resources Commission, the Division of Parks and Recreation in the Department of Environment and Natural Resources, and the Division of Marine Fisheries in the Department of Environment and Natural Resources shall deliver to the Governor by February 1 of each year detailed information on the agency's litter enforcement, litter prevention, and litter removal efforts. The Administrative Office of the Courts shall deliver to the Governor, by February 1 of each year, detailed information on the enforcement of the littering laws of the State, including the number of charges and convictions under the littering laws of the State. The Governor shall gather the information submitted by the respective agencies and deliver a consolidated annual report, on or before March 1 of each year, to the Environmental Review Commission, the Joint Legislative Transportation Oversight Committee, and the House of Representatives and the Senate Appropriations Subcommittees on Natural and Economic Resources. (1868-9, c. 270, s. 27; 1870-1, c. 111; 1883, c. 71; Code, s. 3320; 1895, c. 28, s. 5; 1905, c. 446; Rev., s. 5328; C.S., s. 7636; 1955, c. 910, s. 3; 1959, c. 285; 1967, c. 1253; 1973, c. 1148; 1981 (Reg. Sess., 1982), c. 1191, ss. 3, 4, 68; 1983, c. 913, s. 46; 1985, c. 122, s. 5; c. 757, s. 181(a); 1985 (Reg. Sess., 1986), c. 955, ss. 106, 107; 1997-14, s. 3; 1997-443, s. 32.30(j); 1999-260, s. 4;

2001-487, s. 92; 2001-512, s. 9; 2001-513, s. 29(a); 2006-6, s. 6; 2006-79, s. 15; 2006-203, s. 114; 2006-259, s. 33(a); 2009-281, s. 1; 2011-145, ss. 19.1(g), (h); 2012-83, s. 58.)

§ 147-13. May convene Council of State; quorum; journal.

(a) The Governor may convene the Council for consultation whenever he may deem it proper. In all meetings of the Council of State, five members exclusive of the Governor shall constitute a quorum.

(b) The advice and proceedings of the Council of State shall be entered in a journal, to be kept for this purpose exclusively and signed by all members present. Any member of the Council may have entered in the journal his dissent to any part of the journal. The journal shall be maintained by the Governor and shall be placed before the General Assembly when called for by either house. (1868-9, c. 270, s. 40; Code, s. 3335; Rev., s. 5329; C.S., s. 7637; 1971, cc. 32, 151.)

§ 147-13.1. Governor's power to consolidate State agencies.

(a) The Governor is hereby authorized to direct the inauguration of studies to determine which agencies of the State conduct operations which are so nearly related to the operations of one or more other agencies that a consolidation would produce the same or a more efficient operational result at a reduction in cost, and to prepare recommendations to be presented to the 1971 General Assembly to effect such consolidations.

(b) For purposes of conducting the study, the Governor is authorized to utilize funds available to him from private sources, or from federal or other governmental grants, to be matched, as may be required, by funds available within the existing Department of Administration budget.

(c) The Governor shall direct that agencies which should be consolidated with or absorbed into other agencies having similar responsibilities and duties, as determined by the outcome of the study, shall be so consolidated or absorbed when, in his opinion, efficiency in State governmental operations will be increased thereby, or when such consolidation will result in a reduction in the cost of administering State activities without a reduction in the effectiveness of such operations; provided, however, that the Governor shall not direct such consolidation or combination as would diminish the duty or authority of any State agency or institution created by act of the General Assembly. (1969, c. 1209, ss. 1-3.)

§ 147-14. Appointment of private secretary; official correspondence preserved; books produced before General Assembly.

The Governor shall appoint a private secretary, who shall enter in books kept for that purpose all such letters, written by and to the Governor, as are official and important, and such other letters as the Governor shall think necessary. Such books shall be deposited in the office of the executive by the private secretary, and there carefully preserved, and the Governor shall produce the same before the General Assembly whenever requested. (1868-9, c. 270, ss. 33, 34; Code, ss. 3326, 3327; Rev., s. 5330; C.S., s. 7638.)

§ 147-15. Salary of private secretary.

The salary of the private secretary to the Governor shall be fixed by the Governor. (R.C., c. 102, s. 12; 1856-7, p. 71, res.; 1881, c. 346; Code, ss. 1689, 3721; P.R. 1901, c. 405; 1903, c. 729; Rev., s. 2737; 1907, c. 830; 1911, c. 95; 1913, c. 1; 1915, c. 50; 1917, c. 214; C.S., s. 3859; 1921, c. 227; 1929, c. 322, ss. 1, 2; 1945, c. 45; 1953, c. 675, s. 22; 1955, c. 910, s. 4; c. 1313, s. 8; 1961, c. 738, s. 1; 1983, c. 717, s. 88.)

§ 147-15.1: Repealed by Session Laws 1995, c. 379, s. 11.

§ 147-16. Records kept; certain original applications preserved; notice of commutations.

(a)   The Governor shall cause to be kept the following records:

(1)   A register of all applications for pardon, or for commutation of any sentence, with a list of the official signatures and recommendations in favor of such application.

(2)   An account of all his official expenses and disbursements, including the incidental expenses of his department, and the rewards offered by him for the apprehension of criminals.

These records and the originals of all applications, petitions, and recommendations and reports therein mentioned shall be preserved in the office of the Governor, but when applications for offices are refused he may, in his discretion, return the papers referring to the application.

(b)   The Governor shall, unless otherwise requested by any person listed in subdivisions (1) through (4) of this subsection, provide notice of the commutation of any sentence within 20 days after the commutation by first-class mail to the following at the last known address:

(1)   The victim or victims of the crime for which the sentence was imposed;

(2)   The victims' spouse, children, and parents;

(3)   Any other members of the victims' family who request in writing to be notified; and

(4)   The Chairs of the Joint Legislative Oversight Committee on Justice and Public Safety. (1868-9, c. 270, ss. 29, 30; 1870-1, c. 111; Code, ss. 3322, 3323; Rev., s. 5331; C.S., s. 7639; 1983, c. 913, s. 47; 1995, c. 507, s. 19.3(a); 1997-443, s. 21.4(b); 2001-138, s. 2; 2011-291, s. 2.54.)

§ 147-16.1. Publication of executive orders.

The Governor must submit Executive Orders to the Secretary of State, who must compile, index, and publish the Executive Orders. The Governor's office shall also send a copy of each executive order to the President of the Senate, to the Speaker of the House of Representatives, to the Principal Clerk of the House of Representatives and to the Principal Clerk of the Senate. (1971, c. 1196; 1985, c. 479, ss. 150-152; c. 746, s. 8; 1991, c. 418, s. 14.)

§ 147-16.2. Duration of boards and councils created by executive officials; extensions.

(a) Any executive order of the Governor that creates a board, committee, council, or commission expires two years after the effective date of the executive order, unless the Governor specifies an expiration date in the order; provided, however, that any such executive order that was in effect on July 1, 1983, expires on June 30, 1985, unless the Governor specified a different expiration date in any such order. The Governor may extend any such executive order before it expires for additional periods of up to two years by doing so in writing; copies of the writing shall be filed by the Governor with the Secretary of State and the Legislative Library.

(b) Any other State board, committee, council, or commission created by the Governor or by any other State elective officer specified in Article III of the North Carolina Constitution expires two years after it was created; provided, however, that any such board, committee, council, or commission existing as of July 1, 1984, expires on June 30, 1985, unless it was due to expire on an earlier date. The elective officer creating any such board, committee, council, or commission may extend the board, committee, council, or commission before it expires for additional periods of up to two years by doing so in writing; copies of the writing shall be filed by the elective officer with the Secretary of State and the Legislative Library.

(c) Any State board, committee, council, or commission created by any official in the executive branch of State government, other than by those officials specified in subsections (a) and (b) of this section, expires two years after it was created; provided, however, that any board, committee, council, or commission existing as of July 1, 1984, expires on June 30, 1985, unless it was due to expire on an earlier date. The Governor may extend any such board, committee, council, or commission before it expires for additional periods of up to two years by executive order; copies of the executive order shall be filed by the Governor with the Secretary of State and the Legislative Library.

The words, "official in the executive branch of State government," as used in this section, do not include officials of counties, cities, towns, villages, other municipal corporations or political subdivisions of the State or any agencies of such subdivision, or local boards of education, other local public districts, units or bodies of any kind, or community colleges as defined in G.S. 115D-2(2), or private corporations created by act of the General Assembly.

(d) Any elective officer specified in subsection (b) of this section and any other official in the executive branch of State government who creates a board, committee, council, or commission shall do so in writing and shall file copies of the writing with the Secretary of State and the Legislative Library. (1983, c. 733, s. 1; 1983 (Reg. Sess., 1984), c. 1053; 2004-203, s. 50(b).)

§ 147-16.3. Timely nominations if legislative body must confirm.

Notwithstanding any other provision of law, whenever:

(1) A statute specifies that an office shall be filled by nomination by the Governor and confirmation by the General Assembly or by one house thereof, and

(2) The statute specifies that the nominee shall take office without legislative action if the General Assembly adjourns without action being taken or fails to take action within a specified time, and

(3) The Governor fails to nominate a person for the office by May 15 of a regular session of the General Assembly during an odd-numbered year or by June 7 of a regular session of the General Assembly during an even-numbered year, and

(4) The appropriate legislative body does not act on the nomination before it next adjourns for more than 10 days or sine die,

the nominee shall serve only on an interim basis until 60 days after the convening of the next regular session of the General Assembly, subject to rejection or approval by the appropriate legislative body before that time. (1987, c. 867, s. 4.)

§ 147-17. May employ counsel in cases wherein State is interested.

(a) No department, officer, agency, institution, commission, bureau or other organized activity of the State which receives support in whole or in part from the State shall employ any counsel, except with the approval of the Governor. The Governor shall give his approval only if the Attorney General has advised him, as provided in subsection (b) of this section, that it is impracticable for the Attorney General to render the legal services. In any case or proceeding, civil or criminal, in or before any court or agency of this State or any other state or the United States, or in any other matter in which the State of North Carolina is interested, the Governor may employ such special counsel as he may deem proper or necessary to represent the interest of the State, and may fix the compensation for their services.

(b) The Attorney General shall be counsel for all departments, officers, agencies, institutions, commissions, bureaus or other organized activities of the State which receive support in whole or in part from the State. Whenever the Attorney General shall advise the Governor that it is impracticable for him to render legal services to any State agency, officer, institution, commission, bureau or other organized activity, or to defend a State employee or former employee as authorized by Article 31A of Chapter 143 of the General Statutes, the Governor may authorize the employment of such counsel, as in his judgment, should be employed to render such services, and may fix the compensation for their services.

(c) The Governor may direct that the compensation fixed under this section for special counsel shall be paid out of appropriations or other funds credited to the appropriate department, agency, institution, commission, bureau, or other organized activity of the State or out of the Contingency and Emergency Fund.

(d) In those instances when a department, officer, agency, institution, commission, bureau, or other organized activity of the State which receives support in whole or in part from the State shall employ counsel other than the Attorney General as permitted by law, such employed counsel shall allocate authority between counsel and the State client in conformance with Rule 1.2 of the North Carolina Rules of Professional Conduct. In those instances where more than one counsel is providing legal representation, counsel, or service on a legal matter on behalf of a State client, the client shall designate in writing which of its legal counsel possesses final decision-making authority on behalf of the State client, and other co-counsel shall, consistent with the Rules of Professional Conduct, cooperate with such designated lead counsel. (1868-9, c. 270, s. 6; 1870-1, c. 111; 1873-4, c. 160, s. 2; 1883, c. 71; Code, ss. 3320, 3324; 1901, c. 744; Rev., s. 5332; C.S., s. 7640; 1925, c. 207, s. 3; 1961, c. 1007; 1963, c. 1009; 1967, c. 1092, s. 2; 1985, c. 479, s. 136; 2011-145, s. 22.4.)

§ 147-18. To designate "Indian Day."

The Governor of North Carolina is hereby empowered to set aside some day which shall be called "Indian Day" on which Indian lore shall receive emphasis in the public schools of the State and among the citizens of North Carolina. (Resolutions 54, 1937, p. 957.)

§ 147-19. To appoint a day of thanksgiving.

The Governor is directed to set apart a day in every year, and by proclamation give notice thereof, as a day of solemn and public thanksgiving to Almighty God for past blessings and of supplication for His continued kindness and care over us as a State and a nation. (1868-9, c. 270, s. 39; Code, s. 3334; Rev., s. 5333; C.S., s. 7641.)

§ 147-20. Repealed by Session Laws 1955, c. 867, s. 13.

§ 147-21. Form and contents of applications for pardon.

Every application for pardon must be made to the Governor in writing, signed by the party convicted, or by some person in his behalf. And every such application shall contain the grounds and reasons upon which the executive pardon is asked, and shall be in every case accompanied by a certified copy of the indictment, and the verdict and judgment of the court thereon. (1869-70, c. 171; 1870-1, c. 61; Code, s. 3336; Rev., s. 5334; C.S., s. 7642.)

§ 147-22. Repealed by Session Laws 1981, c. 309.

§ 147-23. Conditional pardons may be granted.

In any case in which the Governor is authorized by the Constitution to grant a pardon he may, upon the petition of the prisoner, grant it, subject to such conditions, restrictions, and limitations as he considers proper and necessary, and he may issue his warrant to all proper officers to carry such pardon into effect in such manner as he thinks proper. (1905, c. 356; Rev., s. 5335; C.S., s. 7643.)

§ 147-24. Governor's duties when conditions of pardon violated.

If a prisoner who has been pardoned upon conditions to be observed and performed by him violates such conditions, or any of them, the Governor, upon receiving information of such violation, shall forthwith cause him to be arrested and detained until the case can be examined by him. The Governor shall examine the case of such prisoner, and if it appears by his own admission or by such evidence as the Governor may require that he has violated the conditions of his pardon, the Governor shall order him remanded and confined for the unexpired term of his sentence; said confinement, if the prisoner is under any other sentence of imprisonment at the time of said order, to begin upon expiration of such sentence. In computing the period of his confinement the time between the conditional pardon and subsequent arrest shall not be taken to be a part of the time of his sentence. If it appears to the Governor that he has not broken the conditions of his conditional pardon he shall be released and his conditional pardon shall remain in force. (1905, c. 356, ss. 2, 3; Rev., s. 5336; C.S., s. 7644.)

§ 147-25. Duty of sheriff and clerk on pardon granted.

If a prisoner is pardoned conditionally or unconditionally, or his punishment is commuted, the officer to whom the warrant for such purpose is issued shall, as soon as may be after executing it, make return thereof, signed by him, with his doing thereon, to the Governor's office, and shall file in the office of the clerk of the court in which the offender was convicted an attested copy of the warrant and return, and the clerk shall file the same in his office and subjoin a brief abstract thereof to the record of the conviction and sentence, and at the next regular term of said court said warrant shall be entered upon the minutes of the court. (1905, c. 356, s. 4; Rev., s. 5337; C.S., s. 7645.)

§ 147-26. To procure great seal of State; its description.

The Governor shall procure for the State a seal, which shall be called the great seal of the State of North Carolina, and shall be two and one-quarter inches in diameter, and its design shall be a representation of the figures of Liberty and Plenty, looking toward each other, but not more than half-fronting each other and otherwise disposed as follows: Liberty, the first figure, standing, her pole with cap on it in her left hand and a scroll with the word "Constitution" inscribed thereon in her right hand. Plenty, the second figure, sitting down, her right arm half extended towards Liberty, three heads of grain in her right hand, and in her left, the small end of her horn, the mouth of which is resting at her feet, and the contents of the horn rolling out.

The background on the seal shall contain a depiction of mountains running from left to right to the middle of the seal and an ocean running from right to left to the middle of the seal. A side view of a three-masted ship shall be located on the ocean and to the right of Plenty. The date "May 20, 1775" shall appear within the seal and across the top of the seal. The date "April 12, 1776" shall appear within the seal and across the bottom of the seal. The words "esse quam videri" shall appear at the bottom around the perimeter. The words "THE GREAT SEAL of the STATE of NORTH CAROLINA" shall appear around the perimeter. No other words, figures or other embellishments shall appear on the seal.

It shall be the duty of the Governor to file in the office of Secretary of State an impression of the great seal, certified to under his hand and attested by the Secretary of State, which impression so certified the Secretary of State shall carefully preserve among the records of his office. (1868-9, c. 270, s. 35; 1883, c. 392; Code, ss. 3328, 3329; 1893, c. 145; Rev., s. 5339; C.S., s. 7646; 1971, c. 167, s. 1; 1983, c. 257, s. 1.)

§ 147-27. Affixing great seal a second time to public papers.

In all cases where any person may find it necessary to have the great seal of the State put again to any public paper, other than a grant for lands, he may prefer his petition to the Governor and Council, who shall, if they deem the same proper, direct the seal to be put thereto. (1868-9, c. 270, s. 38; Code, s. 3333; Rev., s. 5338; C.S., s. 7647.)

§ 147-28. To procure seals for departments and courts.

The Governor shall also procure a seal for each department of the State government to be used for attesting and authenticating grants, proclamations, commissions, and other public acts, in such manner as may be directed by law and the usage established in the public offices; also a seal for every court of record in the State, for the purpose of authenticating the papers and records of such court. All such seals shall be delivered to the proper officers, who shall give a receipt therefor and be accountable for their safekeeping. (1868-9, c. 270, ss. 35, 37; 1883, c. 71; Code, ss. 3328, 3332; Rev., s. 5340; C.S., s. 7648.)

§ 147-29. Seal of Department of State described.

The seal of the Department of State shall be two inches in diameter and shall be of the same design as the great seal of the State, with the words "State of North Carolina, Department of State," surrounding the figures. (1883, c. 238; Code, s. 3330; Rev., s. 5341; C.S., s. 7649.)

§ 147-30. To provide new seals when necessary.

Whenever the great seal of the State shall be lost or so worn or defaced as to render it unfit for use, the Governor shall provide a new one and when such new one is provided the former one, if it can be found, shall be destroyed in the presence of the Governor. Whenever the seal of any department of the State shall be lost or so worn or defaced as to render it unfit for use, a new seal shall be provided by the head of the department and the former one, if it can be found, shall be destroyed in the presence of the head of the department. Whenever the seal of any court of record shall be lost or so worn or defaced as to render it unfit for use, the board of county commissioners of the county in which such court is situate shall provide a new one and the old one, if it can be found, shall be destroyed in the presence of the chairman of the board of county commissioners of such county. (1868-9, c. 270, s. 36; Code, s. 3331; Rev., s. 5342; C.S., s. 7650; 1943, c. 632.)

§ 147-31. Repealed by Session Laws 1983, c. 913, s. 48, effective July 22, 1983.

§ 147-31.1. Office space and expenses for Governor-elect and Lieutenant Governor-elect; and other Council of State members-elect.

(a)   The Department of Administration, upon request of the Governor-elect and Lieutenant Governor-elect, made after the general election for these respective offices, is empowered and directed to provide suitable office space and office staff for each such official for the period between the general election and inauguration.

The Department of Administration shall provide, for the fiscal years in which general election and inauguration of the Governor and Lieutenant Governor shall occur, such sums, not in excess of eighty thousand dollars ($80,000) for the Governor-elect, and not in excess of ten thousand dollars ($10,000) for the Lieutenant Governor-elect, as may be necessary for the salary of the staffs and the payment of office expenses of each such official during such interim.

(b)   The Department of Administration, upon request of any other member-elect of the Council of State who is not an incumbent in that office, shall provide for such persons suitable office space and office staff for each such official for the period between the general election and inauguration.

The Department of Administration shall provide, for the fiscal years in which general election and inauguration of such persons occurs, ten thousand dollars ($10,000) for the salary of the staffs and the payment of office expenses of each such official during such interim. If there are more than two such persons, such services and payments shall be made from the Contingency and Emergency Fund upon approval of the Council of State. (1965, c. 407; 1987 (Reg. Sess., 1988), c. 1086, s. 48.)

§ 147-32. Compensation for surviving spouses of Governors.

All surviving spouses of Governors of the State of North Carolina, who make written request to the Director of the Budget, shall be paid the sum of twelve thousand dollars ($12,000) a year in equal monthly installments, out of the State Treasury upon warrants duly drawn thereon. This compensation shall terminate upon the subsequent remarriage of the surviving spouse. (1937, c. 416; 1947, c. 897, ss. 1, 2; 1955, c. 1314; 1977, c. 554; 1981 (Reg. Sess., 1982), c. 1282, s. 63; 1987, c. 738, s. 40.)

§ 147-33. Compensation and expenses of Lieutenant Governor.

The salary of the Lieutenant Governor shall be set by the General Assembly in the Current Operations Appropriations Act. In addition to this salary, the Lieutenant Governor shall be paid an annual expense allowance in the sum of eleven thousand five hundred dollars ($11,500). In addition to the salary set by the General Assembly in the Current Operations Appropriations Act, longevity pay shall be paid on the same basis as is provided to employees of the State who are subject to the North Carolina Human Resources Act. (1911, c. 103; C.S., s. 3862; 1945, c. 1; 1953, c. 1, s. 1; 1963, c. 1050; 1967, c. 1170, s. 1; 1971, c. 913; 1977, c. 802, s. 42.6; 1977, 2nd Sess., c. 1136, s. 40; 1979, 2nd Sess., c. 1137, s. 32; 1983, c. 761, s. 211; 1983 (Reg. Sess., 1984), c. 1034, s. 164; 1987, c. 738, s. 32(b); 2013-382, s. 9.1(c).)

Article 3A.

Emergency War Powers of Governor.

§ 147-33.1. Short title.

This Article may be cited as the "North Carolina Emergency War Powers Act." (1943, c. 706, s. 1; 1959, c. 337, s. 6.)

§ 147-33.2. Emergency war powers of the Governor.

Upon the Governor's own initiative, or on the request or recommendation of the President of the United States, the United States Army, Navy, or any other branch of the Armed Forces of the United States, the federal Director of Civilian Defense, or any other federal officer, department or agency having duties and responsibilities related to the prosecution of the war or the health, welfare, safety and protection of the civilian population, whenever in the Governor's judgment any such action is in the public interest and is necessary for the protection of the lives or property of the people of the State, or for the defense and security of the State or nation, or for the proper conduct of the war and the successful prosecution thereof, the Governor may, with the approval of the Council of State, at any time and from time to time during the existing state of war:

(1) Formulate and execute plans for:

a. The inventory, mobilization, conservation, distribution or use of food, fuel, clothing and other necessaries of life and health, and of land, labor, materials, industries, facilities and other resources of the State necessary or useful in the prosecution of the war;

b. Organization and coordination of civilian defense in the State in reasonable conformity with the program of civilian defense as promulgated from time to time by the Office of Civilian Defense of the federal government; and, further, to effectuate such plans for civilian defense in such manner as to promote and assure the security, protection and mobilization of the civilian population of the State for the duration of the war and in the interest of State and national defense.

(2) Order and carry out blackouts, radio silences, evacuations and all other precautionary measures against air raids or other forms of enemy action, and suppress or otherwise control any activity which may aid or assist the enemy.

(3) Mobilize, coordinate and direct the activities of the police, fire fighting, health, street and highway repair, public utility, medical and welfare forces and services of the State, of the political subdivisions of the State, and of private agencies and corporations, and formulate and execute plans for the interchange and use of such forces and services for the mutual aid of the people of the State in cases of air raid, sabotage or other enemy action, fire, flood, famine, violence, riot, insurrection, or other catastrophe or emergency.

(4) Prohibit, restrict, or otherwise regulate and control the flow of vehicular and pedestrian traffic, and congregation of persons in public places or buildings, lights and noises of all kinds and the maintenance, extension and operation of public utility and transportation services and facilities.

(5) Accept, or authorize any officer or department of the State to accept, from the federal government or any federal agency or instrumentality, or from any other source, grants of funds and grants or loans of equipment, materials, supplies or other property for war or defense purposes, subject to the terms and conditions appertaining to such grants and loans.

(6) Authorize any department or agency of the State to lease or lend to the United States Army, Navy, or any other branch of the Armed Forces of the United States, any real or personal property of the State upon such terms and

conditions as the Governor may impose, or, on behalf of the State, to make a contract directly therefor.

(7)   Authorize the temporary transfer of personnel of the State for employment by the United States Army, Navy, or any other branch of the Armed Forces of the United States and fix the terms and conditions of such transfers.

(8)   At any time when the General Assembly is not in session, suspend, or modify, in whole or in part, generally or in its application to certain classes of persons, firms, corporations or circumstances, any law, rule or regulation with reference to the subjects hereinafter enumerated, when the Governor shall find and proclaim after such study, investigation or hearings as the Governor may direct, make or conduct, that the operation, enforcement or application of such law, or any part thereof, materially hinders, impedes, delays or interferes with the proper conduct of the war; said subjects being as follows:

a.   The use of the roads, streets, and highways of the State, with particular reference to speed limits, weights and sizes of motor vehicles, regulations of automobile lights and signals, transportation of munitions or explosives and parking or assembling of automobiles on highways or any other public place within the State; provided that any changes in the laws referred to in this subdivision shall be first approved by the Board of Transportation and the Commissioner of Motor Vehicles of the State;

b.   Public health, insofar as suspension or modification of the laws in reference thereto may be stipulated by the United States Public Health Service or other authoritative agency of the United States government as being essential in the interest of national safety and in the successful prosecution of the war effort; provided that such suspension or modification of public health laws shall first be submitted to and approved by the Commission for Public Health;

c.   Labor and industry; provided, however, that any suspension or modification of laws regulating labor and industry shall be only such as are certified by the Commissioner of Labor of the State as being necessary in the interest of national safety and in the furtherance of the war program; and provided further that any such changes as may result in an increase in the hours of employment over and above the limits of the existing statutory provisions shall carry provision for adequate additional compensation; and provided, further, that no changes in such laws or regulations shall be made as affecting existing contracts between labor and management in this State except with the approval of the contracting parties;

d. Whenever it should be certified by the Adjutant General of the State that emergency conditions require such procedure, the Governor, with the approval of the Council of State, shall have the power to call up and mobilize the State militia; to provide transportation and facilities for mobilization and full utilization of the State militia, in such emergency; and to allocate from the Contingency and Emergency Fund such amounts as may be necessary for such purposes during the period of such emergency;

e. Manufacture, sale, transportation, possession and use of explosives or fireworks, or articles in simulation thereof, and the sale, use and handling of firearms;

(9) Cooperate with agencies established by or pursuant to the laws of the United States and the several states for civilian protection and the promotion of the war effort, and coordinate and direct the work of the offices and agencies of the State having duties and responsibilities directly connected with the war effort and the protection of the civilian population.

(10) Aid in the administration and enforcement in this State of any rationing, freezing, price-fixing or similar order or regulation duly promulgated by any federal officer or agency under or pursuant to the authority of any act of Congress or of any order or proclamation of the President of the United States, by making temporarily available personnel and facilities of the State to assist in the administration thereof and/or by adopting and promulgating in this State an order or regulation substantially embodying the provisions of such federal order or regulation, filing the same in the office of the Secretary of State, prescribing the penalties for the violation thereof, and specifying the State and local officers and agencies to be charged with the enforcement thereof.

(11) Formulate and execute plans and adopt rules for:

a. The organization, recruiting, training, maintenance and operation of aircraft warning services, observation and listening posts, information and control centers and such other services and facilities as may be necessary for the prompt and accurate reception and transmission of air-raid warnings and signals;

b. The organization, recruiting, training, equipment, identification, conduct, powers, duties, rights, privileges and immunities of air-raid wardens, auxiliary police, auxiliary firemen and of the members of all other auxiliary defense and civilian protection forces and agencies.

(12) Adopt, promulgate, publicize and enforce such orders, rules and regulations as may be necessary for the proper and effective exercise of the powers granted by this Article, and amend or rescind the same.

(13) Hold and conduct hearings, administer oaths and take testimony, issue subpoenas to compel the attendance of witnesses and the production of relevant books, papers, records or documents, in connection with any investigation made by the Governor under the authority of this Article. (1943, c. 706, s. 2; 1959, c. 337, s. 6; 1973, c. 476, s. 128; c. 507, s. 5; 1999-456, s. 33(f); 2007-182, s. 2; 2011-183, s. 107.)

§ 147-33.3. Orders, rules and regulations.

All orders, rules and regulations promulgated by the Governor pursuant to this Article shall have the full force and effect of law from and after the date of the filing of a duly authenticated copy thereof in the office of the Secretary of State. All laws, ordinances, rules and regulations, insofar as they are inconsistent with the provisions of this Article or of any rule, order or regulation made pursuant to this Article, shall be suspended during the period of time and to the extent that such conflict exists. A violation of any such order, rule or regulation, unless otherwise provided therein, shall be deemed a Class 1 misdemeanor. (1943, c. 706, s. 3; 1959, c. 337, s. 6; 1993, c. 539, s. 1054; 1994, Ex. Sess., c. 24, s. 14(c).)

§ 147-33.4. Immunity.

Neither the State nor any political subdivision thereof, nor the agents or representatives of the State or any political subdivision thereof, under any circumstances, nor any individual, firm, partnership, corporation or other entity, or any agent thereof, in good faith complying with or attempting to comply with any order, rule or regulation made pursuant to this Article, shall be liable for the death or any injury to persons or for any damage to property as the result of any air raid, invasion, act of sabotage, or other form of enemy action, or of any action taken under this Article or such order, rule or regulation. This section shall not be construed to impair or affect the right of any person to receive any benefits or compensation to which he may otherwise be entitled under Workers' Compensation Law, any pension law, or any other law, or any act of Congress, or any contract of insurance or indemnification. (1943, c. 706, s. 4; 1959, c. 337, s. 6; 1991, c. 636, s. 3.)

§ 147-33.5. Federal action controlling.

All action taken under this Article and all orders, rules and regulations made pursuant thereto in any field or with respect to any subject matter over which the United States Army or Navy or any other department or agency of the United States government has duly taken jurisdiction shall be taken or made with due consideration to the orders, rules, regulations, actions, recommendations and requests of such department or agency and shall be consistent therewith. Blackouts, radio silences and evacuations shall be carried out only in such areas, at such times, and for such periods as shall be designated by air-raid warnings or orders with respect thereto issued by the United States Army, or its duly designated agency, and only under such conditions and in such manner as shall be consistent with such warning or order, and practice blackouts shall be held only when and as authorized by the United States Army or its duly designated agency. (1943, c. 706, s. 5; 1959, c. 337, s. 6; 2011-183, s. 127(b).)

§ 147-33.6. Construction of Article.

This Article shall be construed liberally to effectuate its purposes. (1943, c. 706, s. 6; 1959, c. 337, s. 6.)

§§ 147-33.7 through 147-33.11. Reserved for future codification purposes.

Article 3B.

North Carolina Housing Commission.

§§ 147-33.12 through 147-33.21: Repealed by Session Laws 1987, c. 841, s. 5.

Article 3C.

Office of Juvenile Justice.

§§ 147-33.30 through 147-33.71. Repealed by Session Laws 2000-137, s. 1(a), effective July 20, 2000.

§ 147-33.72: Reserved for future codification purposes.

Article 3D.

State Information Technology Services.

Part 1. State Information Technology Management.

§ 147-33.72A. Purpose.

The purposes of this Article are to:

(1) Establish a systematic process for planning and financing the State's information technology resources.

(2) Develop standards and accountability measures for information technology projects, including criteria for adequate project management.

(3) Implement procurement procedures that will result in cost savings on information technology purchases.

(4) Repealed by Session Laws 2011-266, s. 1.9(b), effective July 1, 2011.

(5) Create the Information Technology Fund for statewide information technology efforts. (2004-129, s. 2; 2011-266, s. 1.9(b).)

§ 147-33.72B. Planning and financing State information technology resources.

(a) In order to provide a systematic process for meeting the State's technology needs, the State Chief Information Officer shall develop a biennial State Information Technology Plan (Plan). The Plan shall be transmitted to the General Assembly by February 1 of each regular session.

(b) The Plan shall include the following elements:

(1) An inventory of current information technology assets and major projects currently in progress. As used in this subdivision, the term "major project" includes projects subject to review and approval under G.S. 147-33.72C.

(2) An evaluation and estimation of the significant unmet needs for information technology resources over a five-year time period. The Plan shall rank the unmet needs in priority order according to their urgency.

(3) A statement of the financial requirements posed by the significant unmet needs, together with a recommended funding schedule for each major project currently in progress or recommended for initiation during the upcoming fiscal biennium.

(4) An analysis of opportunities for statewide initiatives that would yield significant efficiencies or improve effectiveness in State programs.

(c) Each executive agency shall biennially develop an agency information technology plan that includes the information required under subsection (b) of this section. The Office of Information Technology Services shall consult with and assist agencies in the preparation of these plans. Each agency shall submit its plan to the State Chief Information Officer by October 1 of each even-numbered year. (2004-129, s. 2; 2013-329, s. 1.)

§ 147-33.72C. Project approval standards.

(a) Project Review and Approval. - The State Chief Information Officer shall:

(1) Review all State agency information technology projects. If the State Chief Information Officer determines a project meets the quality assurance requirements established under this Article, the State Chief Information Officer shall approve the project.

(2) Repealed by Session Laws 2013-329, s. 2, effective July 23, 2013.

(b) Project Implementation. - No State agency shall proceed with an information technology project that is subject to review and approval under subsection (a) of this section until the State CIO approves the project. If a project is not approved, the State CIO shall specify in writing to the agency the grounds for denying the approval. The State CIO shall provide this information to the agency within five business days of the denial.

(c) Suspension of Approval. - The State Chief Information Officer may suspend the approval of any information technology project that does not continue to meet the applicable quality assurance standards. If the State CIO suspends approval of a project, the State CIO shall specify in writing to the agency the grounds for suspending the approval. The State CIO shall provide this information to the agency within five business days of the suspension.

The Office of Information Technology Services shall report any suspension immediately to the Office of the State Controller and the Office of State Budget and Management. The Office of State Budget and Management shall not allow any additional expenditure of funds for a project that is no longer approved by the State Chief Information Officer.

(d) Repealed by Session Laws 2013-329, s. 2, effective July 23, 2013.

(e) Performance Contracting. - All contracts between a State agency and a private party for information technology projects shall include provisions for vendor performance review and accountability. The State CIO may require that these contract provisions require a performance bond, include monetary penalties, or require other performance assurance measures for projects that are not completed or performed within the specified time period or that involve costs in excess of those specified in the contract. The State CIO may utilize cost savings realized on government-vendor partnerships, as defined in G.S. 143-135.9, as performance incentives for an information technology project vendor.

(f) Notwithstanding the provisions of G.S. 114-2.3, any State agency developing and implementing an information technology project with a total cost of ownership in excess of five million dollars ($5,000,000) may be required by the State Chief Information Officer to engage the services of private counsel or subject matter experts with the appropriate information technology and intellectual property expertise. The private counsel or subject matter expert may review requests for proposals; review and provide advice and assistance during the evaluation of proposals and selection of any vendors; and review and negotiate contracts associated with the development, implementation, operation, and maintenance of the project. This requirement may also apply to information technology programs that are separated into individual projects, if the total cost of ownership for the overall program exceeds five million dollars ($5,000,000). (2004-129, s. 2; 2013-188, s. 2; 2013-329, s. 2; 2013-360, s. 7.7(d).)

§ 147-33.72D. Agency/State CIO Dispute Resolution.

(a) Agency Request for Review. - In any instance where the State CIO has denied or suspended the approval of an information technology project, or has denied an agency's request for deviation pursuant to G.S. 147-33.84, the agency may request a committee review of the State CIO's decision. The agency shall submit a written request for review to the State Controller within 15 working days following the agency's receipt of the State CIO's written grounds for denial or suspension. The agency's request for review shall specify the grounds for its disagreement with the State CIO's determination. The agency shall include with its request for review a copy of the State CIO's written grounds for denial or suspension.

(b) Review Process. - The review committee shall consist of the State Controller, the State Budget Officer, and the Secretary of Administration. The State Controller shall serve as the chair of the review committee. If the chair or one of the members of the review committee is an official of the agency that has requested the review, that person is deemed to have a conflict of interest and is ineligible to participate in the consideration of the matter, and the two remaining members of the review committee shall select an alternate official to serve as a member of the review committee for that specific matter. Within 10 business days following receipt of an agency's request for review, the committee shall meet to consider the matter. The committee shall review the information provided, and may request additional information from either the agency or the

State CIO. The committee may affirm, reverse, or modify the decision of the State CIO, or may remand the matter back to the State CIO for additional findings. Within 30 days after initial receipt of the agency's request for review, the committee shall notify the agency and the State CIO of its decision in the matter. The notification shall be in writing, and shall specify the grounds for the committee's decision. The committee may reverse or modify a decision of the State CIO when the committee finds at least one of the following:

(1) The decision of the State CIO is unsupported by substantial evidence that the agency project fails to meet one or more standards of efficiency and quality of State government information technology as required under this Article.

(2) The State CIO did not have the requisite statutory authority or jurisdiction to render the decision.

(3) The decision of the State CIO was rendered in a manner that was arbitrary, capricious, or indicative of an abuse of discretion. (2004-129, s. 2; 2007-282, s. 1.)

§ 147-33.72E. Project management standards.

(a) Agency Responsibilities. - Each agency shall provide for one or more project managers who meet the applicable quality assurance standards for each information technology project that is subject to approval under G.S. 143-33.72C(a). Each project manager shall be subject to the review and approval of the State Chief Information Officer.

Each agency project manager shall provide periodic reports to the project management assistant assigned to the project by the State CIO under subsection (b) of this section. The reports shall include information regarding project costs, issues related to hardware, software, or training, projected and actual completion dates, and any other information related to the implementation of the information technology project.

(b) State Chief Information Officer Responsibilities. - The State Chief Information Officer shall designate a project management assistant from the Office of Information Technology Services for any project that receives approval under. G.S. 147-33.72C(a) if the project costs or is expected to cost more than one million dollars ($1,000,000), whether the project is undertaken in single or multiple phases or components. The State Chief Information Officer may designate a project management assistant for any other information technology project.

The project management assistant shall advise the agency with the initial planning of a project, the content and design of any request for proposals, contract development, procurement, and architectural and other technical reviews. The project management assistant shall also monitor agency progress in the development and implementation of the project and shall provide status reports to the State Chief Information Officer, including recommendations regarding continued approval of the project. (2004-129, s. 2; 2007-281, s. 1.)

§ 147-33.72F. Procurement procedures; cost savings.

Pursuant to Part 4 of this Article, the Office of Information Technology Services shall establish procedures for the procurement of information technology. The procedures may include aggregation of hardware purchases, the use of formal bid procedures, restrictions on supplemental staffing, enterprise software licensing, hosting, and multiyear maintenance agreements. The procedures may require agencies to submit information technology procurement requests to the Office of Information Technology Services on October 1, January 1, and June 1 of each fiscal year in order to allow for bulk purchasing. (2004-129, s. 2; 2006-264, s. 71.)

§ 147-33.72G: Repealed by Session Laws 2011-266, s. 1.9(a), effective July 1, 2011.

§ 147-33.72H. Information Technology Fund.

There is established a special revenue fund to be known as the Information Technology Fund, which may receive transfers or other credits as authorized by the General Assembly. Money shall be appropriated from the Information Technology Fund to support the operation and administration of the Office of the State Chief Information Officer. Money may be appropriated from the

Information Technology Fund to meet statewide requirements, including planning, project management, security, electronic mail, State portal operations, and the administration of systemwide procurement procedures. Expenditures involving funds appropriated to the Office of Information Technology Services from the Information Technology Fund shall be made by the CIO. By October 1 of each year, the State CIO shall submit to the Joint Legislative Oversight Committee on Information Technology a report on all expenditures involving funds appropriated to the Office of Information Technology Services from the Information Technology Fund for the preceding fiscal year. Interest earnings on the Information Technology Fund balance shall be credited to the Information Technology Fund. (2004-129, s. 2; 2011-266, s. 1.9(c); 2013-329, s. 3.)

§ 147-33.73: Reserved for future codification purposes.

§ 147-33.74: Reserved for future codification purposes.

Part 1A. Organization of Office of Information Technology Services.

§ 147-33.75. Office located in the Office of the Governor.

(a) The Office of Information Technology Services ("Office") shall be housed in the Office of the Governor.

(b) The Governor has the authority, powers, and duties over the Office that are assigned to the Governor and the head of department pursuant to Article 1 of Chapter 143B of the General Statutes, G.S. 143A-6(b), and the Constitution and other laws of this State. (1999-434, s. 9; 2000-174, s. 2; 2004-129, ss. 1, 9.)

§ 147-33.76. Qualification, appointment, and duties of the State Chief Information Officer.

(a) The Office of Information Technology Services shall be managed and administered by the State Chief Information Officer ("State CIO"). The State Chief Information Officer shall be qualified by education and experience for the office and shall be appointed by and serve at the pleasure of the Governor.

(b) Repealed by Session Laws 2004-129, s. 3.

(b1) The State CIO shall be responsible for developing and administering a comprehensive long-range plan to ensure the proper management of the State's information technology resources. The State CIO shall set technical standards for information technology, review and approve major information technology projects, review and approve State agency information technology budget requests, establish information technology security standards, provide for the procurement of information technology resources, and develop a schedule for the replacement or modification of major systems. The State CIO is authorized to adopt rules to implement this Article.

(c) The salary of the State Chief Information Officer shall be set by the Governor. The State Chief Information Officer shall receive longevity pay on the same basis as is provided to employees of the State who are subject to the North Carolina Human Resources Act. (1999-434, s. 10; 2000-174, s. 2; 2004-129, ss. 1, 3; 2012-142, s. 25.1(e); 2013-382, s. 9.1(c).)

§ 147-33.77. Office of Information Technology Services; organization and operation.

(a) The State Chief Information Officer may appoint one or more Deputy Chief Information Officers. The salary of a Deputy Information Officer shall be set by the State Chief Information Officer. The State Chief Information Officer may appoint all employees, including legal counsel, necessary to carry out the powers and duties of the office. These employees shall be subject to the North Carolina Human Resources Act, except that employees in positions designated as exempt under G.S. 126-5(d)(1) are not subject to the Act, in accordance with the provisions of that section.

(b) All employees of the office shall be under the supervision, direction, and control of the State Chief Information Officer. Except as otherwise provided by this Article, the State Chief Information Officer may assign any function vested in the State Chief Information Officer or the Office of Information Technology Services to any subordinate officer or employee of the office.

(c) The State Chief Information Officer may, subject to the provisions of G.S. 147-64.7(b)(2), obtain the services of independent public accountants, qualified management consultants, and other professional persons or experts to carry out powers and duties of the office.

(d) The State Chief Information Officer shall have legal custody of all books, papers, documents, and other records of the office.

(e) The State Chief Information Officer shall be responsible for the preparation of and the presentation of the office budget request, including all funds requested and all receipts expected for all elements of the budget.

(f) The State Chief Information Officer may adopt regulations for the administration of the office, the conduct of employees of the office, the distribution and performance of business, the performance of the functions assigned to the State Chief Information Officer and the Office of Information Technology Services, and the custody, use, and preservation of the records, documents, and property pertaining to the business of the office.

(g) The State Chief Information Officer may require background investigations of any employee or prospective employee, including a criminal history record check, which may include a search of the State and National Repositories of Criminal Histories based on the person's fingerprints. A criminal history record check shall be conducted by the State Bureau of Investigation upon receiving fingerprints and other information provided by the employee or prospective employee. If the employee or prospective employee has been a resident of the State for less than five years, the background report shall include a review of criminal information from both the State and National Repositories of Criminal Histories. The criminal background report shall be provided to the State Chief Information Officer and is not a public record under Chapter 132 of the General Statutes. (1989, c. 239, s. 5; c. 770, s. 60; 1989 (Reg. Sess., 1990), c. 1024, s. 36; 1991 (Reg. Sess., 1992), c. 900, s. 14(g); c. 1030, s. 51.14; ; 1997-148, ss. 5, 6; 1999-347, s. 2; 1999-434, s. 27; 2000-174, s. 2; 2004-129, s. 1; 2007-155, s. 1; 2007-189, ss. 1, 5.1; 2013-329, s. 4; 2013-382, ss. 4.2, 9.1(c); 2013-410, s. 47.2(b).)

§ 147-33.78: Repealed by Session Laws 2004-129, ss. 4, 5.

§ 147-33.79. Repealed by Session Laws 2004-129, ss. 4, 5.

Part 2. General Powers and Duties.

§ 147-33.80. Exempt agencies.

Except as otherwise specifically provided by law, this Article shall not apply to the General Assembly, the Judicial Department, or The University of North Carolina and its constituent institutions. These agencies may elect to participate in the information technology programs, services, or contracts offered by the Office, including information technology procurement, in accordance with the statutes, policies, and rules of the Office. (1999-434, s. 10; 2000-174, s. 2.)

§ 147-33.81. Definitions.

As used in this Article:

(1) "Cooperative purchasing agreement" means an agreement between a vendor and one or more states or state agencies providing that the parties may collaboratively or collectively purchase information technology goods and services in order to increase economies of scale and reduce costs.

(1a) "Distributed information technology assets" means hardware, software, and communications equipment not classified as traditional mainframe-based items, including personal computers, local area networks (LANs), servers, mobile computers, peripheral equipment, and other related hardware and software items.

(2) "Information technology" means electronic data processing goods and services, telecommunications goods and services, security goods and services, microprocessors, software, information processing, office systems, any services related to the foregoing, and consulting or other services for design or redesign of information technology supporting business processes.

(3) "Information technology enterprise management" means a method for managing distributed information technology assets from acquisition through retirement so that total ownership costs (purchase, operation, maintenance, disposal, etc.) are minimized while maximum benefits are realized.

(4) "Information technology portfolio management" means a business-based approach for analyzing and ranking potential technology investments and selecting those investments that are the most cost-effective in supporting the strategic business and program objectives of the agency.

(5) "Office" means the Office of Information Technology Services as established in this Article.

(6) "State agency" means any department, institution, commission, committee, board, division, bureau, office, officer, or official of the State. The term does not include any State entity excluded from coverage under this Article by G.S. 147-33.80, unless otherwise expressly provided. (1999-434, s. 9; 2000-174, s. 2; 2001-424, s. 15.2(a); 2013-333, s. 1(a), (b); 2013-410, s. 24.)

§ 147-33.82. Functions of the Office of Information Technology Services.

(a) In addition to any other functions required by this Article, the Office of Information Technology Services shall:

(1) Procure all information technology for State agencies, as provided in Part 4 of this Article.

(2) Submit for approval of the Office of State Budget and Management all rates and fees for common, shared State government-wide technology services provided by the Office on a fee-for-service basis and not covered by another fund.

(3) Conduct an annual assessment of State agencies for compliance with statewide policies for information technology.

(4) Develop standards, procedures, and processes to implement policies approved by the State CIO.

(5) Review State agency management of State information technology resources for compliance with this Article.

(6) Review State agency implementation of statewide information technology management efforts of State government for compliance with this Article.

(7) Repealed by Session Laws 2004-129, s. 13, effective July 1, 2004.

(8) Develop a project management, quality assurance, and architectural review process for projects that require review and approval under G.S. 147-33.72C(a).

(9) Repealed by Session Laws 2004-129, s. 13, effective July 1, 2004.

(10) Provide geographic information systems services through the Center for Geographic Information and Analysis on a cost recovery basis. The Office of Information Technology Services and the Center for Geographic Information and Analysis may contract for funding from federal or other sources to conduct or provide geographic information systems services for public purposes.

(b) Notwithstanding any other provision of law, local governmental entities may use the information technology programs, services, or contracts offered by the Office, including information technology procurement, in accordance with the statutes, policies, and rules of the Office. For purposes of this subsection, "local governmental entities" includes local school administrative units, as defined in G.S. 115C-5, and community colleges. Local governmental entities are not required to comply with otherwise applicable competitive bidding requirements when using contracts established by the Office. Any other State entities may also use the information technology programs, services, or contracts offered by the Office, including information technology procurement, in accordance with the statutes, policies, and rules of the Office.

(c) Recodified as G.S. 147-33.110 by Session Laws 2004-129, s. 12, effective July 1, 2004.

(d) Recodified as G.S. 147-33.111 by Session Laws 2004-129, s. 12, effective July 1, 2004.

(e) Repealed by Session Laws 2004-129, s. 11, effective July 1, 2004.

(e1) Recodified as G.S. 147-33.112 by Session Laws 2004-129, s. 12, effective July 1, 2004.

(f) Recodified as G.S. 147-33.113 by Session Laws 2004-129, s. 12, effective July 1, 2004. (1999-434, s. 10; 2000-174, s. 2; 2001-424, s. 15.2(b); 2002-126, s. 27.2(a); 2003-153, ss. 1(a), 1(b); 2004-129, ss. 10, 11, 12, 13; 2011-266, s. 1.9(d); 2012-142, s. 6A.2.)

§ 147-33.83. Information resources centers and services.

(a) With respect to all executive departments and agencies of State government, except the Department of Justice if they do not elect at their option to participate, the Office of Information Technology Services shall have all of the following powers and duties:

(1) To establish and operate information resource centers and services to serve two or more departments on a cost-sharing basis, if the State CIO, after consultation with the Office of State Budget and Management, decides it is advisable from the standpoint of efficiency and economy to establish these centers and services.

(2) With the approval of the Office of State Budget and Management, to charge each department for which services are performed its proportionate part of the cost of maintaining and operating the shared centers and services.

(3) To require any department served to transfer to the Office ownership, custody, or control of information processing equipment, supplies, and positions required by the shared centers and services.

(4) To adopt reasonable rules for the efficient and economical management and operation of the shared centers, services, and the integrated State telecommunications network.

(5) To adopt plans, policies, procedures, and rules for the acquisition, management, and use of information technology resources in the departments affected by this section to facilitate more efficient and economic use of information technology in these departments.

(6) To develop and promote training programs to efficiently implement, use, and manage information technology resources.

(7) To provide cities, counties, and other local governmental units with access to the Office of Information Technology Services, information resource centers and services as authorized in this section for State agencies. Access shall be provided on the same cost basis that applies to State agencies.

(b) No data of a confidential nature, as defined in the General Statutes or federal law, may be entered into or processed through any cost-sharing information resource center or network established under this section until safeguards for the data's security satisfactory to the department head and the State Chief Information Officer have been designed and installed and are fully operational. Nothing in this section may be construed to prescribe what programs to satisfy a department's objectives are to be undertaken, nor to remove from the control and administration of the departments the responsibility for program efforts, regardless whether these efforts are specifically required by statute or are administered under the general program authority and responsibility of the department. This section does not affect the provisions of G.S. 147-64.6, 147-64.7, or 147-33.91.

(c) Notwithstanding any other provision of law, the Office of Information Technology Services shall provide information technology services on a cost-sharing basis to the General Assembly and its agencies as requested by the Legislative Services Commission. (1989, c. 239, s. 5; c. 770, s. 60; 1989 (Reg. Sess., 1990), c. 1024, s. 36; 1991 (Reg. Sess., 1992), c. 900, s. 14(g); c. 1030, s. 51.14; 1997-148, ss. 5, 6; 1999-347, s. 2; 1999-434, s. 27; 2000-174, s. 2; 2004-129, s. 15.)

§ 147-33.84. Deviations authorized for Department of Revenue; agency requests for deviations.

(a) The Department of Revenue is authorized to deviate from any provision in G.S. 147-33.83(a) that requires departments or agencies to consolidate information processing functions on equipment owned, controlled, or under custody of the Office of Information Technology Services. All deviations by the Department of Revenue pursuant to this section shall be reported in writing within 15 days by the Department of Revenue to the State CIO and shall be consistent with available funding. Any State agency may apply in writing to the State CIO for authority to deviate. If granted, any deviation shall be consistent with available funding and shall be subject to such terms and conditions as may be specified by the State CIO. If the agency's request for deviation is denied by the State CIO, the agency may request a review of the decision pursuant to G.S. 147-33.72D.

(b) The Department of Revenue is authorized to adopt and shall adopt plans, policies, procedures, requirements, and rules for the acquisition, management, and use of information processing equipment, information processing programs, data communications capabilities, and information systems personnel in the Department of Revenue. If the plans, policies, procedures, requirements, rules, or standards adopted by the Department of Revenue deviate from the policies, procedures, or guidelines adopted by the Office of Information Technology Services, those deviations shall be allowed and shall be reported in writing within 15 days by the Department of Revenue to the State CIO. The Department of Revenue and the Office of Information Technology Services shall develop data communications capabilities between the two computer centers utilizing the North Carolina Integrated Network, subject to a security review by the Secretary of Revenue.

(c) The Department of Revenue shall prepare a plan to allow for substantial recovery and operation of major, critical computer applications. The plan shall include the names of the computer programs, databases, and data communications capabilities, identify the maximum amount of outage that can occur prior to the initiation of the plan and resumption of operation. The plan shall be consistent with commonly accepted practices for disaster recovery in the information processing industry. The plan shall be tested as soon as practical, but not later than six months, after the establishment of the Department of Revenue information processing capability.

(d) Notwithstanding the provisions of subsections (a) and (b) of this section, the Department of Revenue shall review and evaluate any deviations and shall, in consultation with the Office of Information Technology Services, adopt a plan to phase out any deviations that are not determined to be necessary in carrying out functions and responsibilities unique to the Department. The plan adopted by the Department shall include a strategy to coordinate its general information processing functions with the Office of Information Technology Services in the manner prescribed by G.S. 147-33.83(a) and provide for its compliance with policies, procedures, and guidelines adopted by the Office of Information Technology Services. The Department of Revenue shall submit its plan to the Office of State Budget and Management by January 15, 2005. (1989, c. 239, s. 5; c. 770, s. 60; 1989 (Reg. Sess., 1990), c. 1024, s. 36; 1991 (Reg. Sess., 1992), c. 900, s. 14(g); c. 1030, s. 51.14; 1997-148, ss. 5, 6; 1999-347, s. 2; 1999-434, s. 27; 2000-174, s. 2; 2004-129, s. 16.)

§ 147-33.85: Repealed by Session Laws 2004-129, ss. 17, 18, effective July 1, 2004.

§147-33.86: Repealed by Session Laws 2004-129, ss. 17, 18, effective July 1, 2004.

§ 147-33.87. Financial reporting and accountability for information technology investments and expenditures.

The Office of Information Technology Services, the Office of State Budget and Management, and the Office of the State Controller shall jointly develop a system for budgeting and accounting of expenditures for information technology operations, services, projects, infrastructure, and assets. The system shall include hardware, software, personnel, training, contractual services, and other items relevant to information technology, and the sources of funding for each. Annual reports regarding information technology shall be coordinated by the Office with the Office of State Budget and Management and the Office of the State Controller, and submitted to the Governor and the General Assembly on or before October 1 of each year. (1999-434, s. 10; 2000-140, s. 93.1(i); 2000-174, s. 2; 2001-424, s. 12.2(b); 2004-129, s. 19.)

§ 147-33.87A. Statewide electronic portal; annual report.

(a)   The Office of the State Chief Information Officer (State CIO) shall plan, develop, implement, and operate a Statewide electronic portal (i) to increase the convenience of members of the public in conducting online transactions with, and obtaining information from, State government and (ii) to facilitate their interactions and communications with government agencies.

(b)   Beginning January 31, 2014, and then annually thereafter, the State CIO shall report to the General Assembly and to the Fiscal Research Division on the following information:

(1)   Services currently provided and associated transaction volumes or other relevant indicators of utilization by user type.

(2)   New services added during the previous year.

(3)   Services added that are currently available in other states.

(4)   The total amount collected for each service.

(5) The total amount remitted to the State for each service.

(6) The total amount remitted to the vendor for each service.

(7) Any other use of State data by the vendor and the total amount of revenue collected per each use and in total.

(8) Customer satisfaction with each service.

(9) Any other issues associated with the provision of each service. (2012-142, s. 6A.12(a), (c).)

§ 147-33.88. Information technology budget development and reports.

(a) The Office of Information Technology Services (ITS) shall develop an annual budget for review and approval by the Office of State Budget and Management (OSBM) in accordance with a schedule prescribed by the Director of the Office of State Budget and Management. The approved Information Technology Internal Service Fund budget shall be included in the Governor's budget recommendations to the General Assembly.

The Office of State Budget and Management shall ensure that State agencies have an opportunity to adjust their budgets based on any rate changes proposed by the Office of Information Technology Services and approved by the Office of State Budget and Management.

(b) The Office shall report to the Joint Legislative Oversight Committee on Information Technology and the Fiscal Research Division on the Office's Internal Service Fund on a quarterly basis, no later than the first day of the second month following the end of the quarter. The report shall include current cash balances, line-item detail on expenditures from the previous quarter, and anticipated expenditures and revenues. The Office shall report to the Joint Legislative Oversight Committee on Information Technology and the Fiscal Research Division on expenditures for the upcoming quarter, projected year-end balance, and the status report on personnel position changes including new positions created and existing positions eliminated. The Office spending reports shall comply with the State Accounting System object codes. (1999-434, s. 10; 2000-174, s. 2; 2004-129, s. 20; 2013-360, s. 7.2(a).)

§ 147-33.89. Business continuity planning.

(a) Each State agency shall develop and continually review and update as necessary a business and disaster recovery plan with respect to information technology. Each agency shall establish a disaster recovery planning team to develop the disaster recovery plan and to administer implementation of the plan. In developing the plan, the disaster recovery planning team shall do all of the following:

(1) Consider the organizational, managerial, and technical environments in which the disaster recovery plan must be implemented.

(2) Assess the types and likely parameters of disasters most likely to occur and the resultant impacts on the agency's ability to perform its mission.

(3) List protective measures to be implemented in anticipation of a natural or man-made disaster.

(b) Each State agency shall submit its disaster recovery plan on an annual basis to the State Chief Information Officer. (2003-153, s. 2; 2004-129, s. 21.)

§ 147-33.90. Analysis of State agency legacy systems.

(a) The Office of Information Technology Services shall analyze the State's legacy information technology systems and develop a plan to ascertain the needs, costs, and time frame required for State agencies to progress to more modern information technology systems.

(b) In conducting the legacy system assessment phase of the analysis, the Office shall:

(1) Examine the hierarchical structure and interrelated relationships within and between State agency legacy systems.

(2) Catalog and analyze the portfolio of legacy applications in use in State agencies and consider the extent to which new applications could be used concurrently with, or should replace, legacy systems.

(3) Consider issues related to migration from legacy environments to Internet-based and client/server environments, and related to the availability of programmers and other information technology professionals with the skills to migrate legacy applications to other environments.

(4) Study any other issue relative to the assessment of legacy information technology systems in State agencies.

(c) Upon completion of the legacy system assessment phase of the analysis, the Office shall ascertain the needs, costs, and time frame required to modernize State agency information technology. The Office shall complete this phase of the assessment by January 31, 2005, and shall report its findings and recommendations to the 2005 General Assembly. The findings and recommendations shall include a cost estimate and time line for modernization of legacy information technology systems in State agencies. The Office shall submit an ongoing, updated report on modernization needs, costs, and time lines to the General Assembly on the opening day of each biennial session. (2003-172, s. 1; 2004-129, s. 22.)

Part 3. Telecommunications Services.

§ 147-33.91. Telecommunications services; duties of State Chief Information Officer with respect to State agencies.

(a) With respect to State agencies, the State Chief Information Officer shall exercise general coordinating authority for all telecommunications matters relating to the internal management and operations of those agencies. In discharging that responsibility, the State Chief Information Officer, in cooperation with affected State agency heads, may:

(1) Provide for the establishment, management, and operation, through either State ownership, contract, or commercial leasing, of the following systems and services as they affect the internal management and operation of State agencies:

a. Central telephone systems and telephone networks.

b. Repealed by Session Laws 2004-129, s. 23, effective July 1, 2004.

c. Repealed by Session Laws 2004-129, s. 23, effective July 1, 2004.

d. Satellite services.

e. Closed-circuit TV systems.

f. Two-way radio systems.

g. Microwave systems.

h. Related systems based on telecommunication technologies.

i. The "State Network", managed by the Office, which means any connectivity designed for the purpose of providing Internet Protocol transport of information to any building.

(2) Coordinate the development of cost-sharing systems for respective user agencies for their proportionate parts of the cost of maintenance and operation of the systems and services listed in subdivision (1) of this subsection.

(3) Assist in the development of coordinated telecommunications services or systems within and among all State agencies and recommend, where appropriate, cooperative utilization of telecommunication facilities by aggregating users.

(4) Perform traffic analysis and engineering for all telecommunications services and systems listed in subdivision (1) of this subsection.

(5) Establish telecommunications specifications and designs so as to promote and support compatibility of the systems within State agencies.

(6) Coordinate the review of requests by State agencies for the procurement of telecommunications systems or services.

(7) Coordinate the review of requests by State agencies for State government property acquisition, disposition, or construction for telecommunications systems requirements.

(8) Provide a periodic inventory of telecommunications costs, facilities, systems, and personnel within State agencies.

(9) Promote, coordinate, and assist in the design and engineering of emergency telecommunications systems, including, but not limited to, the 911 emergency telephone number program, Emergency Medical Services, and other emergency telecommunications services.

(10) Perform frequency coordination and management for State agencies and local governments, including all public safety radio service frequencies, in accordance with the rules and regulations of the Federal Communications Commission or any successor federal agency.

(11) Advise all State agencies on telecommunications management planning and related matters and provide through the State Personnel Training Center or the Office of Information Technology Services training to users within State agencies in telecommunications technology and systems.

(12) Assist and coordinate the development of policies and long-range plans, consistent with the protection of citizens' rights to privacy and access to information, for the acquisition and use of telecommunications systems, and base such policies and plans on current information about State telecommunications activities in relation to the full range of emerging technologies.

(13) Repealed by Session Laws 2013-188, s. 3, effective June 26, 2013.

(b) The provisions of this section shall not apply to the Criminal Information Division of the Department of Justice or to the Judicial Information System in the Judicial Department. (1985 (Reg. Sess., 1986), c. 1024, s. 1; 1987, c. 738, s. 59(a)(2); 1989, c. 239, s. 4; 1989 (Reg. Sess., 1990), c. 1024, s. 37; 1991, c. 542, s. 14; 1993, c. 512, s. 2; 1993 (Reg. Sess., 1994), c. 777, s. 1(a); 1997-148, ss. 3, 6; 1999-347, s. 4; 1999-434, s. 29; 2000-174, s. 2; 2004-129, s. 23; 2013-188, s. 3.)

§ 147-33.92. Telecommunications services for local governmental entities and other entities.

(a) The State Chief Information Officer shall provide cities, counties, and other local governmental entities with access to a central telecommunications system or service established under G.S. 147-33.91 for State agencies. Access shall be provided on the same cost basis that applies to State agencies.

(b) The State Chief Information Officer shall establish broadband telecommunications services and permit, in addition to State agencies, cities, counties, and other local government entities, the following organizations and entities to share on a not-for-profit basis:

(1) Nonprofit educational institutions.

(2) Repealed by Session Laws 2013-188, s. 4, effective June 26, 2013.

(3) MCNC and research affiliates of MCNC for use only in connection with research activities sponsored or funded, in whole or in part, by MCNC, if such research activities relate to health care or education in North Carolina.

(4) Agencies of the United States government operating in North Carolina for use only in connection with activities that relate to health care or education in North Carolina.

(5) Hospitals, clinics, and other health care facilities for use only in connection with activities that relate to health care or education in North Carolina.

Provided, however, that sharing of the broadband telecommunications services by State agencies with entities or organizations in the categories set forth in this subsection shall not cause the State, the Office of Information Technology Services, or the MCNC to be classified as a public utility as that term is defined in G.S. 62-3(23)a.6. Nor shall the State, the Office of Information Technology Services, or the MCNC engage in any activities that may cause those entities to be classified as a common carrier as that term is defined in the Communications Act of 1934, 47 U.S.C. § 153(10). Provided further, authority to share the broadband telecommunications services with the non-State agencies set forth in subdivisions (1) through (5) of this subsection shall terminate one year from the effective date of a tariff that makes the broadband services available to any customer. (1985 (Reg. Sess., 1986), c. 1024, s. 1; 1987, c. 738, s. 59(a)(2); 1989, c. 239, s. 4; 1989 (Reg. Sess., 1990), c. 1024, s. 37; 1991, c. 542, s. 14; 1993, c. 512, s. 2; 1993 (Reg. Sess., 1994), c. 777, s. 1(a); 1997-148, ss. 3, 6; 1999-347, s. 4; 1999-434, s. 29; 2000-174, s. 2; 2004-203, s. 37(b); 2013-188, s. 4.)

§ 147-33.93. Fees; dispute resolution panel.

In addition to the powers granted pursuant to Article 6B of this Chapter or by any other provision of law, the Office of Information Technology Services may go before a panel consisting of the State Treasurer, the State Controller, and the State Budget Officer, or their designees, to resolve disputes concerning services, fees, and charges incurred by State government agencies receiving information technology services from the Office. The State Treasurer shall adopt rules for the dispute resolution process. The decisions of the panel shall be final in the settlement of all fee disputes that come before it. (2001-142, s. 1; 2009-136, s. 1.)

§ 147-33.94. Reserved for future codification purposes.

Part 4. Procurement of Information Technology.

§ 147-33.95. Procurement of information technology.

(a) Notwithstanding any other provision of law, the Office of Information Technology Services shall procure all information technology for State agencies. The Office shall integrate technological review, cost analysis, and procurement for all information technology needs of those State agencies in order to make procurement and implementation of technology more responsive, efficient, and cost-effective. All contract information shall be made a matter of public record after the award of contract. Trade secrets, test data, similar proprietary information, and security information protected under G.S. 132-6.1(c) may remain confidential.

(b) The Office shall have the authority and responsibility, subject to the provisions of this Part, to:

(1) Purchase or contract for all information technology in the State government, or any of its departments, institutions, or agencies covered by this Part. The Office may authorize any State agency covered by this Part to purchase or contract for information technology. The Office or a State agency may use any authorized means, including negotiations, reverse auctions, and the solicitation, offer, and acceptance of electronic bids. G.S. 143-135.9 shall apply to these procedures.

(2) Establish processes, specifications, and standards that shall apply to all information technology to be purchased, licensed, or leased in the State

government or any of its departments, institutions, or agencies covered by this Part.

(2a)   Establish procedures to permit State agencies and local government agencies to use the General Services Administration (GSA) Cooperative Purchasing Program to purchase information technology (i) awarded under General Services Administration Supply Schedule 70 Information Technology and (ii) from contracts under the GSA's Consolidated Schedule containing information technology special item numbers.

(3)   Comply with the State government-wide technical architecture, as required by the State CIO.

(4)   If a State agency wishes to enter into a cooperative purchasing agreement, the agency must first obtain approval by the State CIO. Upon receiving a request to use a cooperative purchasing agreement, the State CIO must evaluate the need for goods or services available through the agreement, review the specifications, terms, and conditions of the agreement, and obtain legal advice on the use of the agreement. Prior to granting approval, the State CIO must find that the agreement was awarded pursuant to a competitive bidding process and that the agency will obtain the best value pursuant to G.S. 143-135.9 by using the agreement. Upon approval by the State CIO, a State agency may use the agreement without further approval. Agencies must report periodically to the CIO regarding the use of these agreements.

(5)   The State CIO shall establish procedures for the utilization of cooperative purchasing agreements.

(c)   For purposes of this section, "reverse auction" means a real-time purchasing process in which vendors compete to provide goods or services at the lowest selling price in an open and interactive electronic environment. The vendor's price may be revealed during the reverse auction. The Office may contract with a third-party vendor to conduct the reverse auction.

(d)   For purposes of this section, "electronic bidding" means the electronic solicitation and receipt of offers to contract. Offers may be accepted and contracts may be entered by use of electronic bidding.

(e)   The Office may use the electronic procurement system established by G.S. 143-48.3 to conduct reverse auctions and electronic bidding. All requirements relating to formal and competitive bids, including advertisement, seal, and signature, are satisfied when a procurement is conducted or a contract is entered in compliance with the reverse auction or electronic bidding requirements established by the Office.

(f) The Office shall adopt rules consistent with this section.

(g) No contract subject to the provisions of this Part may be entered into unless the contractor and the contractor's subcontractors comply with the requirements of Article 2 of Chapter 64 of the General Statutes. (1999-434, s. 10; 2000-174, s. 2; 2002-107, s. 4; 2002-159, s. 64(a); 2004-129, s. 24; 2009-451, s. 6.14A(a); 2013-333, s. 2; 2013-418, s. 2(e).)

§ 147-33.96. Restriction on State agency contractual authority with regard to information technology; local governments.

(a) All State agencies covered by this Part shall use contracts for information technology acquired by the Office for any information technology required by the State agency that is provided by these contracts. Notwithstanding any other statute, the authority of State agencies to procure or obtain information technology shall be subject to compliance with the provisions of this Part. The Office shall have the authority to exercise the authority of State agencies to procure or obtain information technology as otherwise provided by statute.

(b) Local governmental entities are not required to comply with otherwise applicable competitive bidding requirements when using contracts offered by the Office. (1999-434, s. 10; 2000-174, s. 210-241.)

§ 147-33.97. Information technology procurement policy; reporting requirements.

(a) Policy. - In order to further the policy of the State to encourage and promote the use of small, minority, physically handicapped, and women contractors in State purchasing of goods and services, all State agencies covered by this Part shall cooperate with the Office in efforts to encourage the use of small, minority, physically handicapped, and women contractors in achieving the purpose of this Part, which is to provide for the effective and economical acquisition, management, and disposition of information technology.

(a1)   A vendor submitting a bid shall disclose in a statement, provided contemporaneously with the bid, where services will be performed under the contract sought, including any subcontracts and whether any services under that contract, including any subcontracts, are anticipated to be performed outside the United States. Nothing in this section is intended to contravene any existing treaty, law, agreement, or regulation of the United States.

(a2)   The State Chief Information Officer shall retain the statements required by subsection (a1) of this section regardless of the State entity that awards the contract and shall report annually to the Secretary of Administration on the number of contracts which are anticipated to be performed outside the United States.

(b)   Reporting. - Every State agency that makes a direct purchase of information technology using the services of the Office shall report directly to the Department of Administration all information required by G.S. 143-48(b).

(c)   The Department of Administration shall collect and compile the data described in this section and report it annually to the Office. (1999-434, s. 10; 2000-174, s. 2; 2006-264, s. 72(a).)

§ 147-33.98. Unauthorized use of public purchase or contract procedures for private benefit prohibited.

(a)   It shall be unlawful for any person, by the use of the powers, policies, or procedures described in this Part or established hereunder, to purchase, attempt to purchase, procure, or attempt to procure any property or services for private use or benefit.

(b)   This prohibition shall not apply if:

(1)   The department, institution, or agency through which the property or services are procured had theretofore established policies and procedures permitting such purchases or procurement by a class or classes of persons in order to provide for the mutual benefit of such persons and the department, institution, or agency involved, or the public benefit or convenience; and

(2) Such policies and procedures, including any reimbursement policies, are complied with by the person permitted thereunder to use the purchasing or procurement procedures described in this Part or established thereunder.

(c) Any violation of this section is a Class 1 misdemeanor. (1999-434, s. 10; 2000-174, s. 2.)

§ 147-33.99. Financial interest of officers in sources of supply; acceptance of bribes.

Neither the State Chief Information Officer nor the Chief Deputy State Information Officer shall be financially interested, or have any personal beneficial interest, either directly or indirectly, in the purchase of, or contract for, any information technology, nor in any firm, corporation, partnership, or association furnishing any information technology to the State government, or any of its departments, institutions, or agencies, nor shall either of these persons or any other Office employee accept or receive, directly or indirectly, from any person, firm, or corporation to whom any contract may be awarded, by rebate, gifts, or otherwise, any money or anything of value whatsoever, or any promise, obligation, or contract for future reward or compensation. Violation of this section is a Class F felony, and any person found guilty of a violation of this section shall, upon conviction, be removed from State office or employment. (1999-434, s. 10; 2000-174, s. 2.)

§ 147-33.100. Certification that information technology bid submitted without collusion.

The Office shall require bidders to certify that each bid on information technology contracts overseen by the Office is submitted competitively and without collusion. False certification is a Class I felony. (1999-434, s. 10; 2000-174, s. 2.)

§ 147-33.101. Award recommendation; State Chief Information Officer action.

(a) Award Recommendation. - When the dollar value of a contract for the procurement of information technology equipment, materials, and supplies exceeds the benchmark established by the State Chief Information Officer, an award recommendation shall be submitted to the State Chief Information Officer for approval or other action. The State Chief Information Officer shall promptly notify the agency or institution making the recommendation, or for which the purchase is to be made, of the action taken.

(b) Review. - Prior to submission for review pursuant to this section of any contract for information technology being acquired for the benefit of the Office and not on behalf of any other State agency, the Director of the Budget shall review and approve the procurement to ensure compliance with the established processes, specifications, and standards applicable to all information technology purchased, licensed, or leased in State government, including established procurement processes, and compliance with the State government wide technical architecture as established by the State CIO.

(c) Reporting. - The State CIOs shall provide a report of all contract awards approved through the Statewide IT Procurement Office as indicated below. The report shall include the amount of the award, the contract term, the award recipient, the using agency, and a short description of the nature of the award:

(1) For contract awards greater than twenty-five thousand dollars ($25,000), to the Cochairs of the Joint Legislative Oversight Committee on Information Technology on a monthly basis.

(2) For all contract awards outside the established purchasing system, to the Secretary of the Department of Administration on a quarterly basis. (1999-434, s. 10; 2000-174, s. 2; 2004-129, s. 25; 2007-484, s. 20; 2013-234, s. 5.)

§ 147-33.102. Penalty for violations; costs.

Any employee or official of the State who violates this Part shall be liable to the State to repay any amount expended in violation of this Part, together with any court costs. (1999-434, s. 10; 2000-174, s. 2.)

§ 147-33.103. Attorney General contract assistance; rule-making authority.

(a) At the request of the State Chief Information Officer, the Attorney General shall provide legal advice and services necessary to implement this Part.

(b) Repealed by Session Laws 2004-129, s. 26, effective July 1, 2004. (1999-434, s. 10; 2000-174, s. 2; 2004-129, s. 26.)

§ 147-33.104: Repealed by Session Laws 2010-67, s. 1(a)-(d), effective July 1, 2010.

§ 147-33.104A. Purchase by State agencies and governmental entities of certain computer equipment and televisions prohibited.

(a) The exemptions set out in G.S. 147-33.80 do not apply to this section.

(b) No State agency, political subdivision of the State, or other public body shall purchase computer equipment or televisions, as defined in G.S. 130A-309.131, or enter into a contract with any manufacturer that the Secretary determines is not in compliance with the requirements of G.S. 130A-309.134 or G.S. 130A-309.135 as determined from the list provided by the Department of Environment and Natural Resources pursuant to G.S. 130A-309.138. The Secretary shall issue written findings upon a determination of noncompliance. A determination of noncompliance by the Secretary is reviewable under Article 3 of Chapter 150B of the General Statutes.

(c) The Office of Information Technology Services shall make the list available to political subdivisions of the State and other public bodies. A manufacturer that is not in compliance with the requirements of G.S. 130A-309.134 or G.S. 130A-309.135 shall not sell or offer for sale computer equipment or televisions to the State, a political subdivision of the State, or other public body. (2010-67, s. 5(a).)

§ 147-33.105: Reserved for future codification purposes.

§ 147-33.106: Reserved for future codification purposes.

§ 147-33.107: Reserved for future codification purposes.

§ 147-33.108: Reserved for future codification purposes.

§ 147-33.109: Reserved for future codification purposes.

Part 5. Security for Information Technology Services.

§ 147-33.110. Statewide security standards.

The State Chief Information Officer shall establish a statewide set of standards for information technology security to maximize the functionality, security, and interoperability of the State's distributed information technology assets, including communications and encryption technologies. The State CIO shall review and revise the security standards annually. As part of this function, the State Chief Information Officer shall review periodically existing security standards and practices in place among the various State agencies to determine whether those standards and practices meet statewide security and encryption requirements. The State Chief Information Officer may assume the direct responsibility of providing for the information technology security of any State agency that fails to adhere to security standards adopted under this Article. (2001-424, s. 15.2(b); 2004-129, ss. 12, 14; 2011-266, s. 1.9(e).)

§ 147-33.111. State CIO approval of security standards and security assessments.

(a)   Notwithstanding G.S. 143-48.3 or any other provision of law, and except as otherwise provided by this section, all information technology security purchased using State funds, or for use by a State agency or in a State facility, shall be subject to approval by the State Chief Information Officer in accordance with security standards adopted under this Article.

(a1)   The State Chief Information Officer shall conduct assessments of information system security, network vulnerability, including network penetration or any similar procedure. The State Chief Information Officer may contract with another party or parties to perform the assessments. Detailed reports of the security issues identified shall be kept confidential as provided in G.S. 132-6.1(c).

(b)   If the legislative branch, the judicial branch, The University of North Carolina and its constituent institutions, local school administrative units as defined by G.S. 115C-5, or the North Carolina Community Colleges System develop their own security standards, taking into consideration the mission and functions of that entity, that are comparable to or exceed those set by the State Chief Information Officer under this section, then these entities may elect to be governed by their own respective security standards, and approval of the State Chief Information Officer shall not be required before the purchase of information technology security. The State Chief Information Officer shall consult with the legislative branch, the judicial branch, The University of North Carolina and its constituent institutions, local school administrative units, and the North Carolina Community Colleges System in reviewing the security standards adopted by those entities.

(c)   Before a State agency may enter into any contract with another party for an assessment of information system security or network vulnerability, the State agency shall notify the State Chief Information Officer and obtain approval of the request. If the State agency enters into a contract with another party for assessment and testing, after approval of the State Chief Information Officer, the State agency shall issue public reports on the general results of the reviews. The contractor shall provide the State agency with detailed reports of the security issues identified that shall not be disclosed as provided in G.S. 132-6.1(c). The State agency shall provide the State Chief Information Officer with copies of the detailed reports that shall not be disclosed as provided in G.S. 132-6.1(c).

(d)   Nothing in this section shall be construed to preclude the Office of the State Auditor from assessing the security practices of State information technology systems as part of that Office's duties and responsibilities. (2001-424, s. 15.2(b); 2004-129, ss. 10, 12, 14; 2010-31, s. 6.15(a); 2013-188, s. 5.)

§ 147-33.112. Assessment of agency compliance with security standards.

The State Chief Information Officer shall assess periodically the ability of each agency and each agency's contracted vendors to comply with the current security enterprise-wide set of standards established pursuant to this section.

The assessment shall include, at a minimum, the rate of compliance with the enterprise-wide security standards and an assessment of security organization, security practices, security industry standards, network security architecture, and current expenditures of State funds for information technology security. The assessment of an agency shall also estimate the cost to implement the security measures needed for agencies to fully comply with the standards. Each agency subject to the standards shall submit information required by the State Chief Information Officer for purposes of this assessment. The State Chief Information Officer shall include the information obtained from the assessment in the State Information Technology Plan required under G.S. 147-33.72B.

The State Chief Information Officer shall assess the ability of each agency to comply with the current security enterprise-wide set of standards established pursuant to this section. The assessment shall include, at a minimum, the rate of compliance with the standards in each agency and an assessment of each agency's security organization, network security architecture, and current expenditures for information technology security. The assessment shall also estimate the cost to implement the security measures needed for agencies to fully comply with the standards. Each agency subject to the standards shall submit information required by the State Chief Information Officer for purposes of this assessment. The State Chief Information Officer shall include the information obtained from the assessment in the State Information Technology Plan required under G.S. 147-33.72B. (2003-153, s. 1(a); 2004-129, ss. 12, 14; 2013-188, s. 6.)

§ 147-33.113. State agency cooperation.

(a) The head of each State agency shall cooperate with the State Chief Information Officer in the discharge of his or her duties by:

(1) Providing the full details of the agency's information technology and operational requirements and of all the agency's information technology security incidents within 24 hours of confirmation.

(2) Providing comprehensive information concerning the information technology security employed to protect the agency's information technology.

(3) Forecasting the parameters of the agency's projected future information technology security needs and capabilities.

(4) Designating an agency liaison in the information technology area to coordinate with the State Chief Information Officer. The liaison shall be subject to a criminal background report from the State Repository of Criminal Histories, which shall be provided by the State Bureau of Investigation upon its receiving fingerprints from the liaison. If the liaison has been a resident of this State for less than five years, the background report shall include a review of criminal information from both the State and National Repositories of Criminal Histories. The criminal background report shall be provided to the State Chief Information Officer and the head of the agency. In addition, all personnel in the Office of State Auditor who are responsible for information technology security reviews pursuant to G.S. 147-64.6(c)(18) shall be subject to a criminal background report from the State Repository of Criminal Histories, which shall be provided by the State Bureau of Investigation upon receiving fingerprints from the personnel designated by the State Auditor. For designated personnel who have been residents of this State for less than five years, the background report shall include a review of criminal information from both the State and National Repositories of Criminal Histories. The criminal background reports shall be provided to the State Auditor. Criminal histories provided pursuant to this subdivision are not public records under Chapter 132 of the General Statutes.

(b) The information provided by State agencies to the State Chief Information Officer under this section is protected from public disclosure pursuant to G.S. 132-6.1(c). (2001-424, s. 15.2(b); 2003-153, s. 1(a); 2004-129, ss. 12, 14; 2007-155, s. 2; 2007-189, ss. 2, 5.1.)

Part 6. Purchase of Refurbished Computer Equipment.

§ 147-33.120. Definitions.

The following definitions apply in this act:

(1) Computer equipment. - Any desktop computer, notebook or laptop computer, monitor or video display unit for a computer system, and the keyboard, mice, other peripheral equipment, and a printing device such as a printer, a scanner, a combination print-scanner-fax machine, or other device designed to produce hard paper copies from a computer.

(2) Computer equipment refurbisher. - A person in the business of restoring pre-owned computer equipment to original equipment standards, meeting the manufacturers' warranty requirements and any software licensing requirements.

(3) Refurbished computer equipment. - Computer equipment that has been reformatted to remove any preexisting software and data, and then cleaned, repaired, inspected, and tested as necessary to ensure that the equipment has been restored to "like new" full functionality that meets or exceeds the manufacturers' original equipment standards and warranty requirements.

(4) Registered computer equipment refurbisher. - A person certified by the original equipment manufacturer to restore pre-owned computer equipment to original equipment standards meeting the manufacturers' warranty requirements, and any software licensing requirements, in accordance with the manufacturers' and software makers' official refurbisher programs.

(5) State and local governmental entities. - The executive, legislative, and judicial branches of government; any local political subdivisions of the State; community colleges; local boards of educations; and The University of North Carolina. (2013-128, s. 1.)

§ 147-33.121. Refurbished computer equipment purchasing program.

(a) The Office of the State Chief Information Officer and the Department of Administration, with the administrative support of the Information Technology Procurement Office, shall offer State and local governmental entities the option of purchasing refurbished computer equipment from registered computer equipment refurbishers whenever most appropriate to meet the needs of State and local governmental entities.

(b) State and local governmental entities shall document savings resulting from the purchase of the refurbished computer equipment, including, but not limited to, the initial acquisition cost as well as operations and maintenance costs. These savings shall be reported quarterly to the Office of the State Chief Information Officer.

(c) The Information Technology Procurement Office shall administer the refurbished computer equipment program by establishing a competitive purchasing process to support this initiative that meets all State information technology procurement laws and procedures and ensures that agencies receive the best value.

(d)   Participating computer equipment refurbishers must meet all procurement requirements established by the Office of the State Chief Information Officer and the Department of Administration. (2013-128, s. 2.)

§ 147-33.122. Configuration and specification requirements same as for new computers.

Refurbished computer equipment purchased under this act must conform to the same standards as the State may establish as to the configuration and specification requirements for the purchase of new computers. (2013-128, s. 3.)

§ 147-33.123. Data on reliability and other issues; report.

The Office of the State Chief Information Officer shall maintain data on equipment reliability, potential cost savings, and any issues associated with the refurbished computer equipment initiative and shall report the results of the initiative to the Joint Legislative Oversight Committee on Information Technology and the Fiscal Research Division by March 1, 2014, and then quarterly thereafter. (2013-128, s. 4.)

Article 4.

Secretary of State.

§ 147-34. Office and office hours.

The Secretary of State shall attend at his office, in the City of Raleigh, between the hours of 10 o'clock A.M. and three o'clock P.M., on every day of the year, Sundays and legal holidays excepted. (1868-9, c. 270, s. 44; 1870-1, c. 111; Code, s. 3339; Rev., s. 5344; C.S., s. 7652.)

§ 147-35. Salary of Secretary of State.

The salary of the Secretary of State shall be set by the General Assembly in the Current Operations Appropriations Act. In addition to the salary set by the General Assembly in the Current Operations Appropriations Act, longevity pay shall be paid on the same basis as is provided to employees of the State who are subject to the North Carolina Human Resources Act. (1879, c. 240, s. 6; 1881, p. 632, res.; Code, s. 3724; Rev., s. 2741; 1907, c. 994; 1919, c. 247, s. 2; C.S., s. 3863; Ex. Sess. 1920, c. 49, s. 4; 1921, c. 11, s. 1; 1931, c. 277; 1933, c. 46; 1935, c. 304; 1941, c. 1; 1947, c. 1041; 1949, c. 1278; 1953, c. 1, s. 2; 1957, c. 1; 1963, c. 1178, s. 1; 1967, c. 1130; c. 1237, s. 1; 1969, c. 1214, s. 1; 1971, c. 912, s. 1; 1973, c. 778, s. 1; 1975, 2nd Sess., c. 983, s. 14; 1977, c. 802, s. 42.7; 1983, c. 761, s. 212; 1983 (Reg. Sess., 1984), c. 1034, s. 164; 1987, c. 738, s. 32(b); 2013-382, s. 9.1(c).)

§ 147-36. Duties of Secretary of State.

It is the duty of the Secretary of State:

(1)   To perform such duties as may then be devolved upon the Secretary by resolution of the two houses of the General Assembly or either of them;

(2)   To attend the Governor, whenever required by the Governor, for the purpose of receiving documents which have passed the great seal;

(3)   To receive and keep all conveyances and mortgages belonging to the State;

(4)   To distribute annually the statutes and the legislative journals;

(5)   To distribute the acts of Congress received at the Secretary's office in the manner prescribed for the statutes of the State;

(6)   To keep a receipt book, in which the Secretary shall take from every person to whom a grant shall be delivered, a receipt for the same; but may inclose grants by mail in a registered letter at the expense of the grantee, unless otherwise directed, first entering the same upon the receipt book;

(7) To issue charters and all necessary certificates for the incorporation, domestication, suspension, reinstatement, cancellation and dissolution of corporations as may be required by the corporation laws of the State and maintain a record thereof;

(8) To issue certificates of registration of trademarks, labels and designs as may be required by law and maintain a record thereof;

(9) To maintain a Division of Publications to compile data on the State's several governmental agencies and for legislative reference;

(10) To receive, enroll and safely preserve the Constitution of the State and all amendments thereto;

(11) To serve as a member of such boards and commissions as the Constitution and laws of the State may designate;

(12) To administer the Securities Law of the State, regulating the issuance and sale of securities, as is now or may be directed;

(13) To receive and keep all oaths of public officials required by law to be filed in the Secretary's office, and as Secretary of State, is fully empowered to administer official oaths to any public official of whom an oath is required;

(14) To receive and maintain a journal of all appointments made to any State board, agency, commission, council or authority which is filed in the office of the Secretary of State;

(15) To regulate the solicitation of contributions pursuant to Chapter 131F of the General Statutes; and

(16) To apply for and accept grants from the federal government and its agencies and from any foundation, corporation, association, or individual in order to effectuate the purposes of the Nonprofit Corporation Act, Chapter 55A of the General Statutes, and to further aid in the operation and development of nonprofit corporations. The Secretary shall comply with the terms, conditions, and limitations of grants applied for and accepted and shall expend grant funds pursuant to Chapter 143C of the General Statutes, The State Budget Act. (1868-9, c. 270, s. 45; 1881, c. 63; Code, s. 3340; Rev., s. 5345; C.S., s. 7654; 1941, c. 379, s. 6; 1943, cc. 480, 543; 1967, c. 691, s. 53; 1973, c. 1379, s. 1; 1995, c. 20, s. 9; 1998-212, s. 12.14(c); 1999-316, s. 1; 2006-203, s. 115.)

§ 147-36.1. Deputy Secretary of State.

The duly classified Deputy Secretary of State as reflected by the records of the State Department of Personnel, appointed by the Secretary of State to aid him in the discharge of his duties, shall have the authority to perform all acts and duties of the office in the absence of his chief, or in the case of his inability to act, or under his direction. In exercising such authority, certificates relating to documents and other filings, shall be issued in the name of the Secretary of State, printed, typed, stamped or facsimile signature, and signed by the Deputy Secretary of State.

Employees in the office of the Secretary of State designated as deputy or director of specific divisions in the Department, are empowered to issue certificates relating to documents and other filings within the scope of their division. In exercising such authority the certificates shall be issued in the name of the Secretary of State, printed, typed, stamped or facsimile signature, and signed by the deputy or director indicating his approved title. Provided, however, that if the volume of documents or certificates to be issued makes an embossed seal and the autograph signature of the deputy or director impractical, the documents may be certified and certificates issued under the facsimile signature and seal of the Secretary of State only. (1967, c. 1265; 1987, c. 349.)

§ 147-37. Secretary of State; fees to be collected.

When no other charge is provided by law, the Secretary of State shall collect such fees for copying any document or record on file in his office which in his discretion bears a reasonable relation to the quantity of copies supplied and the cost of purchasing or leasing and maintaining copying equipment. These fees may be changed from time to time, but a schedule of fees shall be available on request at all times. In addition to copying charges, the Secretary of State shall collect a fee of ten dollars ($10.00) for certifying any document or record on file in his office or for issuing any certificate as to the facts shown by the records on file in his office, except that if two or more certificates for foreign adoption are requested concurrently, the fee for the second and subsequent certificates is five dollars ($5.00). (R.C., c. 102, s. 13; 1870-1, c. 81, s. 3; 1881, c. 79; Code, s. 3725; Rev., s. 2742; C.S., s. 3864; 1979, c. 85, s. 2; 1991, c. 429, s. 1; 1998-212, s. 29A.9(e); 2002-126, s. 29A.32.)

§ 147-38. Repealed by Session Laws 1979, c. 85, s. 3.

§ 147-39. Custodian of statutes, records, deeds, etc.

The Secretary of State is charged with the custody of all statutes and joint resolutions of the legislature, all documents which pass under the great seal, and of all the books, records, deeds, parchments, maps, and papers now deposited in his office or which may hereafter be there deposited pursuant to law, and he shall from time to time make all necessary provisions for their arrangement and preservation. Every deed, conveyance, or other instrument whereby the State or any State agency or institution has acquired title to any real property and which is deposited with the Secretary of State shall be filed by him, and indexed according to the county or counties wherein the real property is situated and the name or names of the grantor or grantors and of the grantee; and the real property shall be briefly described in the index. (R.C., c. 104, s. 105; 1868-9, c. 270, s. 41; 1873-4, c. 129; Code, s. 3337; Rev., s. 5347; C.S., s. 7656; 1957, c. 584, s. 5.)

§ 147-40. Repealed by Session Laws 1969, c. 1184, s. 8.

§ 147-41. To keep records of oyster grants.

The Secretary of State shall keep books of records in which shall be recorded a full description of all grounds granted for oyster beds under the provisions of Chapter 119 of the Laws of 1887, and laws amendatory thereof, and shall keep a map or maps showing the position and limits of all public and private grounds. (1887, c. 119, s. 14; Rev., s. 2381; C.S., s. 7657.)

§ 147-42. Binding original statutes, resolutions, and documents.

The original statutes and joint resolutions passed at each session of the General Assembly the Secretary of State shall immediately thereafter cause to be bound in volumes of convenient size. Each such volume shall be lettered on the back with its title and the date of its session. (1866-7, c. 71; 1868-9, c. 270, s. 46; Code, s. 3343; Rev., s. 5348; C.S., s. 7658.)

§ 147-43. Reports of State officers.

The Secretary of State shall file and keep in his office one copy of each of the reports of State officers in the best binding in which any such report is issued, and the State Librarian shall likewise keep five similarly bound copies of each such report. (Rev., s. 5101; 1911, c. 211, s. 7; C.S., s. 7300.)

§§ 147-43.1 through 147-43.3: Repealed by Session Laws 1969, c. 1184, s. 8.

§ 147-44. Repealed by Session Laws 1943, c. 48, s. 2.

§ 147-45. Distribution of copies of State publications.

The Secretary of State shall, at the State's expense, as soon as possible after publication, provide such number of copies of the Session Laws and Senate and House Journals to federal, State, and local governmental officials, departments and agencies, and to educational institutions of instruction and exchange use, as is determined by the Legislative Services Commission in consultation with the Principal Clerks of the House of Representatives and the Senate. These publications shall be made available in hardbound and electronic format. Each agency or institution entitled to more than one copy shall receive only one of the copies in hardbound format with the remainder in electronic format, unless that agency or institution requests additional hardbound copies from the Secretary of State by August 1 of the calendar year. The Legislative Services Commission, in consultation with the Principal Clerks of the House of Representatives and the Senate, shall determine each year the total number of bound volumes of each publication to be printed and the total number of the electronic copies of each publication to be produced.

Any State agency, department, institution, commission, committee, board, division, bureau, officer, or official that does not receive a copy of the Session Laws may, upon written request from their respective department head to the Secretary of State, and upon the discretion of the Secretary of State as to need, be issued copies of the Session Laws on a permanent loan basis with the understanding that should said copies be needed they will be recalled. (1941, c. 379, s. 1; 1943, c. 48, s. 4; 1945, c. 534; 1949, c. 1178; 1951, c. 287; 1953, cc. 245, 266; 1955, c. 505, s. 6; cc. 989, 990; 1957, c. 269, s. 1; cc. 1061, 1400; 1959, c. 215; c. 1028, s. 3; 1965, c. 503; 1967, c. 691, s. 54; cc. 695, 777, 1038, 1073, 1200; 1969, c. 355; c. 608, s. 1; c. 801, s. 2; c. 852, ss. 1, 2; c. 1190, s. 54; c. 1285; 1973, c. 476, ss. 48, 84, 128, 138, 143, 193; c. 507, s. 5; c. 731, s.

1; c. 762; c. 798, ss. 1, 2; c. 1262, ss. 10, 38; 1975, c. 19, s. 59; c. 879, s. 46; 1975, 2nd Sess., c. 983, s. 115; 1977, c. 379, s. 1; c. 679, s. 8; c. 771, s. 4; 1979, c. 358, s. 27; 1981, c. 412, ss. 4, 5; 1981 (Reg. Sess., 1982), c. 1348, s. 2; 1983, c. 842; 1987, c. 827, s. 59; 1989, c. 727, s. 223(b); c. 751, s. 9(b); 1991 (Reg. Sess., 1992), c. 959, s. 74; 1993, c. 522, s. 18; c. 553, s. 53; 1995, c. 166, s. 2; c. 509, s. 100; 1995 (Reg. Sess., 1996), c. 603, s. 5; c. 743, s. 22; 1997-443, ss. 11A.118(a), 11A.119(a); 1998-202, s. 4(bb); 2000-137, s. 4(ff); 2001-513, s. 16(a).)

§ 147-46. Repealed by Session Laws 1955, c. 987.

§ 147-46.1. Publications furnished State departments, bureaus, institutions and agencies.

Upon request of any State department, bureau, institution or agency, and upon authorization by the Governor and Council of State, the Secretary of State shall supply to such department, bureau, institution or agency copies of any State publications then available to replace worn, damaged or lost copies and such additional sets or parts of sets as may be requested to meet the reasonable needs of such departments, bureaus, institutions or agencies, disclosed by the request.

This section shall not authorize the reprinting of any State publications which would not be ordered without reference to the provisions hereof. (1947, c. 639.)

§ 147-47. Repealed by Session Laws 1955, c. 748.

§ 147-48. Sale of Laws and Journals.

Such Laws and Journals as may be printed in excess of the number directed to be distributed, the Secretary of State may sell at such price as he deems reasonable, not exceeding cost plus ten percent (10%). All proceeds received from sales made pursuant to this section shall be paid into the State treasury. (1941, c. 379, s. 4; 1943, c. 48, s. 4; 1955, c. 978, s. 2; 1967, c. 691, s. 55; 1977, c. 802, s. 50.30.)

§ 147-49. Disposition of damaged and unsaleable publications.

The Secretary of State is hereby authorized and empowered to dispose of damaged and unsaleable House and Senate Journals and Session Laws of various years at a price to be determined by the Secretary of State. (1939, c. 345; 1967, c. 691, s. 56; 2001-487, s. 93.)

§ 147-50. Publications of State officials and department heads furnished to certain institutions, agencies, etc.

Every State official and every head of a State department, institution or agency issuing any printed report, bulletin, map, or other publication shall, on request, furnish copies of such reports, bulletins, maps or other publications to the following institutions in the number set out below:

University of North Carolina at Chapel Hill copies;	25
University of North Carolina at Charlotte copies;	2
University of North Carolina at Greensboro copies;	2
North Carolina State University at Raleigh copies;	2
East Carolina University at Greenville copies;	2
Duke University copies;	25
Wake Forest College copies;	2
Davidson College copies;	2

North Carolina Supreme Court Library copies;	2
North Carolina Central University copies;	5
Western Carolina University copies;	2
Appalachian State University copies;	2
University of North Carolina at Wilmington copies;	2
North Carolina Agricultural and Technical State University copies;	2
Legislative Library copies;	2

and to governmental officials, agencies and departments and to other educational institutions, in the discretion of the issuing official and subject to the supply available, such number as may be requested: Provided that five sets of all such reports, bulletins and publications heretofore issued, insofar as the same are available and without necessitating reprinting, shall be furnished to the North Carolina Central University. The provisions in this section shall not be interpreted to include any of the appellate division reports or advance sheets distributed by the Administrative Office of the Courts. Except for reports, bulletins, and other publications issued for free distribution, this section shall not apply to the North Carolina State Museum of Natural Sciences. (1941, c. 379, s. 5; 1955, c. 505, s. 7; 1967, cc. 1038, 1065; 1969, c. 608, s. 1; c. 852, s. 3; 1973, c. 476, s. 84; c. 598; c. 731, s. 2; c. 776; 1977, c. 377; 1979, c. 591, s. 1; 1981, c. 435; 1993, c. 561, s. 116(j).)

§ 147-50.1. Repealed by Session Laws 1987, c. 771, s. 1.

§ 147-51. Clerks of superior courts responsible for Appellate Division Reports; lending prohibited.

From and after March 9, 1927, the clerks of the superior courts of the State of North Carolina are held officially responsible for the volumes of the North Carolina Appellate Division Reports furnished and to be furnished them by the State.

The said clerks of the various courts shall not lend or permit to be taken from their custody the said Reports, nor shall any person with or without the permission of the said clerks take them from their possession. (1927, c. 259; 1969, c. 1190, s. 55.)

§ 147-52. Transferred to § 7A-14 by Session Laws 1975, c. 328.

§ 147-53. Superseded by Session Laws 1943, c. 716.

§ 147-54. Printing, distribution and sale of the North Carolina Manual.

The Secretary of State shall have printed biennially for distribution and sale, two thousand three hundred fifty (2,350) copies of the North Carolina Manual, and shall make distribution to the State agencies, individuals, institutions and others as herein set forth.

NORTH CAROLINA STATE GOVERNMENT:

Members of the General Assembly .... 1 ea.

Officers of the General Assembly .... 1 ea.

Offices of the Clerk of each House of the General Assembly .... 1 ea.

Legislative Services Officer 1

Legislative Library 6

Members of the Council of State .... 2 ea.

Appointed Secretaries of Executive Departments .... 2 ea.

Personnel of the Department of the Secretary of State .... 1 ea.

State Board of Elections 2

Divisions of Archives and History, Director 1

Search Room 3

Publications Section 2

State Library 10

Libraries within State Agencies .... 1 ea.

Justices of the North Carolina Supreme Court .... 1 ea.

Judges of the North Carolina Court of Appeals .... 1 ea.

Judges of the North Carolina Superior Court .... 1 ea.

Supreme Court Library 12

Court of Appeals Library 2

Clerk of the Supreme Court 1

Clerk of the Court of Appeals 1

Reporter of the Supreme Court and Court of Appeals 1

Administrative Office of the Courts 5

NORTH CAROLINA EDUCATIONAL INSTITUTIONS:

University of North Carolina System

General Administration Offices 12

Chancellors of the Constituent Institutions .... 1 ea.

University of North Carolina - Chapel Hill Library 15

North Carolina State University Library 5

East Carolina University Library 5

North Carolina Central University Library 5

Appalachian State University Library 4

University of North Carolina - Charlotte Library 4

University of North Carolina - Greensboro Library 4

Western Carolina University Library 4

Other Constituent Institutions Libraries .... 3 ea.

North Carolina School of the Arts, redesignated effective August 1, 2008, as the "University of North Carolina School of the Arts" 2

University of North Carolina Chapel Hill School of Government 2

Community Colleges and Technical Institutes .... 2 ea.

Private Colleges and Universities

Duke University Library 6

Wake Forest University 6

Campbell University Library 5

Davidson College Library 4

All other Libraries of Senior and Junior Colleges .... 2 ea.

Public and Private Schools containing grades 8-12 .... 1 ea.

COUNTY GOVERNMENT:

Clerks of Court
.... 1 ea.

Registers of Deeds
.... 1 ea.

Public Libraries of North Carolina
.... 1 ea.

FEDERAL GOVERNMENT:

President of the United States
.... 1

North Carolina Members of the Presidential Cabinet
.... 1 ea.

North Carolina Members of the United States Congress
.... 2 ea.

Library of Congress
.... 3

Resident Judges of the Federal Judiciary

and United States Attorneys in North Carolina
.... 1 ea.

Secretaries of State of the United States

and
Territories..
.. 1 ea.

After making the above distribution, the remainder shall be sold at the cost of publication plus tax and postage and the proceeds from such sales deposited with the State Treasurer for use by the Publications Division of the Secretary of State's Office to defray the expense of publishing the North Carolina Manual. Libraries and educational institutions not covered in the above distribution shall be entitled to a twenty percent (20%) discount on the cost of any purchase(s). (1933, c. 115, s. 2; 1977, c. 378; 1995, c. 509, s. 101; 2001-424, s. 14F.1; 2006-264, s. 29(p); 2008-192, s. 10.)

§ 147-54.1. Division of Publications; duties.

The Secretary of State is authorized to set up a division to be designated as the Division of Publications and to appoint a director thereof who shall be known as the Director of Publications. This Division shall publish the North Carolina Manual, Directory, Index of Local Legislation and such other publications as may be useful to the members and committees of the General Assembly and other officials of the State and of the various counties and cities. Unless otherwise required by law, the Secretary may publish electronically information permitted or required by this section. The Secretary may sell these publications at such prices as the Secretary deems reasonable; the proceeds of sale shall be paid into the State treasury.

The Division shall also perform all such other duties as may be assigned by the Secretary of State. (1915, c. 202, ss. 1, 2; C.S., ss. 6147, 6148; 1939, c. 316; 1971, c. 685, s. 3; 1977, c. 802, s. 50.31; 1999-260, s. 2.)

§ 147-54.2. Repealed by Session Laws 1979, c. 477, s. 2.

§ 147-54.3. Land records management program.

(a) The Secretary of State shall administer a land records management program for the purposes (i) of advising registers of deeds, local tax officials, and local planning officials about sound management practices, and (ii) of establishing greater uniformity in local land records systems. The management program shall consist of the activities provided for in subsections (b) through (e) of this section, and other related activities essential to the effective conduct of the management program.

(b) The Secretary of State, in cooperation with the Secretary of Cultural Resources and in accordance with G.S. 121-5(c) and G.S. 132-8.1, shall establish minimum standards and provide advice and technical assistance to local governments in implementing and maintaining minimum standards with regard to the following aspects of land records management:

(1)   Uniform indexing of land records;

(2)   Uniform recording and indexing procedures for maps, plats and condominiums; and

(3)   Security and reproduction of land records.

(b1)   The Department of Secretary of State, in cooperation with the North Carolina Association of Registers of Deeds, Inc., and the Real Property Section of the North Carolina Bar Association, shall adopt, pursuant to Chapter 150B of the General Statutes, rules specifying the minimum indexing standards established pursuant to subsection (b) of this section and procedures for complying with those minimum standards in land records management. A copy of the standards adopted shall be posted in the office of the register of deeds in each county of the State.

(c)   The Secretary of State shall conduct a program for the preparation of county base maps pursuant to standards prepared by the Secretary.

(c1)   The Secretary of State, shall, in cooperation with the Secretary of Revenue, conduct a program for the preparation of county cadastral maps pursuant to standards prepared by the Secretary of State.

(d)   Upon the joint request of any board of county commissioners and the register of deeds and subject to available resources of personnel and funds, the Secretary shall make a management study of the office of register of deeds, using assistance from the Office of State Human Resources. At the conclusion of the study, the Secretary shall make nonbinding recommendations to the board, the register of deeds, and to the General Assembly.

(d1)   The Secretary of State shall make comparative salary studies periodically of all registers of deeds offices and at the conclusion of each study the Secretary of State shall present his written findings and shall make recommendations to the board of county commissioners and register of deeds of each county.

(e)   The Secretary of State, in cooperation with the Secretary of Cultural Resources and in accordance with G.S. 121-5(c) and G.S. 132-8.1, shall undertake research and provide advice and technical assistance to local governments on the following aspects of land records management:

(1) Centralized recording systems;

(2) Filming, filing, and recording techniques and equipment;

(3) Computerized land records systems; and

(4) Storage and retrieval of land records.

(f) An advisory committee on land records is created to assist the Secretary in administering the land records management program. The Secretary of State shall appoint 12 members to the committee; one member shall be appointed from each of the organizations listed below from persons nominated by the organization:

(1) The North Carolina Association of Assessing Officers;

(2) The North Carolina Section of the American Society of Photogrammetry;

(3) The North Carolina Chapter of the American Institute of Planners;

(4) The North Carolina Section of the American Society of Civil Engineers;

(5) The North Carolina Property Mappers' Association;

(6) The North Carolina Association of Registers of Deeds;

(7) The North Carolina Bar Association;

(8) The North Carolina Society of Land Surveyors; and

(9) The North Carolina Association of County Commissioners.

In addition, three members from the public at large shall be appointed. The members of the committee shall be appointed for four-year terms, except that the initial terms for members listed in positions (1) through (4) above and for two of the members-at-large shall be two years; thereafter all appointments shall be for four years. The Secretary of State shall appoint the chairman, and the committee shall meet at the call of the chairman. The Secretary of State in making the appointments shall try to achieve geographical and population balance on the advisory committee; one third of the appointments shall be persons from the most populous counties in the State containing approximately one third of the State's population, one third from the least populous counties containing approximately one third of the State's population, and one third shall be from the remaining moderately populous counties containing approximately one third of the State's population. Each organization shall nominate one nominee each from the more populous, moderately populous, and less populous counties of the State. The members of the committee shall receive per diem and subsistence and travel allowances as provided in G.S. 138-5. (1977, c. 771, s. 4; c. 932, s. 1; 1985, c. 479, s. 165(d), (e); 1987, c. 738, s. 158(a); 1989, c. 523, s. 8; c. 727, ss. 169, 218(116a); c. 751, s. 14; 1991, c. 689, ss. 181(b), 181(c); c. 697, s. 1; 1993, c. 258, s. 1; 2013-382, s. 9.1(c).)

§ 147-54.4. Certification of local government property mappers.

(a) Definitions. - The following definitions apply in this section:

(1) Department. - The Department of the Secretary of State.

(2) Large-scale. - A scale that uses an inch to represent no more than 400 feet.

(3) Local government. - A county as defined in G.S. 153A-10 and a city as defined in G.S. 160A-1.

(4) Property mapper. - A person who is employed by a local government and is responsible for creating and maintaining large-scale cadastral maps.

(b) Certification. - The Department shall establish a certification program for property mappers. The purpose of the program is to protect and enhance the State's investment in local government large-scale cadastral maps. To be certified as a property mapper, an applicant must meet the following minimum requirements and the additional requirements set by the Department:

(1) Be at least 18 years old.

(2) Hold a high school diploma or certificate of equivalency.

(3) Achieve a passing score in courses of instruction approved by the Department covering the following topics:

a. The principles and techniques of property mapping.

b. The laws of North Carolina governing the listing, appraisal, and assessment of real property for taxation.

The Department shall establish requirements for certification as a property mapper that are in addition to these minimum requirements. The additional requirements shall ensure that an applicant who is certified as a property mapper has the minimum skills necessary to create and maintain large-scale cadastral maps. In establishing these additional requirements, the Department may consult with the advisory committee on land records created by G.S. 147-54.3(f), the North Carolina Property Mappers' Association, and other relevant professional groups. The additional requirements may include mapping experience and a passing score on an examination administered by the Department.

(c) Renewal. - A certification as a property mapper must be renewed every two years. Attendance of 24 hours of continuing education approved by the Department is a condition of renewal of a certification. The Department shall publish a list of courses acceptable for meeting this continuing education requirement.

(d) Application and Fees. - An applicant for certification as a property mapper or renewal of certification as a property mapper must file an application with the Department. The applicant must submit a fee of twenty dollars ($20.00) with the application. Fees collected under this section shall be credited to the General Fund.

(e) Rules. - The Department may adopt rules to implement this section. Chapter 150B of the General Statutes governs the adoption of rules by the Department. (1993, c. 326, s. 1.)

§ 147-54.5. Investor Protection and Education Trust Fund; administration; limitations on use of the Fund.

(a) The Investor Protection and Education Trust Fund created in the Department of the Secretary of State as an expendable trust account to be used by the Secretary of State only for the purposes set forth in this section.

(b) The proceeds of the Investor Protection and Education Trust Fund shall be used by the Secretary of State to provide investor protection and education to the general public and to potential securities investors in the State through:

(1) The use of the media, including television and radio public service announcements and printed materials; and

(2) The sponsorship of educational seminars, whether live, recorded, or through other electronic means.

(c) The proceeds of the Investor Protection and Education Trust Fund shall not be used for:

(1) Travel expenses of the Secretary of State or staff of the Department of the Secretary of State, unless those expenses are directly related to specific investor protection and education activities performed in accordance with this section.

(2) General operating expenses of the Department of the Secretary of State, or to supplement General Fund appropriations to the Department of the Secretary of State for other than investor education and protection activities.

(3) Promoting the Secretary of State or the Department of the Secretary of State.

(d) Expenditures from the Investor Protection and Education Trust Fund shall be made in compliance with State purchasing and contracting requirements for competitive bidding in accordance with the provisions of Article 3 of Chapter 143 of the General Statutes.

(e) Revenues derived from consent orders resulting from negotiated settlements of securities investigations by the Secretary of State shall be credited to the Fund. The State Treasurer shall invest the assets of the Fund according to law. Any interest or other investment income earned by the Investor Protection and Education Trust Fund shall remain in the Fund. The balance of the Investor Protection and Education Trust Fund at the end of each fiscal year shall not revert to the General Fund.

(f) Beginning January 1, 1997, the Department of the Secretary of State shall report annually to the General Assembly's Fiscal Research Division and to the Joint Legislative Commission on Governmental Operations on the expenditures from the Investor Protection and Education Trust Fund and on the effectiveness of investor awareness education efforts of the Department of the Secretary of State. (1996, 2nd Ex. Sess., c. 18, s. 13.)

§ 147-54.6. International relations assistance.

(a) The Secretary of State may offer direct and indirect assistance in matters relating to international relations and protocol to other governmental agencies and units of the State of North Carolina. The assistance may be provided upon request of the intended recipient when resources are available for these purposes.

(b) The Secretary of State, on behalf of the State, may accept gifts, donations, devises, or other forms of voluntary contributions, apply for grants from public and private sources, and may expend funds received under this subsection for the purpose of promoting international relations and hosting foreign dignitaries and leaders in North Carolina. All funds and gifts received pursuant to this subsection shall be subject to audit by the Office of the State Auditor and all funds shall be expended in conformity with the Executive Budget Act and shall become the property of the State. (1999-260, s. 3; 2011-284, s. 104.)

§ 147-54.7. Abrogation of offensive geographical place-names.

(a) The General Assembly finds that certain geographical place-names are offensive or insulting to the State's people, history, and heritage. These place-names should be replaced by names that reflect the State's people, history, and heritage without resorting to offensive stereotypes, names, words, or phrases.

(b) The Secretary of State, in consultation with the North Carolina Geographic Information Coordinating Council, and pursuant to federal guidelines, shall adopt procedures to effect the change of geographical place-names that are offensive or insulting. The procedures shall include a notification to the governing body of the county where the offensive or insulting place-name is deemed to exist that the Council intends to make application to change the name. The county governing body shall have 90 days in which to respond to the Council, and no action to affect a change in the place-name shall be undertaken by the Council until it has reviewed the county's response, or the expiration of the 90-day period, whichever comes first.

(c) The procedures adopted by the Secretary pursuant to this section shall include the consideration of resolutions, if any, passed by the governing body of any county regarding the changing of a geographical place-name within the county. (2003-211, s. 1.)

§ 147-54.7A: Repealed by Session Laws 2006-201, s. 19, effective January 1, 2007.

Article 4A.

Constitutional Amendments Publication Commission.

§ 147-54.8. Constitutional Amendments Publication Commission.

(a) There is established within the Department of the Secretary of State the Constitutional Amendments Publication Commission (hereinafter "Commission").

(b) The Commission shall consist of three members who shall serve ex officio as follows: The Secretary of State, the Attorney General, and the Legislative Services Officer. (1983, c. 844, s. 1.)

§ 147-54.9. Officers; meetings; quorum.

(a) The Secretary of State shall be the Chairman of the Commission.

(b) A quorum shall consist of all three members.

(c) The Commission shall meet on the call of the Chairman or any two members. (1983, c. 844, s. 1.)

§ 147-54.10. Powers.

At least 60 days before an election in which a proposed amendment to the Constitution, or a revised or new Constitution, is to be voted on, the Commission shall prepare an explanation of the amendment, revision, or new Constitution in simple and commonly used language.

The summary prepared by the Commission shall be printed by the Secretary of State, in a quantity determined by the Secretary of State. A copy shall be sent along with a news release to each county board of elections, and a copy shall be available to any registered voter or representative of the print or broadcast media making request to the Secretary of State. The Secretary of State may make copies available in such additional manner as he may determine. (1983, c. 844, s. 1.)

Article 4B.

Business License Information Office.

§§ 147-54.11 through 147-54.19: Repealed by Session Laws 2004-124, s. 13.9A(a), effective July 1, 2004.

§§ 147-54.20 through 147-54.30: Reserved for future codification purposes.

Article 4C.

Executive Branch Lobbying.

§§ 147-54.31 through 147-54.44: Repealed by Session Laws 2006-201, s. 19, effective January 1, 2007.

Article 5.

Auditor.

§ 147-55: Repealed by Session Laws 1983, c. 913, s. 1.

§ 147-56. Repealed by Session Laws 1983, c. 913, s. 1, effective July 22, 1983.

§ 147-57. Repealed by Session Laws 1981, c. 884, s. 12.

§ 147-58. Repealed by Session Laws 1983, c. 913, s. 1, effective July 22, 1983.

§§ 147-59 through 147-61. Repealed by Session Laws 1981, c. 302.

§ 147-62: Recodified as § 143-3.3 by Session Laws 1983, c. 913, s. 49.

§§ 147-63 through 147-64: Recodified as § 143-3.4 by Session Laws 1983, c. 913, ss. 50, 51.

Article 5A.

Auditor.

§ 147-64.1. Salary of State Auditor.

(a)   The salary of the State Auditor shall be set by the General Assembly in the Current Operations Appropriations Act.

(b)   In addition to the salary set by the General Assembly in the Current Operations Appropriations Act, longevity pay shall be paid on the same basis as is provided to employees of the State who are subject to the North Carolina Human Resources Act. (1983, c. 761, s. 214; c. 913, s. 2; 1983 (Reg. Sess., 1984), c. 1034, s. 164; 1987, c. 738, s. 32(b); 2013-382, s. 9.1(c).)

§ 147-64.2. Legislative policy and intent.

The General Assembly is ultimately responsible for authorizing the expenditure of public moneys, designating the sources from which moneys may be collected, and shaping the administrative structure to perform the work of government throughout the State, and is held finally accountable for how the funds are spent and what is accomplished with them. The legislature should, therefore, provide the basic direction for audits of State agencies.

In the interest of reducing audit overlap and expense at all levels of government, the General Assembly and the Auditor should promote, to the extent possible, coordinated nonduplicating audits of public programs and activities of all governmental levels throughout the State.

It is the intent of this Article that all State agencies, and entities supported, partially or entirely, by public funds be subject to audit under the policy guidance of the Auditor. Such audits shall be made to assist in furnishing the General Assembly, the Governor, the executive departments and agencies of the State, the governing bodies and executive departments of the political subdivisions of the State, and the public in general with an independent evaluation of public program performance. (1983, c. 913, s. 2.)

§ 147-64.3. Legislative and management control system.

It is the intent of this Article that the State Auditor shall perform or coordinate all audit functions for State government. As appropriate, all State agencies are encouraged to establish, maintain, and use effective systems of management control. The adequacy of these control systems will be reviewed by the Auditor. The Auditor may, at his discretion, use such reviews to limit his audit activity or to suggest guidelines, make recommendations, and provide assistance where necessary within the resources available. (1983, c. 913, s. 2.)

§ 147-64.4. Definitions.

The words and phrases used in this Article have the following meanings:

(1) "Audit". - An independent review or examination of government organizations, programs, activities, and functions. The purpose of an audit is to help ensure full accountability and assist government officials and employees in carrying out their responsibilities. The elements of such an audit are:

a. Financial and compliance: to determine whether financial operations are properly conducted, whether the financial reports of an audited entity are presented fairly, and whether the entity has complied with applicable laws and regulations; and,

b. Economy and efficiency: to determine whether the entity is managing or utilizing its resources (such as personnel and property) in an economical and efficient manner and the causes of any inefficiencies or uneconomical practices, including inadequacies in laws and regulations, management information systems, administrative policies and procedures, or organizational structures; and,

c. Program results: to determine whether the desired results or benefits are being achieved, whether the objectives established by the General Assembly or other authorizing body are being met, and whether the agency has considered alternatives which might yield desired results at lower costs.

d. An audit may include all three elements or only one or two. It is not intended or desirable that every audit include all three. Economy and efficiency and program result audits should be selected when their use will meet the needs of expected users of audit results.

(2) "Accounting system". - The total structure of records and procedures which discover, record, classify, and report information on the financial position and operating results of a governmental unit or any of its funds, balanced account groups, and organizational components.

(3) "Federal agency". - Any department, agency, or instrumentality of the federal government and any federally owned or controlled corporation.

(4) "State agency". - Any department, institution, board, commission, committee, division, bureau, officer, official or any other entity for which the State has oversight responsibility, including but not limited to, any university, mental or specialty hospital, community college, or clerk of court. (1983, c. 913, s. 2; 1987, c. 564, s. 31.)

§ 147-64.5. Cooperation with Joint Legislative Commission on Governmental Operations and other governmental bodies.

(a) Joint Legislative Commission on Governmental Operations. - The Auditor shall furnish copies of any and all audits only when requested by the Joint Legislative Commission on Governmental Operations. The copies shall be in written or electronic form, as requested. Accordingly, the Auditor shall, upon request by the chairmen, appear before the Commission to present findings and answer questions concerning the results of these audits. The Commission is hereby authorized to use these audit findings in its inquiries concerning the operations of State agencies and is empowered to require agency heads to advise the Commission of actions taken or to be taken on any recommendations made in the report or explain the reasons for not taking action.

(b) Requests for Auditor Assistance. - Committees of the General Assembly, the Governor, and other State officials may make written requests that the Auditor undertake, to the extent deemed practicable and within the resources provided, a specific audit or investigation; provide technical assistance and advice; and provide recommendations on management systems, finance, accounting, auditing, and other areas of management interest. The Auditor may request the advice of the Joint Legislative Commission on Governmental Operations in prioritizing these requests and in determining whether the requests are practicable and can be undertaken within the resources provided.

(c) Cooperation with Other Governmental Bodies. - The Auditor shall cooperate, act, and function with other audit or evaluation organizations in the State, with appropriate councils or committees of other states, with governing bodies of the political subdivisions of the State, and with federal agencies in an effort to maximize the extent of intergovernmental audit coordination and thereby avoid unnecessary duplication and expense of audit effort. Nothing in this Article is intended nor shall it be construed as giving the Auditor control over the internal auditors of any agency. (1983, c. 913, s. 2; 1997-443, s. 25; 2001-424, s. 9.1(b).)

§ 147-64.6. Duties and responsibilities.

(a) It is the policy of the General Assembly to provide for the auditing of State agencies by the impartial, independent State Auditor.

(b) The duties of the Auditor are independently to examine into and make findings of fact on whether State agencies:

(1) Have established adequate operating and administrative procedures and practices; systems of accounting, reporting and auditing; and other necessary elements of legislative or management control.

(2) Are providing financial and other reports which disclose fairly, consistently, fully, and promptly all information needed to show the nature and scope of programs and activities and have established bases for evaluating the results of such programs and operations.

(3) Are promptly collecting, depositing, and properly accounting for all revenues and receipts arising from their activities.

(4) Are conducting programs and activities and expending funds made available in a faithful, efficient, and economical manner in compliance with and in furtherance of applicable laws and regulations of the State, and, if applicable, federal law and regulation.

(5) Are determining that the authorized activities or programs effectively serve the intent and purpose of the General Assembly and, if applicable, federal law and regulation.

(c) The Auditor shall be responsible for the following acts and activities:

(1) Audits made or caused to be made by the Auditor shall be conducted in accordance with generally accepted auditing standards as prescribed by the American Institute of Certified Public Accountants, the United States General Accounting Office, or other professionally recognized accounting standards-setting bodies.

(2) Financial and compliance audits may be made at the discretion of the Auditor without advance notice to the organization being audited. Audits of economy and efficiency and program results shall be discussed in advance with the prospective auditee unless an unannounced visit is essential to the audit.

(3) The Auditor, on his own initiative and as often as he deems necessary, or as requested by the Governor or the General Assembly, shall, to the extent deemed practicable and consistent with his overall responsibility as contained in

this act, make or cause to be made audits of all or any part of the activities of the State agencies.

(4) The Auditor, at his own discretion, may, in selecting audit areas and in evaluating current audit activity, consider and utilize, in whole or in part, the relevant audit coverage and applicable reports of the audit staffs of the various State agencies, independent contractors, and federal agencies. He shall coordinate, to the extent deemed practicable, the auditing conducted within the State to meet the needs of all governmental bodies.

(5) The Auditor is authorized to contract with federal audit agencies, or any governmental agency, on a cost reimbursable basis, for the Auditor to perform audits of federal grants and programs administered by the State Departments and institutions in accordance with agreements negotiated between the Auditor and the contracting federal audit agencies or any governmental agency. In instances where the grantee State agency shall subgrant these federal funds to local governments, regional councils of government and other local groups or private or semiprivate institutions or agencies, the Auditor shall have the authority to examine the books and records of these subgrantees to the extent necessary to determine eligibility and proper use in accordance with State and federal laws and regulations.

The Auditor shall charge and collect from the contracting federal audit agencies, or any governmental agencies, the actual cost of all the audits of the grants and programs contracted by him to do. Amounts collected under these arrangements shall be deposited in the State Treasury and be budgeted in the Department of State Auditor and shall be available to hire sufficient personnel to perform these contracted audits and to pay for related travel, supplies and other necessary expenses.

(6) The Auditor is authorized and directed in his reports of audits or reports of special investigations to make any comments, suggestions, or recommendations he deems appropriate concerning any aspect of such agency's activities and operations.

(7) The Auditor shall charge and collect from each examining and licensing board the actual cost of each audit of such board. Costs collected under this subdivision shall be based on the actual expense incurred by the Auditor's office in making such audit and the affected agency shall be entitled to an itemized statement of such costs. Amounts collected under this subdivision shall be deposited into the general fund as nontax revenue.

(8) The Auditor shall examine as often as may be deemed necessary the accounts kept by the Treasurer, and if he discovers any irregularity or deficiency therein, unless the same be rectified or explained to his satisfaction, report the same forthwith in writing to the General Assembly, with copy of such report to the Governor and Attorney General. In addition to regular audits, the Auditor shall check the treasury records at the time a Treasurer assumes office (not to succeed himself), and therein charge him with the balance in the treasury, and shall check the Treasurer's records at the time he leaves office to determine that the accounts are in order.

(9) The Auditor may examine the accounts and records of any bank or financial institution relating to transactions with the State Treasurer, or with any State agency, or he may require banks doing business with the State to furnish him information relating to transactions with the State or State agencies.

(10) The Auditor may, as often as he deems advisable, conduct a detailed review of the bookkeeping and accounting systems in use in the various State agencies which are supported partially or entirely from State funds. Such examinations will be for the purpose of evaluating the adequacy of systems in use by these agencies and institutions. In instances where the Auditor determines that existing systems are outmoded, inefficient, or otherwise inadequate, he shall recommend changes to the State Controller. The State Controller shall prescribe and supervise the installation of such changes, as provided in G.S. 143B-426.39(2).

(11) The Auditor shall, through appropriate tests, satisfy himself concerning the propriety of the data presented in the Comprehensive Annual Financial Report and shall express the appropriate auditor's opinion in accordance with generally accepted auditing standards.

(12) The Auditor shall provide a report to the Governor and Attorney General, and other appropriate officials, of such facts as are in his possession which pertain to the apparent violation of penal statutes or apparent instances of malfeasance, misfeasance, or nonfeasance by an officer or employee.

(13) At the conclusion of an audit, the Auditor or his designated representative shall discuss the audit with the official whose office is subject to audit and submit necessary underlying facts developed for all findings and recommendations which may be included in the audit report. On audits of economy and efficiency and program results, the auditee's written response

shall be included in the final report if received within 30 days from receipt of the draft report.

(14) The Auditor shall notify the General Assembly, the Governor, the Chief Executive Officer of each agency audited, and other persons as the Auditor deems appropriate that an audit report has been published, its subject and title, and the locations, including State libraries, at which the report is available. The Auditor shall then distribute copies of the report only to those who request a report. The copies shall be in written or electronic form, as requested. He shall also file a copy of the audit report in the Auditor's office, which will be a permanent public record; Provided, nothing in this subsection shall be construed as authorizing or permitting the publication of information whose disclosure is otherwise prohibited by law.

(15) It is not the intent of the audit function, nor shall it be so construed, to infringe upon or deprive the General Assembly and the executive or judicial branches of State government of any rights, powers, or duties vested in or imposed upon them by statute or the Constitution.

(16) The Auditor shall be responsible for receiving reports of allegations of the improper governmental activities as provided in G.S. 147-64.6B. The Auditor shall adopt policies and procedures necessary to provide for the investigation or referral of these allegations.

(17) Repealed by Session Laws 2009-136, s. 2, effective June 19, 2009.

(18) Repealed by Session Laws 2010-31, s. 6.15(b), effective July 1, 2010.

(19) Whenever the Auditor believes that information received or collected by the Auditor may be evidence of a violation of any of the provisions of Chapter 138A of the General Statutes, Chapter 120C of the General Statutes, or Article 14 of Chapter 120 of the General Statutes, the Auditor shall report that information to the State Ethics Commission and the Secretary of State as appropriate. The Auditor shall be bound by interpretations issued by the State Ethics Commission as to whether or not any information reported by the Auditor under this subdivision involves or may involve a violation of Chapter 138A of the General Statutes, Chapter 120C of the General Statutes, or Article 14 of Chapter 120 of the General Statutes. Nothing in this subdivision shall be construed to limit the Auditor's authority under subdivision (1) of this subsection.

(d) Reports and Work Papers. - The Auditor shall maintain for 10 years a complete file of all audit reports and reports of other examinations, investigations, surveys, and reviews issued under the Auditor's authority. Audit work papers and other evidence and related supportive material directly pertaining to the work of the Auditor's office shall be retained according to an agreement between the Auditor and State Archives. To promote intergovernmental cooperation and avoid unnecessary duplication of audit effort, and notwithstanding the provisions of G.S. 126-24, pertinent work papers and other supportive material related to issued audit reports may be, at the discretion of the Auditor and unless otherwise prohibited by law, made available for inspection by duly authorized representatives of the State and federal government who desire access to and inspection of such records in connection with some matter officially before them, including criminal investigations.

Except as provided in this section, or upon an order issued in Wake County Superior Court upon 10 days' notice and hearing finding that access is necessary to a proper administration of justice, audit work papers and related supportive material shall be kept confidential, including any interpretations, advisory opinions, or other information or materials furnished to or by the State Ethics Commission under this section. (1983, c. 913, s. 2; 1985 (Reg. Sess., 1986), c. 1024, ss. 24, 25; 1987, c. 738, s. 62; 1989, c. 236, s. 2; 1999-188, s. 2; 2001-142, s. 2; 2001-424, ss. 9.1(a), 15.2(c); 2002-126, s. 27.2(b); 2002-159, s. 48; 2004-129, s. 46; 2008-215, ss. 1(a), 2, 3; 2009-136, s. 2; 2010-31, s. 6.15(b); 2010-194, s. 27.)

§ 147-64.6A: Repealed by Session Laws 2012-142, s. 8.4, effective July 1, 2012.

§ 147-64.6B. Reports of improper governmental activities.

(a) The Auditor shall provide various means, including a telephone hotline, electronic mail, and Internet access to receive reports of allegations of improper governmental activities. The Auditor shall periodically publicize the hotline telephone number, electronic mail address, Internet Web site address, and any other means by which the Auditor may receive reports of allegations of improper governmental activities. Individuals who make a report under this section may choose to remain anonymous until the individual affirmatively consents to having his or her identity disclosed.

(b) The Auditor shall investigate reports of allegations of improper governmental activities of State agencies and State employees within the scope of authority set forth in G.S. 147-64.6, including misappropriation, mismanagement, or waste of State resources, fraud, violations of State or federal law, rule or regulation by State agencies or State employees administering State or federal programs, and substantial and specific danger to the public health and safety. When the allegation involves issues of substantial and specific danger to the public health and safety, the Auditor shall notify the appropriate State agency immediately. When the Auditor believes that an allegation of improper governmental activity is outside the authority set forth in G.S. 147-64.6, the Auditor shall refer the allegation to the appropriate State agency responsible for the enforcement or administration of the matter for investigation. When the Auditor believes that an allegation of improper governmental activity involves matters set forth in subdivisions (1), (2), or (3) of this subsection, those matters shall be referred as follows:

(1) Allegations of criminal misconduct to either the State Bureau of Investigation or the District Attorney for the county where the alleged misconduct occurred.

(2) Allegations of violations of Chapter 138A, Chapter 120C, and Article 14 of Chapter 120 of the General Statutes to the State Ethics Commission.

(3) Allegations of violations of Chapter 163 of the General Statutes to the State Board of Elections.

(c) All records maintained by the Auditor of reports of unsubstantiated allegations of improper governmental activities shall be destroyed within four years from the date the unsubstantiated allegation was received. (2008-215, s. 1(b).)

§ 147-64.6C. Cost of audit report published.

Each audit report shall itemize the number of staff hours used in conducting the audit and in preparation of the audit report and the total cost of conducting the audit and preparing the audit report. (2012-142, s. 17.3.)

§ 147-64.6D. Cost of CPA audit report published.

Each audit report prepared for a State agency by a Certified Public Accountant shall itemize the number of hours used in conducting the audit and in preparation of the audit report and the total cost of conducting the audit and preparing the audit report. (2012-142, s. 17.4.)

§ 147-64.7. Authority.

(a) Access to Persons and Records. -

(1) The Auditor and the Auditor's authorized representatives shall have ready access to persons and may examine and copy all books, records, reports, vouchers, correspondence, files, personnel files, investments, and any other documentation of any State agency. The review of State tax returns shall be limited to matters of official business and the Auditor's report shall not violate the confidentiality provisions of tax laws. Notwithstanding confidentiality provisions of tax laws, the Auditor may use and disclose information related to overdue tax debts in support of the Auditor's statutory mission.

(2) The Auditor and the Auditor's duly authorized representatives shall have such access to persons, records, papers, reports, vouchers, correspondence, books, and any other documentation which is in the possession of any individual, private corporation, institution, association, board, or other organization which pertain to:

a. Amounts received pursuant to a grant or contract from the federal government, the State, or its political subdivisions.

b. Amounts received, disbursed, or otherwise handled on behalf of the federal government or the State. In order to determine that payments to providers of social and medical services are legal and proper, the providers of such services will give the Auditor, or the Auditor's authorized representatives, access to the records of recipients who receive such services.

(3) The Auditor shall, for the purpose of examination and audit authorized by this act, have the authority, and will be provided ready access, to examine and inspect all property, equipment, and facilities in the possession of any State agency or any individual, private corporation, institution, association, board, or

other organization which were furnished or otherwise provided through grant, contract, or any other type of funding by the State of North Carolina, or the federal government.

(4) All contracts or grants entered into by State agencies or political subdivisions shall include, as a necessary part, a clause providing access as intended by this section.

(5) The Auditor and his authorized agents are authorized to examine all books and accounts of any individual, firm, or corporation only insofar as they relate to transactions with any agency of the State.

(b) Experts; Contracted Audits. -

(1) The Auditor may obtain the services of independent public accountants, qualified management consultants, or other professional persons and experts as he deems necessary or desirable to carry out the duties and functions assigned under the act.

(2) No State agency may enter into any contract for auditing services which may impact on the State's comprehensive annual financial report without consultation with, and the prior written approval of, the Auditor, except in instances where audits are called for by the Governor under G.S. 143C-2-1 and he shall so notify the Auditor. The Auditor shall prescribe policy and establish guidelines containing appropriate criteria for selection and use of independent public accountants, qualified management consultants, or other professional persons by State agencies and governing bodies to perform all or part of the audit function.

(c) Authority to Administer Oaths, Subpoena Witnesses and Records, and Take Depositions. -

(1) For the purposes of this Article the Auditor or his authorized representative shall have the power to subpoena witnesses, to take testimony under oath, to cause the deposition of witnesses (residing within or without the State) to be taken in a manner prescribed by law, and to assemble records and documents, by subpoena or otherwise. The subpoena power granted by this section may be exercised only at the specific written direction of the Auditor or his chief deputy.

(2) In case any person shall refuse to obey a subpoena, the Auditor shall invoke the aid of any North Carolina court within the jurisdiction of which the investigation is carried on or where such person may be, in requiring the attendance and testimony of witnesses and the production of books, papers, correspondence, memoranda, contracts, agreements, and other records. Such court may issue an order requiring such person to appear before the Auditor or officers designated by the Auditor, there to produce records, if so ordered, or to give testimony touching the matter under investigation or in question; and any failure to obey such order of the court may be punished by such court as a contempt thereof. (1983, c. 913, s. 2; 1999-188, s. 1; 2006-203, s. 116; 2007-484, s. 34.5.)

§ 147-64.7A. Obstruction of audit.

Any person who shall willfully make or cause to be made to the State Auditor or his designated representatives any false, misleading, or unfounded report for the purpose of interfering with the performance of any audit, special review, or investigation, or to hinder or obstruct the State Auditor or the State Auditor's designated representatives in the performance of their duties, shall be guilty of a Class 2 misdemeanor. (1997-526, s. 1.)

§ 147-64.8. Independence.

The Auditor shall maintain independence in the performance of his authorized duties. Except as otherwise provided by law, neither the General Assembly nor the Governor nor any department or agency of the executive or judicial branches of State government shall have the authority to limit the scope, direction, or report of an audit undertaken by the Auditor. No State regulatory agency shall by any fiscal or administrative requirements attempt to limit the scope, direction, or report of an audit undertaken by the Auditor. (1983, c. 913, s. 2.)

§ 147-64.9. Rules and regulations.

The Auditor shall make and enforce such reasonable rules and regulations as are necessary for the operation of his office. The Auditor shall install an adequate accounting system for his office and shall keep or cause to be kept a complete, accurate, and adequate record of all fiscal transactions of his office. (1983, c. 913, s. 2.)

§ 147-64.10. Powers of appointment.

The Auditor may, subject to the provisions of the North Carolina Human Resources Act, appoint all employees necessary to perform the duties and functions assigned to him by the provisions of this Article.

Except where otherwise provided in this Article, all powers and duties vested in the Auditor may be delegated by him to deputies, assistants, employees, or other auditors, consultants, professionals, and experts, whose services are obtained in accordance with the provisions of this act; but the Auditor shall retain responsibility for the powers and duties so delegated. (1983, c. 913, s. 2; 2013-382, s. 9.1(c).)

§ 147-64.11. Review of office.

The Auditor may, on his own initiative and as often as he deems necessary, or as requested by the General Assembly, cause to be made a quality review audit of the operations of his office. Such a "peer review" shall be conducted in accordance with standards prescribed by the accounting profession. Upon the recommendation of the Joint Legislative Commission on Governmental Operations may contract with an independent public accountant, qualified management consultant, or other professional person to conduct a financial and compliance, economy and efficiency, and program result audit of the State Auditor. (1983, c. 913, s. 2; 2006-203, s. 117.)

§ 147-64.12. Conflict of interest.

(a) To preserve the independence and objectivity of the audit function, the Auditor and his employees may not, unless otherwise expressly authorized by statute, serve in any capacity on an administrative board, commission, or agency of government of a political subdivision of the State or any other organization that, under the provisions of this act, they have the responsibility or authority to audit. Nor shall they have a material, direct or indirect financial, or other economic interest in the transactions of any State agency.

(b) The Auditor shall not conduct an audit on a program or activity for which he had management responsibility or in which he has been employed during the preceding two years. The General Assembly shall otherwise provide for the necessary audit of programs and activities within the meaning of this subsection.

If the Auditor's hotline receives a report of allegations of improper governmental activities in a program or activity that the Auditor is prohibited by this subsection from auditing, the Hotline Manager shall transmit the report to the Legislative Services Officer or his designee. The report shall retain the same confidentiality after transmittal to the General Assembly that it had in the possession of the Auditor. (1983, c. 913, s. 2; 1993, c. 152, s. 1; 1996, 2nd Ex. Sess., c. 18, s. 8(n).)

§ 147-64.13. Construction.

This Article shall be construed liberally in the aid of its declared purpose. It is the intent of this Article that the establishment of the Office of the Auditor and the duties, powers, qualifications, and purposes herein specified shall take precedence over any conflicting part or application of any other law. (1983, c. 913, s. 2.)

§ 147-64.14. Severability.

If any provision of this Article or the application thereof to any person, State agency, political subdivision, or circumstance is held invalid, such invalidation shall not affect other provisions or applications of this Article which can be given effect without the invalid provision of application, and to this end the provisions of this Article are declared severable. (1983, c. 913, s. 2.)

Article 6.

Treasurer.

§ 147-65. Salary of State Treasurer.

The salary of the State Treasurer shall be as established in the Current Operations Appropriations Act. In addition to the salary set by the General Assembly in the Current Operations Appropriations Act, longevity pay shall be paid on the same basis as is provided to employees of the State who are subject to the North Carolina Human Resources Act. (Code, s. 3723; 1891, c. 505; Rev., s. 2739; 1907, c. 830, s. 3; c. 994, s. 2; 1917, c. 161; 1919, c. 233; c. 247, s. 3; C.S., s. 3868; Ex. Sess. 1920, c. 49, s. 2; 1921, c. 11, s. 1; 1935, c. 249; 1941, c. 1; 1947, c. 1041; 1949, c. 1278; 1953, c. 1, s. 2; 1957, c. 1; 1963, c. 1178, s. 1; 1967, c. 1130; c. 1237, s. 1; 1969, c. 1214, s. 1; 1971, c. 912, s. 1; 1973, c. 778, s. 1; 1975, 2nd Sess., c. 983, s. 16; 1977, c. 802, s. 42.9; 1983, c. 761, s. 215; 1983 (Reg. Sess., 1984), c. 1034, s. 164; 1987, c. 738, s. 32(b); 2013-382, s. 9.1(c).)

§ 147-66. Office and office hours.

The Treasurer shall keep his office at the City of Raleigh, and shall attend there between the hours of 10 o'clock A.M. and three o'clock P.M., Sundays and legal holidays excepted. He shall be allowed such office room as may be necessary. (1868-9, c. 270, ss. 80, 81; Code, s. 3362; Rev., s. 5369; C.S., s. 7679.)

§ 147-67. Repealed by Session Laws 1981, c. 884, s. 14.

§ 147-68. To receive and disburse moneys; to make reports.

(a) It is the duty of the Treasurer to receive all moneys which shall from time to time be paid into the treasury of this State; and to pay all warrants legally drawn on the Treasurer.

(b) No moneys shall be paid out of the treasury except on warrant unless there is a legislative appropriation or authority to pay the same.

(c) It shall be the responsibility of the Treasurer to determine that all warrants presented to him for payment are valid and legally drawn on the Treasurer.

(d) The Treasurer shall report to the Governor annually and to the General Assembly at the beginning of each biennial session the exact balance in the treasury to the credit of the State, with a summary of the receipts and payments of the treasury during the preceding fiscal year, and so far as practicable an account of the same down to the termination of the current calendar year.

(d1) The Treasurer shall report to the Joint Legislative Commission on Governmental Operations, the chairs of the House of Representatives and Senate Appropriations Committees, the chairs of the House of Representatives and Senate Finance Committees, and the Fiscal Research Division of the General Assembly, on a quarterly basis, concerning all investments and deposits made by and through his office. The report shall include a listing of all investments with or on behalf of the State or any of its agencies or institutions and shall include the particular agency or institution, fund, rate of return, duration of the investment, and the amount of deposit on all noninterest bearing accounts. The first report is due 90 days after July 1, 1982, and shall include all investments and deposits made during the 1981-82 fiscal year and all investments made during the first quarter of the 1982-83 fiscal year; thereafter, reports shall be made on a quarterly basis including all investments and deposits made during that reporting period. The report shall include a specific listing of all investments made with certified green managers and companies and funds that support sustainable practices, including the names of the companies, managers, and funds, the amount invested, and the State's return on investment.

(d2) After consulting with the Select Committee on Information Technology and the Joint Legislative Commission on Governmental Operations and after consultation with and approval of the Information Resources Management Commission, the Department of State Treasurer may spend departmental receipts for the 2000-2001 fiscal year to continue improvement of the Department's investment banking operations system, retirement payroll systems, and other information technology infrastructure needs. The Department of State Treasurer shall report by January 1, 2001, and annually thereafter to the following regarding the amount and use of the departmental receipts: the Joint Legislative Commission on Governmental Operations, the Chairs of the General Government Appropriations Subcommittees of both the

House of Representatives and the Senate, and the Joint Legislative Committee on Information Technology.

(e) The State Treasurer, in carrying out the responsibilities of this section, shall be independent of any fiscal control exercise by the Director of the Budget or the Department of Administration and shall be responsible to the General Assembly and the people of North Carolina for the efficient and faithful exercise of the responsibilities of his office. The State Treasurer, for all other purposes, is subject to Chapter 143C of the General Statutes. (1868-9, c. 270, s. 71; Code, s. 3356; Rev., s. 5370; C.S., s. 7682; 1955, c. 577; 1957, c. 269, s. 1; 1981 (Reg. Sess., 1982), c. 1282, s. 65; 1983, c. 913, s. 52; 2000-67, s. 24A; 2003-284, s. 28.2(a); 2004-129, s. 46A; 2006-203, s. 118; 2007-323, s. 13.2(b).)

§ 147-68.1. Banking operations.

The cost of administration, management, and operations of the banking operations of the Department of State Treasurer shall be apportioned equitably among the funds and programs using these services, and the costs so apportioned shall be deposited with the State Treasurer as a general fund nontax revenue. The cost of administration, management and operations of the banking operations of the Department of State Treasurer shall be covered by an appropriation to the State Treasurer for this purpose in the Current Operations Appropriations Act. (1983 (Reg. Sess., 1984), c. 1034, s. 118.)

§ 147-69. Deposits of State funds in banks and savings and loan associations regulated.

Banks and savings and loan associations having State deposits shall furnish to the Auditor of the State, upon the Auditor's request, a statement of the moneys which have been received and paid by them on account of the treasury. The Treasurer shall keep in the Treasurer's office a full account of all moneys deposited in and drawn from all banks and savings and loan associations in which the Treasurer may deposit or cause to be deposited any of the public funds, and these accounts shall be open to the inspection of the Auditor. The Treasurer shall sign all checks, and no depository bank or savings and loan association shall be authorized to pay checks not bearing the Treasurer's official signature. The Treasurer is authorized to use a facsimile signature machine or device in affixing the Treasurer's signature to warrants, checks or any other instrument the Treasurer is required by law to sign. The Commissioner of Banks, the bank examiners, and the savings and loan examiners, when so required by the State Treasurer, shall keep the State Treasurer fully informed at all times as to the condition of all these depository banks and savings and loan associations, so as to fully protect the State from loss. The State Treasurer shall, before making deposits in any bank or savings and loan association, require ample security from the bank or savings and loan association for these deposits. (1905, c. 520; Rev., s. 5371; 1915, c. 168; 1917, c. 159; C.S., s. 7684; 1931, c. 127, s. 1; c. 243, s. 5; 1933, c. 175, s. 1; 1945, c. 644; 1949, c. 1183; 1967, c. 398, s. 2; 1977, c. 401, s. 1; 1983, c. 158, s. 4; 1987, c. 751, s. 1; 1989, c. 76, s. 27; 2001-193, s. 16; 2004-203, s. 11.)

§ 147-69.1. Investments authorized for General Fund and Highway Funds assets.

(a) The Governor and Council of State, with the advice and assistance of the State Treasurer, shall adopt such rules and regulations as shall be necessary and appropriate to implement the provisions of this section.

(b) This section applies to funds held by the State Treasurer to the credit of:

(1) The General Fund;

(2) The Highway Fund and Highway Trust Fund.

(c) It shall be the duty of the State Treasurer to invest the cash of the funds enumerated in subsection (b) of this section in excess of the amount required to meet the current needs and demands on such funds, selecting from among the following:

(1) Obligations of the United States or obligations fully guaranteed both as to principal and interest by the United States.

(2) Obligations of the Federal Financing Bank, the Federal Farm Credit Bank, the Federal Home Loan Banks, the Federal Home Loan Mortgage Corporation, Fannie Mae, the Government National Mortgage Association, the Federal Housing Administration, the Farmers Home Administration, the United States Postal Service, the Export-Import Bank, the International Bank for

Reconstruction and Development, the International Finance Corporation, the Inter-American Development Bank, the Asian Development Bank, the African Development Bank, and the Student Loan Marketing Association.

(3) Repurchase Agreements with respect to securities issued or guaranteed by the United States government or its agencies or other securities eligible for investment by this section executed by a bank or trust company or by primary or other reporting dealers to the Federal Reserve Bank of New York.

(4) Obligations of the State of North Carolina.

(5) Certificates of deposit and other deposit accounts of financial institutions under any of the following conditions:

a. With financial institutions with a physical presence in the State for the purpose of receiving commercial or retail deposits; provided that any principal amount of such deposit in excess of the amount insured by the federal government or any agency thereof, be fully secured by surety bonds, or be fully collateralized; provided further that the rate of return or investment yield may not be less than that available in the market on United States government or agency obligations of comparable maturity.

b. With financial institutions with a physical presence inside or outside the State, in accordance with all of the following conditions:

1. The funds are initially deposited through a bank or savings and loan association in the State that is an official depository and that is selected by the State Treasurer, provided that the rate of return or investment yield shall not be less than that available in the market on United States government or agency obligations of comparable maturity.

2. The selected bank or savings and loan association arranges for the redeposit of the funds in deposit accounts of the State in one or more federally insured banks or savings and loan associations wherever located, provided that no State funds shall be deposited in a bank or savings and loan association that at the time holds other deposits from the State.

3. The full amount of principal and any accrued interest of each deposit account are covered by federal deposit insurance.

4. The selected bank or savings and loan association acts as custodian for the State with respect to the deposit in the State's account.

5. On the same date that the State funds are redeposited, the selected bank or savings and loan association receives an amount of federally insured deposits from customers of other financial institutions wherever located equal to or greater than the amount of the funds invested by the State through the selected bank or savings and loan association pursuant to this sub-subdivision.

(6) Repealed by Session Laws 1989 (Regular Session, 1990), c. 813, s. 10.

(7) Prime quality commercial paper bearing the highest rating of at least one nationally recognized rating service and not bearing a rating below the highest by any nationally recognized rating service which rates the particular obligation.

(8) Bills of exchange or time drafts drawn on and accepted by a commercial bank and eligible for use as collateral by member banks in borrowing from a federal reserve bank, provided that the accepting bank or its holding company is either (i) incorporated in the State of North Carolina or (ii) has outstanding publicly held obligations bearing the highest rating of at least one nationally recognized rating service and not bearing a rating below the highest by any nationally recognized rating service which rates the particular obligations.

(9) Asset-backed securities (whether considered debt or equity) provided they bear the highest rating of at least one nationally recognized rating service and do not bear a rating below the highest rating by any nationally recognized rating service which rates the particular securities.

(10) Corporate bonds and notes provided they bear the highest rating of at least one nationally recognized rating service and do not bear a rating below the highest by any nationally recognized rating service which rates the particular obligation.

(d) Unless otherwise provided by law, the interest or income received and accruing from all deposits or investments of such cash balances shall be paid into the State's General Fund, except that all interest or income received and accruing on the monthly balance of the Highway Fund and Highway Trust Fund shall be paid into the State Highway Fund and Highway Trust Fund. The cash balances of the several funds may be combined for deposit or investment purposes; and when such combined deposits or investments are made, the interest or income received and accruing from all deposits or investments shall be prorated among the funds in conformity with applicable law and the rules and regulations adopted by the Governor and Council of State.

(e)   The State Treasurer shall cause to be prepared quarterly statements on or before the tenth day of February, May, August, and November in each year, which shall show the amount of cash on hand, the amount of money on deposit, the name of each depository, and all investments for which he is in any way responsible. Each quarterly statement shall be delivered to the Governor, Council of State, President Pro Tempore of the Senate, and Speaker of the House of Representatives; and a copy shall be posted in the office of the State Treasurer for the information of the public.

(f)   Repealed by Session Laws 1989 (Regular Session, 1990), c. 813, s. 10.

(g)   Repealed by Session Laws 2001-444, s. 1, effective October 1, 2001. (1943, c. 2; 1949, c. 213; 1957, c. 1401; 1961, c. 833, s. 2.2; 1967, c. 398, s. 1969, c. 125; 1975, c. 482; 1979, c. 467, s. 1; c. 717, s. 1; 1981, c. 801, ss. 1, 2; 1985, c. 313, s. 3; 1987, c. 751, ss. 2-4; 1987 (Reg. Sess., 1988), c. 882, s. 5; 1989, c. 76, s. 28; c. 751, s. 7(43); 1989 (Reg. Sess., 1990), c. 813, s. 10; 1991 (Reg. Sess., 1992), c. 959, s. 75; 1993, c. 105, s. 2; 1999-251, s. 1; 2001-444, s. 1; 2001-487, s. 14(m); 2005-394, s. 1; 2013-305, s. 3.)

§ 147-69.2. Investments authorized for special funds held by State Treasurer.

(a)   This section applies to funds held by the State Treasurer to the credit of each of the following:

(1)   The Teachers' and State Employees' Retirement System.

(2)   The Consolidated Judicial Retirement System.

(3)   The State Health Plan for Teachers and State Employees.

(4)   The General Assembly Medical and Hospital Care Plan.

(5)   The Disability Salary Continuation Plan.

(6)   The Firefighters' and Rescue Workers' Pension Fund.

(7) The Local Governmental Employees' Retirement System.

(8) The Legislative Retirement System.

(9) The Escheat Fund.

(10) The Legislative Retirement Fund.

(11) The State Education Assistance Authority.

(12) The State Property Fire Insurance Fund.

(13) The Stock Workers' Compensation Fund.

(14) The Mutual Workers' Compensation Fund.

(15) The Public School Insurance Fund.

(16) The Liability Insurance Trust Fund.

(16a) The University of North Carolina Hospitals at Chapel Hill funds, except appropriated funds, deposited with the State Treasurer pursuant to G.S. 116-37.2.

(17) Trust funds of The University of North Carolina and its constituent institutions deposited with the State Treasurer pursuant to G.S. 116-36.1.

(17a) North Carolina Veterans Home Trust Fund.

(17b) North Carolina National Guard Pension Fund.

(17c) Retiree Health Benefit Fund.

(17d) The Election Fund.

(17e) The North Carolina State Lottery Fund.

(17f) Funds deposited with the State Treasurer by public hospitals pursuant to G.S. 159-39(g).

(17g) Funds deposited with the State Treasurer by Local Government Other Post-Employment Benefits Trusts pursuant to G.S. 159-30.1.

(17h) The Local Government Law Enforcement Special Separation Allowance Fund.

(17i) The North Carolina Conservation Easement Endowment Fund.

(17j) The Conservation Grant Fund.

(18) Any other special fund created by or pursuant to law for purposes other than meeting appropriations made pursuant to the Executive Budget Act.

(19) The Swain County Settlement Trust Fund.

(20) Institutional funds of the colleges of the North Carolina Community College System.

(b) It shall be the duty of the State Treasurer to invest the cash of the funds enumerated in subsection (a) of this section in excess of the amount required to meet the current needs and demands on such funds. The State Treasurer may invest the funds as provided in this subsection. If an investment was authorized by this subsection at the time the investment was made or contractually committed to be made, then that investment shall continue to be authorized by this subsection, and none of the percentage or other limitation on investments set forth in this subsection shall be construed to require the State Treasurer to subsequently dispose of the investment or fail to honor any contractual commitments as a result of changes in market values, ratings, or other investment qualifications. For purposes of computing market values on which percentage limitations on investments in this subsection are based, all investments shall be valued as of the last date of the most recent fiscal quarter.

(1) Investments authorized by G.S. 147-69.1(c)(1)-(7).

(2) General obligations of other states of the United States.

(3) General obligations of cities, counties and special districts in North Carolina.

(4) Obligations of any company, other organization or legal entity incorporated or otherwise created or located within or outside the United States,

including obligations that are convertible into equity securities, if the obligations bear one of the four highest ratings of at least one nationally recognized rating service when acquired.

(5) Repealed by Session Laws 2001-444, s. 2, effective October 1, 2001.

(6) Asset-backed securities (whether considered debt or equity) provided they bear ratings by nationally recognized rating services as provided in G.S. 147-69.2(b)(4).

(6a) In addition to the limitations and requirements with respect to the investments of the Retirement Systems set forth in this subsection, the State Treasurer shall select investments of the assets of the Retirement Systems such that investments made pursuant to subdivisions (b)(1) through (6) of this section shall at all times equal or exceed twenty percent (20%) of the market value of all invested assets of the Retirement Systems.

(6b) Investments pursuant to subdivisions (b)(1) through (6) of this section may be made directly by the State Treasurer or through contractual arrangements in which the investment manager has full and complete discretion and authority to invest assets specified in such arrangements in investments authorized by subdivisions (b)(1) through (6) of this section, provided for each indirect investment, the investment manager has assets under management of at least one hundred million dollars ($100,000,000).

(6c) With respect to Retirement Systems' assets referred to in subdivision (b)(8), they may be invested in obligations, debt securities, and asset-backed securities, whether considered debt or equity, including obligations and securities convertible into other securities, that do not meet the requirements of any of subdivisions (b)(1) through (6) of this section nor subdivision (b)(7) of this section, provided such investments are made through investment companies registered under the Investment Company Act of 1940, individual, common, or collective trust funds of banks and trust companies, group trusts and limited partnerships, limited liability companies or other limited liability investment vehicles that invest primarily in investments authorized by this subdivision and through contractual arrangements in which the investment manager has full and complete discretion and authority to invest assets specified in such arrangements in investments authorized by this subdivision, provided the investment manager for each investment pursuant to this subdivision has assets under management of at least one hundred million dollars ($100,000,000) and provided that the investments authorized under this subdivision shall not exceed seven and one-half percent (7.5%) of the market value of all invested assets of the Retirement Systems.

(7) With respect to Retirement Systems' assets referred to in subdivision (8) of this subsection, (i) insurance contracts that provide for participation in individual or pooled separate accounts of insurance companies, (ii) group trusts, (iii) individual, common, or collective trust funds of banks and trust companies, (iv) real estate investment trusts, (v) investment companies registered under the Investment Company Act of 1940, (vi) limited partnerships, limited liability companies, or other limited liability investment vehicles, and (vii) contractual arrangements in which the investment manager has discretion and authority to invest assets specified in such arrangements in investments authorized by this subsection; provided the investment manager has assets under management of at least one hundred million dollars ($100,000,000); provided such investment assets are managed primarily for the purpose of investing in or owning real estate or related debt financing, excluding asset-backed financing, located within or outside the United States; and provided that the investments authorized by this subdivision shall not exceed ten percent (10%) of the market value of all invested assets of the Retirement Systems.

(8) With respect to assets of the Teachers' and State Employees' Retirement System, the Consolidated Judicial Retirement System, the Firefighters' and Rescue Workers' Pension Fund, the Local Governmental Employees' Retirement System, the Legislative Retirement System, the North Carolina National Guard Pension Fund, and the Retiree Health Benefit Fund (hereinafter referred to collectively as the Retirement Systems), and assets invested pursuant to subdivision (b2) of this section, they may be invested in equity securities traded on a public securities exchange or market organized and regulated pursuant to the laws of the jurisdiction of such exchange or market and issued by any company incorporated or otherwise created or located within or outside the United States; provided the investments meet the conditions of this subdivision. The investments authorized for the Retirement Systems under this subdivision cannot exceed sixty-five percent (65%) of the market value of all invested assets of the Retirement Systems.

The assets authorized under this subdivision may be invested directly by the State Treasurer in any equity securities authorized by this subdivision for the primary purpose of approximating the movements of a nationally recognized and published market benchmark index. No more than one and one-half percent (1.5%) of the market value of the Retirement Systems' assets that may be invested directly under this subdivision can be invested in the stock of a single corporation, and the total number of shares in that single corporation cannot exceed eight percent (8%) of the issued and outstanding stock of that corporation.

So long as each investment manager has assets under management of at least one hundred million dollars ($100,000,000), the assets authorized under this subdivision may also be invested through any of the following:

a. Investment companies registered under the Investment Company Act of 1940; individual, common, or collective trust funds of banks and trust companies; and group trusts that invest primarily in investments authorized by this subdivision.

b. Limited partnerships, limited liability companies, or other limited liability investment vehicles that are not publicly traded and invest primarily in investments authorized by this subdivision. Investments under this sub-subdivision shall not exceed eight and one-half percent (8.5%) of the market value of all invested assets of the Retirement Systems.

c. Contractual arrangements in which investment managers have full and complete discretion and authority to invest assets specified in such contractual arrangements in investments authorized by this subdivision.

(9) With respect to Retirement Systems' assets, as defined in subdivision (b)(8) of this subsection, they may be invested in interests in limited partnerships, limited liability companies, or other limited liability investment vehicles that are not publicly traded if the primary purpose of the limited partnership, limited liability company, or other limited liability investment vehicle is (i) to invest in private equity, or corporate buyout transactions, within or outside the United States or (ii) to engage in other strategies not expressly authorized by any other subdivision of this subsection. The amount invested under this subdivision shall not exceed eight and three-quarters percent (8.75%) of the market value of all invested assets of the Retirement Systems.

(9a) With respect to Retirement Systems' assets, as defined in subdivision (b)(8) of this subsection, they may be invested in inflation-linked bonds, timberlands, commodities, and other investments that are acquired by the Treasurer for the primary purpose of providing protection against risks associated with inflation, provided such investments are made through investment companies registered under the Investment Company Act of 1940, individual, common or collective trust funds of banks and trust companies, group trusts and limited partnerships, limited liability companies or other limited liability investment vehicles that invest primarily in investments authorized by this subdivision and through contractual arrangements in which the investment manager has full and complete discretion and authority to invest assets specified in such arrangements in investments authorized by this subdivision, provided the investment manager for each investment pursuant to this subdivision has assets under management of at least one hundred million dollars ($100,000,000) and provided that the investments authorized under this subdivision shall not exceed seven and one-half percent (7.5%) of the market value of all invested assets of the Retirement Systems. Notwithstanding anything in this subsection to the contrary, the investments authorized by this subdivision shall not be included in any subdivision other than this subdivision for purposes of the percentage investment limitations therein or otherwise.

(10) Recodified as part of subdivision (b)(9) by Session Laws 2000-160, s. 2.

(10a) With respect to Retirement Systems' assets, as defined in subdivision (8) of this subsection, the market value of any of subdivision (6c) or (7), sub-subdivision b. of subdivision (8), or subdivision (9) or (9a) of this subsection shall not exceed ten percent (10%) of the market value of all invested assets of the Retirement Systems; and the aggregate market value of all assets invested pursuant to subdivisions (6c) and (7), sub-subdivision b. of subdivision (8), and subdivisions (9) and (9a) of this subsection shall not exceed thirty-five percent (35%) of the market value of all invested assets of the Retirement Systems. The quarterly report provided by the Treasurer pursuant to G.S. 147-68(d1) shall include a specific listing of all direct and indirect placement fees, asset fees, performance fees, and any other money management fees incurred by the State in the management of subdivisions (6c) and (7), sub-subdivision b. of subdivision (8), and subdivisions (9) and (9a) of this subsection. In the event that the market value of any of subdivision (6c) or (7), sub-subdivision b. of subdivision (8), or subdivision (9) or (9a) of this subsection increases during a fiscal year by an amount greater than three percent (3%) of the market value of all invested assets of the Retirement Systems as of the prior fiscal year end, then the quarterly report provided by the Treasurer pursuant to G.S. 147-68(d1) shall describe how that increase complies with the duties described in G.S. 147-69.7 and the consequent expected impact on the risk profile of the Retirement Systems' assets.

(11) Repealed by Session Laws 2013-360, s. 6.3(c), effective July 1, 2013.

(12) With respect to assets of the Escheat Fund, in addition to those investments authorized by subdivisions (1) through (6) of this subsection, up to twenty percent (20%) of such assets may be invested in the investments authorized under subdivisions (7) through (9) of this subsection, notwithstanding the percentage limitations imposed on the Retirement Systems' investments under those subdivisions.

(b1) With respect to investments authorized by subdivisions (b)(7), (b)(8), and (b)(9) of this section, the State Treasurer shall appoint an Investment Advisory Committee, which shall consist of seven members: the State Treasurer, who shall be chairman ex officio; two members selected from among the members of the boards of trustees of the Retirement Systems; and four members selected from the general public. The four public members must have experience in areas relevant to the administration of a large, diversified investment program, including, but not limited to, investment management, securities law, real estate development, or absolute return strategies. The State Treasurer shall also appoint a Secretary of the Investment Advisory Committee who need not be a member of the committee. Members of the committee shall receive for their services the same per diem and allowances granted to members of the State boards and commissions generally. The committee shall have advisory powers only and membership shall not be deemed a public office within the meaning of Article VI, Section 9 of the Constitution of North Carolina or G.S. 128-1.1.

(b2) The State Treasurer may invest funds deposited pursuant to subdivision (a)(17f) of this section in any of the investments authorized under subdivisions (b)(1) through (6), subdivision (b)(6c), and subdivision (b)(8) of this section, notwithstanding the percentage limitations imposed on the Retirement Systems' investments therein. The State Treasurer may require a minimum deposit, up to one hundred thousand dollars ($100,000), and may assess reasonable fees, not to exceed 15 basis points per annum, as a condition of participation pursuant to this subsection. Funds deposited pursuant to this subsection by a hospital shall remain the funds of that hospital, and interest or other investment income earned thereon shall be prorated and credited to the contributing hospital on the basis of the amounts thereof contributed, figured according to sound accounting principles. Fees assessed by the State Treasurer may be used to defray the cost of administering investments pursuant to this subsection.

(b3) The State Treasurer may invest funds deposited pursuant to subdivision (a)(16a) of this section in any of the investments authorized under subdivisions (1) through (6), subdivision (6c) and subdivision (b)(8) of this section, notwithstanding the percentage limitations imposed on the Retirement Systems' investments therein. The State Treasurer may require a minimum deposit, up to one hundred thousand dollars ($100,000), and may assess reasonable fees, not to exceed 15 basis points per annum, as a condition of participation pursuant to this subsection. Funds deposited pursuant to this subsection by the University of North Carolina Hospitals at Chapel Hill shall remain the funds of the University of North Carolina Hospitals at Chapel Hill, and interest or other investment income earned thereon shall be prorated and credited to the University of North Carolina Hospitals at Chapel Hill on the basis of the amounts thereof contributed, figured according to sound accounting principles. Fees assessed by the State Treasurer may be used to defray the cost of administering investments pursuant to this subsection.

(b4) In addition to the investments authorized under subdivisions (b)(1) through (6) of this section, the State Treasurer may invest funds deposited pursuant to subdivision (17g) of subsection (a) of this section in any of the investments authorized under subdivisions (b)(6c) and (b)(8) of this section, notwithstanding the percentage limitations imposed on the Retirement Systems' investments therein. Funds deposited pursuant to this subsection by a Local Government Other Post-Employment Benefits Trust and interest or other investment income earned from those funds shall be prorated and credited to the contributing trust on the basis of the amounts contributed, figured according to sound accounting principles. For investments under subdivisions (b)(6c) and (b)(8) of this section, the State Treasurer may require a minimum deposit of up to one hundred thousand dollars ($100,000) and may assess fees of up to 15 basis points per annum as a condition of participation pursuant to this subsection. Fees assessed by the State Treasurer may be used to defray the costs of administering the Fund.

(b5) In addition to the investments authorized under subdivisions (b)(1) through (6) of this section, the State Treasurer may invest funds deposited in the Local Government Law Enforcement Special Separation Allowance Fund in any of the investments authorized under subdivisions (b)(6c) and (b)(8) of this section, notwithstanding the percentage limitations imposed on the Retirement Systems' investments therein. For investments from that Fund made under subdivisions (b)(6c) and (b)(8) of this section, the State Treasurer may require a minimum deposit of up to one hundred thousand dollars ($100,000) and may assess fees of up to 15 basis points per annum as a condition of making the investment. The fee may be used to defray the costs of administering the Fund.

(c) Repealed by Session Laws 1995, c. 501, s. 2.

(d) The State Treasurer may invest funds deposited pursuant to subdivision (a)(17i) of this section in any of the investments authorized under subdivisions (1) through (6) and subdivision (8) of subsection (b) of this section. The State Treasurer may require a minimum deposit, up to one hundred thousand dollars ($100,000), and may assess a reasonable fee, not to exceed 15 basis points, as a condition of participation pursuant to this subsection. Funds deposited pursuant to this subsection shall remain the funds of the North Carolina Conservation Easement Endowment Fund, and interest or other investment income earned thereon shall be prorated and credited to the North Carolina Conservation Easement Endowment Fund on the basis of the amounts thereof contributed, figured according to sound accounting principles. (1979, c. 467, s. 2; 1983, c. 702, ss. 1-9; 1987, c. 446, s. 1; c. 751, s. 5; 1987 (Reg. Sess., 1988), c. 1070; 1989, c. 770, s. 54; 1989 (Reg. Sess., 1990), c. 813, s. 11; c. 848, s. 5; 1991, c. 542, s. 16; c. 636, s. 3; c. 749, s. 8; 1993 (Reg. Sess., 1994), c. 777, s. 4(i); 1995, c. 346, s. 2; c. 501, s. 2; 1997-456, s. 27; 1999-237, s. 27.16; 1999-251, s. 2; 2000-160, s. 2; 2001-444, ss. 2, 3; 2003-12, s. 2; 2004-124, s. 30.22(b); 2005-144, s. 7; 2005-201, s. 2; 2005-252, s. 1; 2005-276, s. 28.17; 2005-344, s. 10; 2005-417, s. 2; 2007-323, s. 27.7; 2007-384, ss. 2, 3, 7, 8; 2008-13, s. 2; 2008-107, ss. 12.9(b), (c), 12.13; 2009-98, s. 1; 2009-283, s. 2; 2009-451, s. 25.2(a); 2010-175, ss. 3, 4; 2011-145, ss. 6.10(a), 8.20(c); 2011-211, s. 1; 2011-340, s. 4(a), (b); 2012-130, s. 10; 2012-142, s. 6.4; 2012-178, s. 6; 2013-284, s. 1(d); 2013-360, s. 6.3(c); 2013-398, s. 1.)

§ 147-69.3. Administration of State Treasurer's investment programs.

(a) The State Treasurer shall establish, maintain, administer, manage, and operate within the Department of State Treasurer one or more investment programs for the deposit and investment of assets pursuant to the provisions of G.S. 147-69.1 and G.S. 147-69.2.

(b) Any official, board, commission, other public authority, local government, school administrative unit, local ABC board, or community college of the State having custody of any funds not required by law to be deposited with and invested by the State Treasurer may deposit all or any portion of those funds with the State Treasurer for investment in one of the investment programs established pursuant to this section, subject to any provisions of law with respect to eligible investments, provided that any occupational licensing board as defined in G.S. 93B-1 may participate in one of the investment programs established pursuant to this section regardless of whether or not the funds were required by law to be deposited with and invested by the State Treasurer. In the absence of specific statutory provisions to the contrary, any of those funds may be invested in accordance with the provisions of G.S. 147-69.2 and 147-69.3. Upon request from any depositor eligible under this subsection, the State Treasurer may authorize moneys invested pursuant to this subsection to be withdrawn by warrant on the State Treasurer.

(c) The State Treasurer's investment programs shall be so managed that in the judgment of the State Treasurer funds may be readily converted into cash when needed.

(d) Except as provided by G.S. 147-69.1(d), the total return earned on investments shall accrue pro rata to the fund whose assets are invested according to the formula prescribed by the State Treasurer with the approval of the Governor and Council of State.

(e) The State Treasurer has full powers as a fiduciary to hold, purchase, sell, assign, transfer, lend and dispose of any of the securities or investments in which any of the programs created pursuant to this section have been invested, and may reinvest the proceeds from the sale of those securities or investments and any other investable assets of the program.

(f) The cost of administration, management, and operation of investment programs established pursuant to this section shall be apportioned equitably among the programs in such manner as may be prescribed by the State Treasurer, such costs to be paid from each program, and to the extent not otherwise chargeable directly to the income or assets of the specific investment program or pooled investment vehicle, shall be deposited with the State Treasurer as a General Fund nontax revenue. The cost of administration, management, and operation of investment programs established pursuant to this section and not directly paid from the income or assets of such program shall be covered by an appropriation to the State Treasurer for this purpose in the Current Operations Appropriations Act.

(g) The State Treasurer is authorized to retain the services of independent appraisers, auditors, actuaries, attorneys, investment counseling firms, statisticians, custodians, or other persons or firms possessing specialized skills or knowledge necessary for the proper administration of investment programs created pursuant to this section.

(h) The State Treasurer shall prepare, as of the end of each fiscal year, a report on the financial condition of each investment program created pursuant to this section. A copy of each report shall be submitted within 30 days following the end of the fiscal year to the official, institution, board, commission or other agency whose funds are invested, the State Auditor, and the chairs of the Finance Committees of the House of Representatives and the Senate.

(i) The State Treasurer shall report at least twice a year to the General Assembly, through the Finance Committees of the House of Representatives and the Senate, on the investment programs created under this section. The Treasurer shall present the reports to a joint meeting of the Finance Committees. The chairs of the Finance Committees may receive the reports and call the meetings. The Finance Committees may meet during the interim as necessary to hear the reports from the State Treasurer. The State Treasurer's report and presentation to the Finance Committees shall include all of the following:

(1) A full and complete statement of all moneys invested by virtue of the provisions of G.S. 147-69.1 and G.S. 147-69.2.

(2) The nature and character of the investments.

(3) The revenues derived from the investments.

(4) The costs of administering, managing, and operating the investment programs, including the recapture of any investment commissions.

(5) A statement of the investment policies for the revenues invested.

(6) Any other information that may be helpful in understanding the State Treasurer's investment policies and investment results.

(7) Any other information requested by the Finance Committees.

(i1) The State Treasurer shall report the incentive bonus paid to the Chief Investment Officer to the Joint Legislative Commission on Governmental Operations by October 1 of each year.

(i2) In order to retain key public employees in the Investment Division, the State Treasurer is authorized to establish compensation including bonuses for the Chief Investment Officer and Investment Directors. The bonuses may be based on compensation studies conducted by a nationally recognized firm specializing in public fund investment compensation and the Pension Plan performance. The salaries and other associated benefits shall be apportioned directly from the investment program. The Treasurer shall report the bonuses paid to the Joint Legislative Commission on Governmental Operations annually.

(j) Subject to the provisions of G.S. 147-69.1(d), the State Treasurer shall adopt any rules necessary to carry out the provisions of this section. (1979, c. 467, s. 3; 1981, c. 445, ss. 4, 5; 1983, c. 515, s. 1; c. 702, s. 10; 1983 (Reg. Sess., 1984), c. 1034, ss. 116, 117; 1987, c. 751, ss. 6-8; 2001-444, s. 4; 2002-126, s. 6.12; 2005-276, s. 27.3; 2006-203, s. 119; 2008-132, s. 5.)

§ 147-69.3A. Liability insurance for State Treasurer.

(a) The State Treasurer may purchase commercial insurance of any kind to cover all risks or potential liability of the State Treasurer, boards in the Department of the State Treasurer, members of boards in the Department of the State Treasurer, and employees and agents of the State Treasurer, including the risks and potential liability related to investments managed by the State Treasurer.

(b) Board members and employees of boards in the Department of the State Treasurer shall be considered State employees for purposes of Articles 31 and 31A of Chapter 143 of the General Statutes. To the extent that the State Treasurer purchases commercial liability insurance coverage in excess of one hundred fifty thousand dollars ($150,000) per claim for liability arising under Article 31 or 31A of Chapter 143 of the General Statutes, the provisions of G.S. 143-299.4 shall not apply. To the extent that the State Treasurer purchases commercial insurance coverage for liability arising under Article 31 or 31A of Chapter 143 of the General Statutes, the provisions of G.S. 143-300.6(a) shall not apply.

(c) The purchase of insurance by the State Treasurer under this section shall not be construed to waive sovereign immunity or any other defense available to the State Treasurer, boards in the Department of the State Treasurer, members of boards in the Department of the State Treasurer, or employees or agents of the State Treasurer in an action or contested matter in any court, agency, or tribunal. The purchase of insurance by the State Treasurer shall not be construed to alter or expand the limitations on claims or payments established in G.S. 143-299.2 or limit the right of the State Treasurer, board members, employees, or agents to defense by the State as provided by G.S. 143-300.3. (2011-300, s. 1.)

§ 147-69.4: Repealed by Session Laws 2010-175, s. 5, effective July 1, 2010.

§ 147-69.5. Local Government Law Enforcement Special Separation Allowance Fund.

The Local Government Law Enforcement Special Separation Allowance Fund is established as a fund in the Office of the State Treasurer under the management of the Treasurer. The Fund consists of contributions made by entities authorized to make contributions to the Fund and interest and other investment income earned by the Fund. Contributions to the Fund are irrevocable. Assets of the Fund may be used only to provide law enforcement special separation allowance benefits to individuals who are former employees of a unit of local government that contributes to the Fund and are entitled to law enforcement special separation allowance payable by the unit. The assets of the Fund are not subject to the claims of creditors of an entity that contributes to the Fund. (2007-384, s. 6.)

§ 147-69.6. Swain County Settlement Trust Fund.

(a)   The Swain County Settlement Trust Fund is established as a special fund in the Office of the State Treasurer under the management of the Treasurer. The Fund shall consist of the proceeds of any payments made by the United States in settlement of the 1943 agreement between Swain County and the United States Department of Interior, such other contributions as Swain County or other entities may choose to make to the Fund, and the interest and other investment income earned by the Fund. Contributions to the Fund are irrevocable. Assets in the Fund may be disbursed only to Swain County.

(b)   On such schedule as the State Treasurer may determine, in consultation with the Board of Commissioners of Swain County, the State Treasurer shall disburse to Swain County amounts requested by the Swain County Board of Commissioners pursuant to a majority vote of that body, provided that disbursements to Swain County under this subsection in any fiscal year shall not exceed the total interest and investment income earned by the Fund in that fiscal year. At the start of each fiscal year, the State Treasurer shall issue a nonbinding opinion and recommendation to the Swain County Board of

Commissioners suggesting an appropriate amount of interest and investment income to be reinvested in the Fund to ensure that the principal investment grows to keep pace with inflation.

(c) No portion of the principal balance of the Fund may be disbursed to Swain County absent a request by the Swain County Board of Commissioners accompanied by a certification by the Swain County Board of Elections that two-thirds of the registered voters of Swain County voted in favor of the disbursement and subsequent expenditure of the amount requested in a referendum conducted under subsection (f) of this section.

(d) Funds disbursed to Swain County under subsections (b) or (c) of this section shall be managed by the county in accordance with the requirements of the Local Government Budget and Fiscal Control Act as amended from time to time.

(e) No part of the principal of the Swain County Settlement Trust Fund or of any interest or other income earned on that principal may be paid to or received by any agent or attorney on account of services rendered in connection with negotiating the settlement agreement between Swain County and the United States Department of Interior or obtaining the monetary settlement from the United States.

(f) The Board of Commissioners of Swain County may direct the Swain County Board of Elections to conduct an advisory referendum on the question of whether any portion of the principal of the Fund should be disbursed to and expended by the county for a particular purpose. The election shall be held in accordance with the procedures of G.S. 163-287. The question to be presented on the ballot shall disclose the specific purpose proposed for expenditure of the principal investment of the Trust Fund and the amount proposed for expenditure.

(g) The Swain County Settlement Trust Fund is subject to the oversight of the State Auditor pursuant to Article 5A of Chapter 147 of the General Statutes.

(h) The Swain County Settlement Trust Fund and the income therefrom shall not take the place of or be counted against any other State appropriations or program providing funds or disbursements to Swain County. (2008-13, s. 3; 2013-381, s. 10.22.)

§ 147-69.7. Discharge of duties to Retirement Systems.

(a) The Treasurer shall discharge his or her duties with respect to the Retirement Systems enumerated in G.S. 147-69.2(b)(8) as follows:

(1) Solely in the interest of the participants and beneficiaries.

(2) For the exclusive purpose of providing benefits to participants and beneficiaries and paying reasonable expenses of administering the Retirement Systems.

(3) With the care, skill, and caution under the circumstances then prevailing which a prudent person acting in a like capacity and familiar with those matters would use in the conduct of an activity of like character and purpose.

(4) Impartially, taking into account any differing interests of participants and beneficiaries.

(5) Incurring only costs that are appropriate and reasonable.

(6) In accordance with a good-faith interpretation of the law governing the Retirement Systems.

(b) In investing and managing assets of the Retirement Systems pursuant to subsection (a) of this section, the Treasurer:

(1) Shall consider the following circumstances:

a. General economic conditions.

b. The possible effect of inflation or deflation.

c. The role that each investment or course of action plays within the overall portfolio of the Retirement Systems.

d. The expected total return from income and the appreciation of capital.

e. Needs for liquidity, regularity of income, and preservation or appreciation of capital.

f. The adequacy of funding for the Retirement Systems based on reasonable actuarial factors.

(2) Shall diversify the investments of the Retirement Systems unless the Treasurer reasonably determines that, because of special circumstances, it is clearly prudent not to do so.

(3) Shall make a reasonable effort to verify facts relevant to the investment and management of assets of the Retirement Systems.

(4) May invest in any kind of property or type of investment consistent with the provisions of Article 6 of Chapter 146 of the General Statutes.

(5) May consider benefits created by an investment in addition to investment return only if the Treasurer determines that the investment providing these collateral benefits would be prudent even without collateral benefits.

(c) Compliance by the Treasurer with this section must be determined in light of the facts and circumstances existing at the time of the Treasurer's decision or action and not by hindsight.

(d) The Treasurer's investment and management decisions must be evaluated not in isolation but in the context of the portfolio of the Retirement Systems as a whole and as part of an overall investment strategy having risk and return objectives reasonably suited to the Retirement Systems. (2009-283, s. 3; 2013-284, s. 1(e); 2013-398, s. 2; 2013-410, s. 27.5.)

§ 147-69.8. Annual report on new investment authority.

Whenever the General Assembly broadens the investment authority of the State Treasurer as to the General Fund, the Teachers' and State Employees' Retirement System, the Consolidated Judicial Retirement System, the Firefighters' and Rescue Squad Workers' Pension Fund, the Local Governmental Employees' Retirement System, the Legislative Retirement System, the North Carolina National Guard Pension Fund, or any idle funds, the State Treasurer shall annually report in detail to the General Assembly the investments made under such new authority, including the returns on those investments, earnings, changes to value, and gains and losses in disposition of such investments. The report shall be made during the first six months of each calendar year, covering performance in the prior calendar year. As to each type of new investment authority, the report shall be made for at least four years. (2009-283, s. 4; 2013-284, s. 1(f).)

§ 147-70. To make short-term notes in emergencies.

Subject to the approval of the Governor and Council of State, the State Treasurer is authorized to make short-term notes for temporary emergencies, but such notes must only be made to provide for appropriations already made by the General Assembly. (1915, c. 168, s. 3; C.S., s. 7685.)

§ 147-71. May demand and sue for money and property of State.

The Treasurer is authorized to demand, sue for, collect and receive all money and property of the State not held by some person under authority of law. (1866, c. 46; Code, s. 3359; Rev., s. 5375; C.S., s. 7688.)

§ 147-72. Ex officio treasurer of State institutions; duties as such.

The Treasurer shall be ex officio the treasurer of the Department of Agriculture and Consumer Services, of the North Carolina State College of Agriculture and Engineering, of the North Carolina School for the Deaf and Dumb at Morganton, of the North Carolina Institution for the Deaf and Dumb and the Blind at Raleigh, for the State hospitals (for the insane) at Raleigh, Morganton and Goldsboro and for the State's prison. He may appoint deputies to act for him at Morganton and Goldsboro, and may pay such deputies reasonable compensation. He shall keep all accounts of the institutions, and shall pay out all moneys, upon the warrant of the respective chief officers or superintendents, countersigned by two members of the board of directors, managers, or trustees. He shall report to the respective boards at such times as they may call on him, showing the amount received on account of the institution, amount paid out, and amount on hand. He shall perform his duties as treasurer of these several institutions under such regulation as shall be prescribed in each case by their respective boards of managers, trustees or directors, with the approval of the Governor; and shall be responsible on his official bond for the faithful discharge of his duties as treasurer of each of the several institutions. As treasurer of such institutions he shall, annually, after the examination, verification, and cancellation of his vouchers, deposit the same with the respective institutions, and the superintendents thereof shall be responsible for their safekeeping. (1879, c. 240, s. 2; 1881, c. 128; c. 211, s. 9; 1883, c. 156, s. 12; c. 405; Code, ss. 2235, 2251, 3723; 1895, c. 434; 1899, c. 1, s. 11; Rev., s. 5376; 1919, c. 314, s. 6; C.S., s. 7689; 1947, c. 781; 1997-261, s. 109.)

§ 147-73. Office of treasurer of each State institution abolished.

The office of treasurer of each of the several State institutions of which the State Treasurer is ex officio treasurer is hereby abolished. (1929, c. 337, s. 3.)

§ 147-74. Office of State Treasurer declared office of deposit and disbursement.

The office of the State Treasurer is declared to be an office of deposit and disbursement and only such records and accounts as may be necessary to disclose the accountability of the State Treasurer shall be kept. The purpose of this section is to prevent duplication in account and record keeping and such accounts as may be necessary shall be prescribed by the Director of the Budget under the terms of the Executive Budget Act. (1929, c. 337, s. 2.)

§ 147-75. Deputy to act for Treasurer.

The Treasurer may authorize a deputy to perform any duties pertaining to the office. The Treasurer may authorize a deputy to affix the Treasurer's signature to any check, warrant or any other instrument the Treasurer is required to sign by use of the facsimile signature machine or device during the Treasurer's absence or disability. The Treasurer shall be responsible for the conduct of his deputies. (1868-9, c. 270, s. 76; Code, s. 3358; Rev., s. 5377; C.S., s. 7690; 1977, c. 401, s. 2.)

§ 147-76. Liability for false entries in his books.

If the Treasurer of the State shall wittingly or falsely make, or cause to be made, any false entry or charge in any book by him as Treasurer, or shall wittingly or falsely form, or procure to be formed, any statement of the treasury, to be by him laid before the Governor, the General Assembly, or any committee thereof, or to be by him used in any settlement which he is required to make with intent, in any of said instances, to defraud the State or any person, such Treasurer shall be guilty of a Class 1 misdemeanor. (R.C., c. 34, s. 68; Code, s. 1119; Rev., s. 3606; C.S., s. 7691; 1983, c. 913, s. 53; 1993, c. 539, s. 1055; 1994, Ex. Sess., c. 24, s. 14(c).)

§ 147-77. Daily deposit of funds to credit of Treasurer.

All funds belonging to the State of North Carolina, in the hands of any head of any department of the State which collects revenue for the State in any form whatsoever, and every institution, agency, officer, employee, or representative of the State or any agency, department, division or commission thereof, except officers and the clerks of the Supreme Court and Court of Appeals, collecting or receiving any funds or money belonging to the State of North Carolina, shall daily deposit the same in some bank, or trust company, selected or designated by the State Treasurer, in the name of the State Treasurer, at noon, or as near thereto as may be, and shall report the same daily to said Treasurer: Provided that the State Treasurer may authorize exemptions from the provisions of this section so long as funds are deposited and reported pursuant to the provisions of this section at least once a week and, in addition, so long as funds are deposited and reported pursuant to the provisions of this section whenever as much as two hundred fifty dollars ($250.00) has been collected and received: Provided, that the Treasurer may refund the amount of any bad checks which have been returned to the department by the Treasurer when the same have not been collected after 30 days' trial. (1925, c. 128, s. 1; 1945, c. 159; 1969, c. 44, s. 77; 1985, c. 708.)

§ 147-78. Treasurer to select depositories.

The State Treasurer is hereby authorized and empowered to select and designate, wherever necessary, in this State some bank or banks, savings and loan association or associations, or trust company as an official depository of the State. (1925, c. 128, s. 2; 1979, c. 637, s. 4; 1983, c. 158, s. 5.)

§ 147-78.1. Good faith deposits; use of master trust.

Notwithstanding any other provision of law, the State Treasurer is authorized to select a bank or trust company as master trustee to hold cash or securities to be pledged to the State when deposited with him pursuant to statute or at the request of another State agency. Securities may be held by the master trustee in any form that, in fact, perfects the security interest of the State in the securities. The State Treasurer shall by rule or regulation establish the manner in which the master trust shall operate. The master trustee may charge reasonable fees for services rendered to each person who deposits the cash or securities with the State. (1985, c. 496, s. 1.)

§ 147-79. Deposits to be secured; reports of depositories.

(a) The amount of funds deposited by the State Treasurer in an official depository shall be adequately secured by deposit insurance, surety bonds, or investment securities of such nature, in such amounts, and in such manner, as may be prescribed by rule or regulation of the State Treasurer with the approval of the Governor and Council of State. No security is required for the protection of funds remitted to and received by a bank or trust company designated by the State Treasurer under G.S. 142-1 and acting as paying agent for the payment of the principal of or interest on bonds or notes of the State.

(b) Each official depository having deposits required to be secured by subsection (a) of this section may be required to report to the State Treasurer on January 1 and July 1 of each year (or such other dates as he may prescribe) a list of all surety bonds or investment securities securing such deposits. If the State Treasurer finds at any time that any funds of the State are not properly secured, he shall so notify the depository. Upon such notification, the depository shall comply with the applicable law or regulations forthwith.

(c) Violation of the provisions of this section shall be a Class 1 misdemeanor. (1933, c. 461, ss. 1, 1 1/2; 1979, c. 637, s. 3; 1993, c. 539, s. 1056; 1994, Ex. Sess., c. 24, s. 14(c).)

§ 147-80. Deposit in other banks unlawful; liability.

It shall be unlawful for any funds of the State to be deposited by any person, institution, or department or agency in any place or bank or trust company, other than those so selected and designated as official depositories of the State of North Carolina by the State Treasurer, and any person so offending or aiding and abetting in such offense shall be guilty of a Class 1 misdemeanor and any person so offending or aiding and abetting in such offense shall also immediately become civilly liable to the State of North Carolina in the amount of the money or funds unlawfully deposited, and, at the instance of the State Treasurer, or at the instance of the Governor, the Attorney General shall forthwith institute the civil action in the name of the State of North Carolina against such person or persons, either in the courts of Wake County, according to their respective jurisdiction, or in the county in which said unlawful deposit has been made, according to the selection made by the officer requesting the institution of such action, for the purpose of recovering the amount of the money so unlawfully deposited, with interest thereon at six percent (6%) per annum, and for the cost of said action, and the court in which said action is tried may also tax, as a part of the cost in said action, to the use of the State of North Carolina, a sum sufficient to reimburse the State of North Carolina for all expense incidental to or connected with the preparation and prosecution of such action. (1925, c. 128, s. 3; 1993, c. 539, s. 1057; 1994, Ex. Sess., c. 24, s. 14(c).)

§ 147-81. Number of depositories; contract.

The State Treasurer is authorized and empowered to select as many depositories in one place and in the State as may appear to him to be necessary and convenient for the various officers, representatives and employees of the State, to comply with the purposes of G.S. 147-77, 147-78, 147-80, 147-81, 147-82, 147-83 and 147-84, and may make such contracts with said depositories for the payment of interest on average daily or monthly balances as may appear advantageous to the State in the opinion of such Treasurer and the Governor. (1925, c. 128, s. 4.)

§ 147-82. Accounts of funds kept separate.

In order to preserve and keep them separate, all funds that are now required by law to be kept separate or to be separately administered, both by State departments, institutions, commissions, and other agencies or divisions of the State which collect or receive funds belonging to the State, or funds handled or maintained as trust funds in any form by such department, division or institution shall be evidenced in daily reports by distribution sheets, which shall reflect and show an exact copy of the accounts, showing the distribution of said money kept by such collecting departments, institutions and agencies, and the same shall be entered in the records of the office of the State Treasurer, so as to keep and maintain in the office where the same is first collected or received the same account thereof, and of the distribution thereof, the same records and accounts as are kept in the office of the State Treasurer relating thereto. (1925, c. 128, s. 5.)

§ 147-83. Receipts from federal government and gifts not affected.

General Statutes 147-77, 147-78, 147-80, 147-81, 147-82, 147-83 and 147-84 shall not be held or construed to affect or interfere with the receipts and disbursements of any funds received by any institution or department of this State from the federal government or any gift or donation to any institution or department of the State or commission or agency thereof when either in the act of Congress, relating to such funds received from the federal government, or in the instrument evidencing the said private donation or gift, a contrary disposition or handling is prescribed or required, and the said sections shall not apply to any moneys paid to any department, institution or agency, or undertaking of the State of North Carolina, as a part of any legislative appropriation, or allotment from any contingent fund, as provided by law, after the same has been paid out of the State treasury. (1925, c. 128, s. 6.)

§ 147-84. Refund of excess payments.

Whenever taxes or other receipts of any kind are or have been by clerical error, misinterpretation of the law, or otherwise, collected and paid into the State treasury in excess of the amount found legally due the State, said excess amount shall be refunded to the person entitled thereto. (1925, c. 128, s. 7; 1983, c. 913, s. 54.)

§ 147-85. Fiscal year.

The fiscal year of the State government shall annually close on the thirtieth day of June. (1868-9, c. 270, s. 77; 1883, c. 60; Code, s. 3360; 1885, c. 334; 1905, c. 430; Rev., s. 5378; C.S., s. 7692; 1921, c. 229; Ex. Sess. 1921, c. 7; 1925, c. 89, s. 21; 1983, c. 913, s. 55.)

§ 147-86. Additional clerical assistance authorized; compensation and duties.

The State Treasurer, by and with the consent and advice of the Governor and Council of State, is authorized to employ an additional clerk in the Treasury Department, whose compensation and duties shall be fixed by the State Treasurer, by and with the consent and advice of the Governor and Council of State. The compensation of such additional clerk as may be employed pursuant to this section shall be paid as other officers and clerks are paid. (1923, c. 172; C.S., s. 7693 (a).)

§ 147-86.1. Pool account for local government unemployment compensation.

(a)   The State Treasurer is authorized to establish a pool account, in accordance with rules of the Division of Employment Security (DES), in cooperation with any one or more units of local government, for the purpose of reimbursing the DES for unemployment benefits paid by the DES and chargeable to each local unit of government participating in the pool account. In the pool account established pursuant to this section, the funds contributed by a unit of local government shall remain the funds of the particular unit, and interest or other investment income earned by the pool account shall be prorated and credited to the various contributing local units on the basis of the amounts thereof contributed, figured according to an average periodic balance or some other sound accounting principle.

(b)   The State Treasurer shall pay to the Division of Employment Security, within 25 days from receipt of a list thereof, all unemployment benefits charged by the DES to each unit of local government participating in the pool account from the funds in the pool account belonging to each such unit, to the extent that said funds are sufficient to do so.

(c) Notwithstanding the participation by a unit of local government in the pool account authorized by this section, such unit shall remain liable to the Division of Employment Security for any benefits duly charged by the Division to the unit which are not paid by the State Treasurer from funds in the pool account belonging to the unit. Notwithstanding its participation in the pool account, each unit of local government shall continue to maintain an individual account with the DES.

(d) The Director of the Budget shall be authorized to transfer from the interest earned on the pool account, to the State Treasurer's departmental budget, such funds as may be necessary to defray the Treasurer's cost of administering the pool account. (1977, c. 1124; 1983, c. 717, s. 89; 2011-401, s. 3.23.)

§ 147-86.2. Information Technology Services fees; dispute resolution panel.

The State Treasurer or the State Treasurer's designee, in conjunction with the State Controller and the State Budget Officer or their designees, shall handle the resolution of fee disputes between the Office of Information Technology Services and the State agencies receiving information technology services from the Office. (2009-136, s. 3.)

§ 147-86.3. Reserved for future codification purposes.

§ 147-86.4. Reserved for future codification purposes.

§ 147-86.5. Reserved for future codification purposes.

§ 147-86.6. Reserved for future codification purposes.

§ 147-86.7. Reserved for future codification purposes.

§ 147-86.8. Reserved for future codification purposes.

§ 147-86.9. Reserved for future codification purposes.

Article 6A.

Cash Management.

§ 147-86.10. Statement of policy.

It is the policy of the State of North Carolina that all agencies, institutions, departments, bureaus, boards, commissions, and officers of the State, whether or not subject to the State Budget Act, Chapter 143C of the General Statutes, shall devise techniques and procedures for the receipt, deposit, and disbursement of moneys coming into their control and custody which are designed to maximize interest-bearing investment of cash, and to minimize idle and nonproductive cash balances. This policy shall apply to the General Court of Justice as defined in Article IV of the North Carolina Constitution, the public school administrative units, and the community colleges with respect to the receipt, deposit, and disbursement of moneys required by law to be deposited with the State Treasurer and with respect to moneys made available to them for expenditure by warrants drawn on the State Treasurer. This policy shall include the acceptance of electronic payments in accordance with G.S. 147-86.22 to the maximum extent possible consistent with sound business practices. (1985, c. 709, s. 1; 1999-434, s. 2; 2006-203, s. 120.)

§ 147-86.11. Cash management for the State.

(a) Uniform Plan. - The State Controller, with the advice and assistance of the State Treasurer, the State Budget Officer, and the State Auditor, shall develop, implement and amend as necessary a uniform statewide plan to carry out the cash management policy for all State agencies. The State Auditor shall report annually to the General Assembly on the implementation of the plan as shown in the audits completed during the prior fiscal year. The State Treasurer shall recommend periodically to the General Assembly any implementing legislation necessary or desirable in the furtherance of the State policy. When used in this section, "State agency" means any agency, institution, bureau, board, commission or officer of the State; however, except as provided in G.S. 147-86.12, 147-86.13, 147-86.14, and 147-86.22, this Article does not apply to the agencies, institutions, bureaus, boards, commissions and officers of the General Court of Justice as defined in Article IV of the North Carolina Constitution or to the local school administrative units and community colleges and their officers and employees.

(b) Duties of Auditor. - The State Auditor pursuant to authority under G.S. 147-64.6 shall monitor agency compliance with this Article, and make any comments, suggestions, and recommendations the Auditor deems advisable to the agencies.

(c) Treasurer's Report. - The State Treasurer shall publish a quarterly report on all funds in the control or custody of the State Treasurer showing cash balances on hand, investments of cash balances and a comparative analysis of earnings and investment performances.

(d) Earnings on Trust Funds. - The statewide cash management plan shall provide that any net earnings on invested funds, whose beneficial owner is not the State or a local governmental unit, shall be paid to the beneficial owners of the funds. "Net earnings" are the amounts remaining after allowance for the cost of administration, management, and operation of the invested funds.

(e) Elements of Plan. - For moneys received or to be received, the statewide cash management plan shall provide at a minimum that:

(1) Except as otherwise provided by law, moneys received by employees of State agencies in the normal course of their employment shall be deposited as follows:

a. Moneys received in trust for specific beneficiaries for which the employee-custodian has a duty to invest shall be deposited with the State Treasurer under the provisions of G.S. 147-69.3.

b. All other moneys received shall be deposited with the State Treasurer pursuant to G.S. 147-77 and G.S. 147-69.1.

(2) Moneys received shall be deposited daily in the form and amounts received, except as otherwise provided by statute.

(3) Moneys due to a State agency by another governmental agency or by private persons shall be promptly billed, collected and deposited.

(4) Unpaid billings due to a State agency other than amounts owed by patients to the University of North Carolina Health Care System or East Carolina University's Division of Health Sciences shall be turned over to the Attorney General for collection no more than 90 days after the due date of the billing, except that a State agency need not turn over to the Attorney General unpaid

billings of less than five hundred dollars ($500.00), or (for institutions where applicable) amounts owed by all patients which are less than the federally established deductible applicable to Part A of the Medicare program, and instead may handle these unpaid bills pursuant to agency debt collection procedures.

(4a) The University of North Carolina Health Care System and East Carolina University's Division of Health Sciences may turn over to the Attorney General for collection accounts owed by patients.

(5) Moneys received in the form of warrants drawn on the State Treasurer shall be deposited by the State agency directly with the State Treasurer and not through the banking system, unless otherwise approved by the State Treasurer.

(6) State agencies shall accept payment by electronic payment in accordance with G.S. 147-86.22 to the maximum extent possible consistent with sound business practices.

(f) Disbursement Requirements. - For the disbursement of money, the statewide cash management plan shall provide at a minimum that:

(1) Moneys deposited with the State Treasurer remain on deposit with the State Treasurer until final disbursement to the ultimate payee.

(2) The order in which appropriations and other available resources are expended shall be subject to the provisions of Chapter 143C of the General Statutes regardless of whether the State agency disbursing or expending the moneys is subject to the State Budget Act.

(3) Federal and other reimbursements of expenditures paid from State funds shall be paid immediately to the source of the State funds.

(4) Billings to the State for goods received or services rendered shall be paid neither early nor late but on the discount date or the due date to the extent practicable.

(5) Disbursement cycles for each agency shall be established to the extent practicable so that the overall efficiency of the warrant disbursement system is maximized while maintaining prompt payment of bills due.

(g) Interest Maximized. - The interest earnings of the General Fund and Highway Fund shall be maximized to the extent practicable. To this end:

(1) Interest earnings shall not be allocated to an account by the State Treasurer unless all of the moneys in the account are expressly eligible by law for receiving interest allocations.

(2) State officers and employees who received moneys in trust or for investment shall be solely responsible for properly segregating such funds for investment in the manner prescribed by law. The officer or employee charged with the responsibility for these moneys shall be under a duty to segregate the funds in a timely manner. No investment income shall be allocated by the State Treasurer to trust or other investment accounts until properly segregated into investment accounts as provided by law and the rules of the State Treasurer.

(h) New Technologies. - The statewide cash management plan shall consider new technologies and procedures whenever the technologies and procedures are economically beneficial to the State as a whole. Where the new technologies and procedures may be implemented without additional legislation, the technologies and procedures shall be implemented in the plan.

(i) Penalty. - A willful or continued failure of an employee paid from State funds or employed by a State agency to follow the statewide cash management plan is sufficient cause for immediate dismissal of the employee. (1985, c. 709, s. 1; 1985 (Reg. Sess., 1986), c. 1024, s. 26; 1987, c. 564, s. 32; c. 738, s. 59(a)(1); 1991, c. 95, s. 1; c. 542, s. 15; 1999-434, s. 4; 2006-203, s. 121; 2007-306, s. 3; 2012-194, s. 68(b).)

§ 147-86.12. Cash management for school administration units.

All school administrative units and their officers and employees are subject to the provision of G.S. 147-86.11 with respect to moneys required by law to be deposited with the State Treasurer and with respect to moneys made available to the school administrative unit for expenditure by warrants drawn on the State Treasurer. (1985, c. 709, s. 1.)

§ 147-86.13. Cash management for community colleges.

All community colleges and their officers and employees are subject to the provisions of G.S. 147-86.11 with respect to moneys required by law to be deposited with the State Treasurer and with respect to moneys made available to them for expenditure by warrants drawn on the State Treasurer. (1985, c. 709, s. 1; 1987, c. 564, s. 9.)

§ 147-86.14. Cash management for the General Court of Justice.

All agencies, institutions, bureaus, boards, commissions, and officers of the General Court of Justice as defined in Article IV of the Constitution are subject to the provisions of G.S. 147-86.11 with respect to moneys required by law to be deposited with the State Treasurer and with respect to moneys made available to them for expenditure by warrants drawn on the State Treasurer; provided, that the provisions of G.S. 147-86.11 shall not apply to any funds deposited with a clerk of superior court unless the beneficial owner of the funds is either the State or a local governmental unit of the State. (1985, c. 709, s. 1.)

§ 147-86.15. Cash management of the Highway Fund and the Highway Trust Fund.

The State Treasurer may combine the balances of the Highway Fund and the Highway Trust Fund for cash management purposes. The State Treasurer may make short-term loans between the Funds to accomplish the purposes of this section. (2001-424, s. 27.23(b).)

§§ 147-86.16 through 147-86.19. Reserved for future codification purposes.

Article 6B.

Statewide Accounts Receivable Program.

§ 147-86.20. Definitions.

The following definitions apply in this Article:

(1) Account receivable. - An asset of the State reflecting a debt that is owed to the State and has not been received by the State agency servicing the debt. The term includes claims, damages, fees, fines, forfeitures, loans, overpayments, taxes, and tuition as well as penalties, interest, and other costs authorized by law. The term does not include court costs or fees assessed in actions before the General Court of Justice or counsel fees and other expenses of representing indigents under Article 36 of Chapter 7A of the General Statutes.

(2) Debtor. - A person who owes an account receivable.

(2a) Electronic payment. - Payment by charge card, credit card, debit card, or by electronic funds transfer as defined in this subsection.

(3) Past Due. - An account receivable is past due if the State has not received payment of it by the payment due date.

(4) Person. - An individual, a fiduciary, a firm, a partnership, an association, a corporation, a unit of government, or another group acting as a unit.

(5) State Agency. - Defined in G.S. 147-64.4(4). The term does not include, however, a community college, a local school administrative unit, an area mental health, developmental disabilities, and substance abuse authority, or the General Court of Justice.

(6) Write-off. - To remove an account receivable from a State agency's accounts receivable records. (1993, c. 512, s. 1; 1999-434, s. 1; 2010-31, s. 31.8(a).)

§ 147-86.21. State agencies to collect accounts receivable in accordance with statewide policies.

A State agency to which an account receivable is owed is responsible for collecting the account receivable. In fulfilling this responsibility, a State agency shall establish internal policies and procedures for the management and collection of accounts receivable and shall submit its internal policies and procedures to the State Controller for review.

The State Controller shall examine the policies and procedures submitted by a State agency to determine whether they are consistent with statewide policies and procedures adopted by the State Controller. The statewide policies and procedures shall ensure that a State agency takes all cost-effective and appropriate actions to collect accounts receivable owed to it. If the State Controller determines that a State agency's policies and procedures are not consistent with the statewide policies and procedures, the State Controller shall discuss the inconsistencies with the State agency to determine whether special circumstances, such as a requirement of federal law, justify the inconsistencies. If the State Controller, after consulting with the Office of the Attorney General, finds that no special circumstances justify the inconsistencies, the State Controller shall notify the State agency and the State agency shall conform its policies and procedures to the statewide policies and procedures. If the State Controller finds that special circumstances justify the inconsistencies, the State agency's internal policies and procedures shall reflect the special circumstances. (1993, c. 512, s. 1.)

§ 147-86.22. Statewide accounts receivable program.

(a) Program. - The State Controller shall implement a statewide accounts receivable program. As part of this program, the State Controller shall do all of the following:

(1) Monitor the State's accounts receivable collection efforts.

(2) Coordinate information, systems, and procedures between State agencies to maximize the collection of past-due accounts receivable.

(3) Adopt policies and procedures for the management and collection of accounts receivable by State agencies.

(4) Establish procedures for writing off accounts receivable.

(b) Electronic Payment. - Notwithstanding the provisions of G.S. 147-86.20 and G.S. 147-86.21, this subsection applies to debts owed a community college, a local school administrative unit, an area mental health, developmental disabilities, and substance abuse authority, and the Administrative Office of the Courts, and to debts payable to or through the office of a clerk of superior court or a magistrate, as well as to debts owed to other State agencies as defined in G.S. 147-86.20.

The State Controller shall establish policies that allow accounts receivable to be payable under certain conditions by electronic payment. These policies shall be established with the concurrence of the State Treasurer. In addition, any policies that apply to debts payable to or through the office of a clerk of superior court or a magistrate shall be established with the concurrence of the Administrative Officer of the Courts. The Administrative Officer of the Courts may also establish policies otherwise authorized by law that apply to these debts as long as those policies are not inconsistent with the Controller's policies.

A condition of payment by electronic payment is receipt by the appropriate State agency of the full amount of the account receivable owed to the State agency. A debtor who pays by electronic payment may be required to pay any fee or charge associated with the use of electronic payment. Fees associated with processing electronic payments may be paid out of the General Fund and Highway Fund if the payment of the fee by the State is economically beneficial to the State and the payment of the fee by the State has been approved by the State Controller and State Treasurer.

The State Controller and State Treasurer shall consult with the Joint Legislative Commission on Governmental Operations before establishing policies that allow accounts receivable to be payable by electronic payment and before authorizing fees associated with electronic payment to be paid out of the General Fund and Highway Fund. A State agency must also consult with the Joint Legislative Commission on Governmental Operations before implementing any program to accept payment under the policies established pursuant to this subsection.

A payment of an account receivable that is made by electronic payment and is not honored by the issuer of the card or the financial institution offering electronic funds transfer does not relieve the debtor of the obligation to pay the account receivable.

(c) Collection Techniques. - The State Controller, in conjunction with the Office of the Attorney General, shall establish policies and procedures to govern techniques for collection of accounts receivable. These techniques may include use of credit reporting bureaus, judicial remedies authorized by law, and administrative setoff by a reduction of a tax refund pursuant to the Setoff Debt Collection Act, Chapter 105A of the General Statutes, or a reduction of another payment, other than payroll, due from the State to a person to reduce or eliminate an account receivable that the person owes the State.

The State Controller shall negotiate a contract with a third party to perform an audit and collection process of inadvertent overpayments by State agencies to vendors as a result of pricing errors, neglected rebates and discounts, miscalculated freight charges, unclaimed refunds, erroneously paid excise taxes, and related errors. The third party shall be compensated only from funds recovered as a result of the audit. Savings realized in excess of costs shall be transferred from the agency to the Office of State Budget and Management and placed in a special reserve account for future direction by the General Assembly. Any disputed savings shall be settled by the State Controller. This paragraph does not apply to the purchase of medical services by State agencies or payments used to reimburse or otherwise pay for health care services. (1993, c. 512, s. 1; 1998-212, s. 26.1; 1999-434, s. 3; 2000-140, s. 93.1(a); 2001-424, s. 12.2(b); 2010-31, s. 31.8(b).)

§ 147-86.23. Interest and penalties.

A State agency shall charge interest at the rate established pursuant to G.S. 105-241.21 on a past-due account receivable from the date the account receivable was due until it is paid. A State agency shall add to a past-due account receivable a late payment penalty of no more than ten percent (10%) of the account receivable. A State agency may waive a late-payment penalty for good cause shown. If another statute requires the payment of interest or a penalty on a past-due account receivable, this section does not apply to that past-due account receivable. This section does not apply to money owed to the University of North Carolina Health Care System or to East Carolina University's Division of Health Sciences for health care services, to the North Carolina Turnpike Authority for money owed to the Authority for tolls, or to the North Carolina State Health Plan for past-due account receivables related to premiums and claims payments. (1993, c. 512, s. 1; 2007-306, s. 4; 2007-491, s. 44(1)a; 2012-78, s. 14; 2012-194, s. 68(c); 2013-324, s. 6.)

§ 147-86.24. Debtor information and skip tracing.

A State agency shall collect from clients and debtors minimum identifying information as prescribed by the State Controller. A State agency shall use all available debtor information to skip trace debtors as prescribed by the State Controller.

The State Controller shall establish procedures to give the State Controller access to information that is in the custody of a State agency and could assist another State agency in the collection of accounts receivable owed to that State agency. A State agency that has this information shall cooperate with the State Controller in giving the State Controller access to the information. If the information is contained in an electronic database, the State agency shall provide the State Controller on-line electronic access upon request. A State agency is not required to give the State Controller access to information when a State or federal law prohibits the disclosure of the information. (1993, c. 512, s. 1.)

§ 147-86.25. Setoff debt collection.

The State Controller shall implement a statewide setoff debt collection program to provide for collection of the following accounts receivable by setoff against payments the State owes to debtors, other than payments of tax refunds and payroll:

(1)   Accounts receivable submitted to the Department of Revenue by a claimant agency under the Setoff Debt Collection Act, Chapter 105A of the General Statutes.

(2)   An overdue tax debt, as defined in G.S. 105-243.1. (1993, c. 512, s. 1; 2010-31, s. 31.8(c).)

§ 147-86.26. Reporting requirements.

A State agency shall provide the State Controller a complete report of the agency's accounts receivable at least quarterly or more frequently as required by the State Controller. The State Controller shall use the information provided by a State agency and any additional information available to compile a summary report of the agency. The State Controller shall provide copies of these summary reports annually to the Governor, the Joint Legislative Commission on Governmental Operations, and each State agency. Each summary report shall include the following:

(1)   The type of accounts receivable owed to the State agency.

(2) An aging of the accounts receivable.

(3) Any attempted collection activity and any costs incurred in the collection process.

(4) Any accounts receivable that have been written off.

(5) Information required by subdivisions (1) through (4) for the previous three years.

(6) Identification of a State agency that is not complying with this Article or Chapter 105A of the General Statutes.

(7) Any additional information the State Controller considers useful. (1993, c. 512, s. 1.)

§ 147-86.27. Rules.

A State agency may adopt rules to implement this Article. (1993, c. 512, s. 1.)

§ 147-86.28. Reserved for future codification purposes.

§ 147-86.29. Reserved for future codification purposes.

Article 6C.

Health and Wellness Trust Fund.

§ 147-86.30: Repealed by Session Laws 2011-145, s. 6.11(a), effective August 14, 2011.

§ 147-86.31: Repealed by Session Laws 2011-145, s. 6.11(a), effective August 14, 2011.

§ 147-86.32: Repealed by Session Laws 2011-145, s. 6.11(a), effective August 14, 2011.

§ 147-86.33: Repealed by Session Laws 2011-145, s. 6.11(a), effective August 14, 2011.

§ 147-86.34: Repealed by Session Laws 2011-145, s. 6.11(a), effective August 14, 2011.

§ 147-86.35: Repealed by Session Laws 2011-145, s. 6.11(a), effective August 14, 2011.

§ 147-86.36: Repealed by Session Laws 2011-145, s. 6.11(a), effective August 14, 2011.

Article 6D.

Sudan (Darfur) Divestment Act.

§ 147-86.41. Legislative findings.

(1) On July 23, 2004, the United States Congress declared that "the atrocities unfolding in Darfur, Sudan, are genocide."

(2) On September 9, 2004, Secretary of State Colin L. Powell told the U.S. Senate Foreign Relations Committee that "genocide has occurred and may still be occurring in Darfur" and "the Government of Sudan and the Janjaweed bear responsibility."

(3) On September 21, 2004, addressing the United Nations General Assembly, President George W. Bush affirmed the Secretary of State's finding and stated, "At this hour, the world is witnessing terrible suffering and horrible crimes in the Darfur region of Sudan, crimes my government has concluded are genocide."

(4) On December 7, 2004, the U.S. Congress noted that the genocidal policy in Darfur has led to reports of "systematic rape of thousands of women and girls, the abduction of women and children, and the destruction of hundreds of ethnically African villages, including the poisoning of their wells and the

plunder of their crops and cattle upon which the people of such villages sustain themselves."

(5) Also on December 7, 2004, Congress found that "the Government of Sudan has restricted access by humanitarian and human rights workers to the Darfur area through intimidation by military and security forces, and through bureaucratic and administrative obstruction, in an attempt to inflict the most devastating harm on those individuals displaced from their villages and homes without any means of sustenance or shelter."

(6) On September 25, 2006, Congress reaffirmed that "the genocide unfolding in the Darfur region of Sudan is characterized by acts of terrorism and atrocities directed against civilians, including mass murder, rape, and sexual violence committed by the Janjaweed and associated militias with the complicity and support of the National Congress Party-led faction of the Government of Sudan."

(7) On September 26, 2006, the U.S. House of Representatives stated that "an estimated 300,000 to 400,000 people have been killed by the Government of Sudan and its Janjaweed allies since the [Darfur] crisis began in 2003, more than 2,000,000 people have been displaced from their homes, and more than 250,000 people from Darfur remain in refugee camps in Chad."

(8) The Darfur crisis represents the first time the United States Government has labeled ongoing atrocities genocide.

(9) The Federal Government has imposed sanctions against the Government of Sudan since 1997. These sanctions are monitored through the U.S. Treasury Department's Office of Foreign Assets Control (OFAC).

(10) According to a former chair of the U.S. Securities and Exchange Commission, "the fact that a foreign company is doing material business with a country, government, or entity on OFAC's sanctions list is, in the SEC staff's view, substantially likely to be significant to a reasonable investor's decision about whether to invest in that company."

(11) Since 1993, the U.S. Secretary of State has determined that Sudan is a country the government of which has repeatedly provided support for acts of international terrorism, thereby restricting United States assistance, defense exports and sales, and financial and other transactions with the Government of Sudan.

(12) A 2006 U.S. House of Representatives report states that "a company's association with sponsors of terrorism and human rights abuses, no matter how large or small, can have a materially adverse result on a public company's operations, financial condition, earnings, and stock prices, all of which can negatively affect the value of an investment."

(13) In response to the financial risk posed by investments in companies doing business with a terrorist-sponsoring state, the Securities and Exchange Commission established its Office of Global Security Risk to provide for enhanced disclosure of material information regarding such companies.

(14) The current Sudan divestment movement encompasses nearly 100 universities, cities, states, and private pension plans.

(15) Companies facing such widespread divestment present further material risk to remaining investors.

(16) It is a fundamental responsibility of the State of North Carolina to decide where, how, and by whom financial resources in its control should be invested, taking into account numerous pertinent factors.

(17) It is the prerogative and desire of the State of North Carolina in respect to investment resources in its control and to the extent reasonable, with due consideration for, among other things, return on investment, on behalf of itself and its investment beneficiaries, not to participate in an ownership or capital-providing capacity with entities that provide significant practical support for genocide, including certain non-United States companies presently doing business in Sudan.

(18) It is the judgment of the General Assembly that this article should remain in effect only insofar as it continues to be consistent with, and does not unduly interfere with, the foreign policy of the United States as determined by the Federal Government.

(19) It is the judgment of this General Assembly that mandatory divestment of public funds from certain companies is a measure that should be employed sparingly and judiciously. A Congressional and Presidential declaration of genocide satisfies this high threshold. (2007-486, s. 1.)

§ 147-86.42. Definitions.

As used in this article, the following definitions apply:

(1) "Active Business Operations" means all Business Operations that are not Inactive Business Operations.

(2) "Business Operations" means engaging in commerce in any form in Sudan, including by acquiring, developing, maintaining, owning, selling, possessing, leasing, or operating equipment, facilities, personnel, products, services, personal property, real property, or any other apparatus of business or commerce.

(3) "Company" means any sole proprietorship, organization, association, corporation, partnership, joint venture, limited partnership, limited liability partnership, limited liability company, or other entity or business association, including all wholly-owned subsidiaries, majority-owned subsidiaries, parent companies, or affiliates of such entities or business associations, that exists for profit-making purposes.

(4) "Complicit" means taking actions during any preceding 20-month period which have directly supported or promoted the genocidal campaign in Darfur, including, but not limited to, preventing Darfur's victimized population from communicating with each other, encouraging Sudanese citizens to speak out against an internationally approved security force for Darfur, actively working to deny, cover up, or alter the record on human rights abuses in Darfur, or other similar actions.

(5) "Direct Holdings" in a Company means all securities of that Company held directly by the Public Fund or in an account or fund in which the Public Fund owns all shares or interests.

(6) "Government of Sudan" means the government in Khartoum, Sudan, which is led by the National Congress Party (formerly known as the National Islamic Front) or any successor government formed on or after October 13, 2006 (including the coalition National Unity Government agreed upon in the Comprehensive Peace Agreement for Sudan), and does not include the regional government of southern Sudan.

(7) "Inactive Business Operations" means the mere continued holding or renewal of rights to property previously operated for the purpose of generating revenues but not presently deployed for such purpose.

(8) "Indirect Holdings" in a Company means all securities of that Company held in an account or fund, such as a mutual fund, managed by one or more persons not employed by the Public Fund, in which the Public Fund owns shares or interests together with other investors not subject to the provisions of this article.

(9) "Marginalized Populations of Sudan" include, but are not limited to, the portion of the population in the Darfur region that has been genocidally victimized; the portion of the population of southern Sudan victimized by Sudan's North-South civil war; the Beja, Rashidiya, and other similarly underserved groups of eastern Sudan; the Nubian and other similarly underserved groups in Sudan's Abyei, Southern Blue Nile, and Nuba Mountain regions; and the Amri, Hamadab, Manasir, and other similarly underserved groups of northern Sudan.

(10) "Military Equipment" means weapons, arms, military supplies, and equipment that readily may be used for military purposes, including, but not limited to, radar systems or military-grade transport vehicles; or supplies or services sold or provided directly or indirectly to any force actively participating in armed conflict in Sudan.

(11) "Mineral Extraction Activities" include exploring, extracting, processing, transporting, or wholesale selling or trading of elemental minerals or associated metal alloys or oxides (ore), including gold, copper, chromium, chromite, diamonds, iron, iron ore, silver, tungsten, uranium, and zinc, as well as facilitating such activities, including by providing supplies or services in support of such activities.

(12) "Oil-Related Activities" include, but are not limited to, owning rights to oil blocks; exporting, extracting, producing, refining, processing, exploring for, transporting, selling, or trading of oil; constructing, maintaining, or operating a pipeline, refinery, or other oil-field infrastructure; and facilitating such activities, including by providing supplies or services in support of such activities, provided that the mere retail sale of gasoline and related consumer products shall not be considered Oil-Related Activities.

(13) "Power Production Activities" means any Business Operation that involves a project commissioned by the National Electricity Corporation (NEC) of Sudan or other similar Government of Sudan entity whose purpose is to facilitate power generation and delivery, including, but not limited to, establishing power-generating plants or hydroelectric dams, selling or installing components for the project, providing service contracts related to the installation or maintenance of the project, as well as facilitating such activities, including by providing supplies or services in support of such activities.

(14) "Public Fund" means any funds held by the State Treasurer to the credit of:

a. The Teachers' and State Employees' Retirement System.

b. The Consolidated Judicial Retirement System.

c. The Firemen's and Rescue Workers' Pension Fund.

d. The Local Governmental Employees' Retirement System.

e. The Legislative Retirement System.

f. The Legislative Retirement Fund.

g. The North Carolina National Guard Pension Fund.

(14a) "Scrutinized Business Operations" means Business Operations that have resulted in a Company becoming a Scrutinized Company.

(15) "Scrutinized Company" means any Company that meets the criteria in sub-subdivisions a., b., or c. below:

a. The Company has Business Operations that involve contracts with and/or provision of supplies or services to the Government of Sudan, to companies in which the Government of Sudan has any direct or indirect equity share, Government of Sudan-commissioned consortiums or projects, or to Companies involved in Government of Sudan-commissioned consortiums or projects and at least one of the following conditions is satisfied:

1. More than ten percent (10%) of the Company's revenues or assets linked to Sudan involve Oil-Related Activities or Mineral Extraction Activities;

less than seventy-five percent (75%) of the Company's revenues or assets linked to Sudan involve contracts with and/or provision of Oil-Related or Mineral Extracting products or services to the regional government of southern Sudan or a project or consortium created exclusively by that regional government; and the Company has failed to take Substantial Action.

2. More than ten percent (10%) of the Company's revenues or assets linked to Sudan involve Power Production Activities; less than seventy-five percent (75%) of the Company's Power Production Activities include projects whose intent is to provide power or electricity to the Marginalized Populations of Sudan; and the Company has failed to take Substantial Action.

b. The Company is Complicit in the Darfur genocide.

c. The Company supplies Military Equipment within Sudan, unless it clearly shows that the Military Equipment cannot be used to facilitate offensive military actions in Sudan or the Company implements rigorous and verifiable safeguards to prevent use of that equipment by forces actively participating in armed conflict, for example, through post-sale tracking of such equipment by the Company, certification from a reputable and objective third party that such equipment is not being used by a party participating in armed conflict in Sudan, or sale of such equipment solely to the regional government of southern Sudan or any internationally recognized peacekeeping force or humanitarian organization.

Notwithstanding anything herein to the contrary, a Social Development Company which is not Complicit in the Darfur genocide shall not be considered a Scrutinized Company.

(16) "Social Development Company" means a Company whose primary purpose in Sudan is to provide humanitarian goods or services, including medicine or medical equipment, agricultural supplies or infrastructure, educational opportunities, journalism-related activities, information or information materials, spiritual-related activities, services of a purely clerical or reporting nature, food, clothing, or general consumer goods that are unrelated to Oil-Related Activities, Mineral Extraction Activities, or Power Production Activities.

(17) "Substantial Action" means adopting, publicizing, and implementing a formal plan to cease Scrutinized Business Operations within one year and to refrain from any such new Business Operations; undertaking significant

humanitarian efforts on behalf of one or more Marginalized Populations of Sudan; or through engagement with the Government of Sudan, materially improving conditions for the genocidally victimized population in Darfur. (2007-486, s. 2.)

§ 147-86.43. Identification of companies.

(a) Within 90 days of August 30, 2007, the Public Fund shall make its best efforts to identify all Scrutinized Companies in which the Public Fund has Direct or Indirect Holdings or could possibly have such holdings in the future. Such efforts shall include, as appropriate:

(1) Reviewing and relying, as appropriate in the Public Fund's judgment, on publicly available information regarding Companies with Business Operations in Sudan, including information provided by nonprofit organizations, research firms, international organizations, and government entities;

(2) Contacting asset managers contracted by the Public Fund that invest in Companies with Business Operations in Sudan; or

(3) Contacting other institutional investors that have divested from and/or engaged with Companies that have Business Operations in Sudan.

(b) By the first meeting of the Public Fund following the 90-day period described in subsection (a), the Public Fund shall assemble all Scrutinized Companies identified into a "Scrutinized Companies List."

(c) The Public Fund shall update the Scrutinized Companies List on a quarterly basis based on evolving information from, among other sources, those listed in subsection (a) of this section. (2007-486, s. 3.)

§ 147-86.44. Required actions.

(a) General. - The Public Fund shall adhere to the procedure for Companies on the Scrutinized Companies List as provided in this section:

(b) Engagement. -

(1) The Public Fund shall immediately determine the Companies on the Scrutinized Companies List in which the Public Fund owns Direct or Indirect Holdings.

(2) For each Company identified in subdivision (1) of this section with only Inactive Business Operations, the Public Fund shall send a written notice informing the Company of this article and encouraging it to continue to refrain from initiating Active Business Operations in Sudan until it is able to avoid Scrutinized Business Operations. The Public Fund shall continue such correspondence on a semiannual basis.

(3) For each Company newly identified in subdivision (1) of this section with Active Business Operations, the Public Fund shall send a written notice informing the Company of its Scrutinized Company status and that it may become subject to divestment by the Public Fund. The notice shall offer the Company the opportunity to clarify its Sudan-related activities and shall encourage the Company, within 90 days, to either cease its Scrutinized Business Operations or convert such operations to Inactive Business Operations in order to avoid qualifying for divestment by the Public Fund.

(4) If, within 90 days following the Public Fund's first engagement with a Company pursuant to subdivision (3) of this section that Company ceases Scrutinized Business Operations, the Company shall be removed from the Scrutinized Companies List and the provisions of this Section shall cease to apply to it unless it resumes Scrutinized Business Operations. If, within 90 days following the Public Fund's first engagement, the Company converts its Scrutinized Active Business Operations to Inactive Business Operations, the Company shall be subject to all provisions relating thereto.

(c) Divestment. -

(1) If, after 90 days following the Public Fund's first engagement with a Company pursuant to subdivision (b)(3) of this section, the Company continues to have Scrutinized Active Business Operations, and only while such Company continues to have Scrutinized Active Business Operations, the Public Fund shall sell, redeem, divest, or withdraw all publicly traded securities of the Company within 15 months after the Company's most recent appearance on the Scrutinized Companies List.

(2) If a Company that ceased Scrutinized Active Business Operations following engagement pursuant to subdivision (b)(3) of this section resumes

such operations, subdivision (1) of this subsection shall immediately apply, and the Public Fund shall send a written notice to the Company. The Company shall also be immediately reintroduced onto the Scrutinized Companies List.

(d) Prohibition. - At no time shall the Public Fund acquire securities of Companies on the Scrutinized Companies List that have Active Business Operations, except as provided below.

(e) Exemption. - No Company which the United States Government affirmatively declares to be excluded from its present or any future federal sanctions regime relating to Sudan shall be subject to divestment or investment prohibition pursuant to subsections (c) and (d) of this section.

(f) Excluded Securities. - Notwithstanding anything herein to the contrary, subsections (c) and (d) of this section shall not apply to Indirect Holdings in actively managed investment funds. The Public Fund shall, however, submit letters to the managers of such investment funds containing Companies with Scrutinized Active Business Operations requesting that they consider removing such Companies from the fund or create a similar actively managed fund with Indirect Holdings devoid of such Companies. If the manager creates a similar fund, the Public Fund shall replace all applicable investments with investments in the similar fund in an expedited time frame consistent with prudent investing standards. For the purposes of this section, "private equity" funds shall be deemed to be actively managed investment funds. (2007-486, s. 4.)

§ 147-86.45. Reporting.

(a) The Public Fund shall file a publicly available report to the General Assembly that includes the Scrutinized Companies List annually.

(b) Annually thereafter, the Public Fund shall file a publicly available report to the General Assembly and send a copy of that report to the United States Presidential Special Envoy to Sudan (or an appropriate designee or successor) that includes:

(1) A summary of correspondence with Companies engaged by the Public Fund under G.S. 147-86.44(b)(2) and (b)(3).

(2) All investments sold, redeemed, divested, or withdrawn in compliance with G.S. 147-86.44(c).

(3) All prohibited investments under G.S. 147-86.44(d); and

(4) Any progress made under G.S. 147-86.44(f). (2007-486, s. 5.)

§ 147-86.46. Expiration of this article.

This article expires upon the occurrence of any of the following:

(1) The Congress or President of the United States declaring that the Darfur genocide has been halted for at least 12 months.

(2) The United States revoking all sanctions imposed against the Government of Sudan.

(3) The Congress or President of the United States declaring that the Government of Sudan has honored its commitments to cease attacks on civilians, demobilize and demilitarize the Janjaweed and associated militias, grant free and unfettered access for deliveries of humanitarian assistance, and allow for the safe and voluntary return of refugees and internally displaced persons.

(4) The Congress or President of the United States, through legislation or executive order, declaring that mandatory divestment of the type provided for in this article interferes with the conduct of United States foreign policy. (2007-486, s. 6.)

§ 147-86.47. Other legal obligations.

With respect to actions taken in compliance with this article, including all good faith determinations regarding Companies as required by this article, the Public Fund shall be exempt from any conflicting statutory or common law obligations, including any such obligations in respect to choice of asset managers, investment funds, or investments for the Public Fund's securities portfolios. (2007-486, s. 7.)

§ 147-86.48. Reinvestment in certain companies with Scrutinized Active Business Operations.

Notwithstanding anything in this article, the Public Fund is permitted to cease divesting from certain Scrutinized Companies pursuant to G.S. 147-86.44(c) and/or reinvest in certain Scrutinized Companies from which it divested pursuant to G.S. 147-86.44(c) if clear and convincing evidence shows that the value for all assets under management by the Public Fund becomes equal to or less than 99.50% (50 basis points) of the hypothetical value of all assets under management by the Public Fund assuming no divestment for any company had occurred under G.S. 147-86.44(c). Cessation of divestment, reinvestment, and/or any subsequent ongoing investment authorized by this section shall be strictly limited to the minimum steps necessary to avoid the contingency set forth in the preceding sentence. For any cessation of divestment, reinvestment, and/or subsequent ongoing investment authorized by this section, the Public Fund shall provide a written report to the General Assembly in advance of initial reinvestment, updated semiannually thereafter as applicable, setting forth the reasons and justification, supported by clear and convincing evidence, for its decisions to cease divestment, reinvest, and/or remain invested in Companies with Scrutinized Active Business Operations. This section has no application to reinvestment in Companies on the ground that they have ceased to have Scrutinized Active Business Operations. (2007-486, s. 8.)

§ 147-86.49. Enforcement.

The Attorney General is charged with enforcing the provisions of this article and, through any lawful designee, may bring such actions in court as are necessary to do so. (2007-486, s. 9.)

Article 7.

Secretary of Revenue.

§ 147-87. Secretary of Revenue; appointment; salary.

A Secretary of Revenue shall be appointed by the Governor on January 1, 1933, and quadrennially thereafter. The term of office of the Secretary shall be four years and until his successor is appointed and qualified. His salary shall be fixed by the General Assembly in the Current Operations Appropriations Act. (1921, c. 40, ss. 2, 6; 1929, c. 232; 1973, c. 476, s. 193; 1983, c. 717, s. 90; 1983 (Reg. Sess., 1984), c. 1034, s. 164.)

§ 147-88: Repealed by Session Laws 1991, c. 10, s. 3.

Article 8.

District Attorneys.

§ 147-89. To prosecute cases removed to federal courts.

It shall be the duty of the district attorneys of this State, in whose jurisdiction the circuit and district courts of the United States are held, having first obtained the permission of the judges of said courts, to prosecute, or assist in the prosecution of, all criminal cases in said courts where the defendants are charged with violations of the laws of this State, and have moved their cases from the State to the federal courts under the provisions of the various acts of Congress on such subjects. (1874-5, c. 164, s. 1; Code, s. 1239; Rev., s. 5381; C.S., s. 7696; 1973, c. 47, s. 2.)

§ 147-90. Investigations of uses of deadly force.

In every instance in which a private citizen is killed as a result of the use of a firearm by a law enforcement officer in the line of duty, the district attorney in the prosecutorial district in which the death occurred shall, upon the request of the surviving spouse or next of kin of the private citizen within 180 days of the death, request the State Bureau of Investigation to conduct an investigation into the incident. For purposes of this section, the term "next of kin" includes only the child, father, mother, sister, or brother of the private citizen.

Statements prepared by or on behalf of a district attorney pursuant to this section are not public records as defined by G.S. 132-1 and may be released by the district attorney only as provided by G.S. 132-1.4 or other applicable law. (2007-129, s. 1.)

Vision Books Order Form

Fax Orders:	1-980-299-5965
Phone Orders:	1-704-898-0770
E-mail Orders:	www.visionbooks.org
Mail Orders:	Vision Books, LLC P.O. Box 42406 Charlotte, NC 28215

Shipp To:
Name_____
Address_____
City_____State_____Zip_____
Phone_____Fax_____
Email_____@_____

Bill To: We can bill a third party on your behalf.
Name_____
Address_____
City_____State_____Zip_____
Phone___(_____)_____Fax_____
Email_____@_____

Pamphlet Number ($15.00 Each)	Qty	Total Cost
_____	_____	_____
_____	_____	_____
_____	_____	_____
_____	_____	_____
_____	_____	_____
_____	_____	_____
_____	_____	_____
_____	_____	_____
<u>Full Volume Set 1-92</u>	<u>92 Pamphlets</u>	<u>1,380.00</u>

Free Shipping & Handling on Full Volume Orders
Add $1.00 Shipping & Handling Per Pamphlet $_____

Total Cost $_____

Thank you for your order. Management!

DID YOU ENJOY THIS BOOK?

Vision Books, LLC would like to hear from you! If you or someone you know has been fasely imprisoned, we would like to hear your story. If the 'North Carolina Criminal Law and Procedure' has had an effect in your life or if you have suggestions, we would like to hear from you. Send your letters to:

Vision Books, LLC
Attn: Staff Writers
P.O. Box 42406
Charlotte, NC 28215
Email: staff@visionbooks.org

Order Additional Copies:

Fax Orders: 1-980-299-5965

Phone Orders: 1-704-898-0770

E-mail Orders: www.visionbooks.org

Mail Orders: Vision Books, LLC
                    P.O. Box 42406
                    Charlotte, NC 28215

www.ingramcontent.com/pod-product-compliance
Lightning Source LLC
Chambersburg PA
CBHW051628170526
45167CB00001B/102